ALLIANCE & LEICESTER   Moreton Morrell Site
A MAJOR UK LEADER IN FINANCIAL SERVICES

...ce & Leicester is ... of the UK's leading fina...
... of products and ...rvices to perso... clients, comme... a... ...atio... and sma...
business customers.

Sustained success and growth
We've enjoyed continued success and growth over a sustained period of time – and
we've been a member of the FTSE 100 Index of leading shares since converting from
our original building society status in 1997.

A wide range of business services
Our business customer services include cash handling for retailers and corporate
clients, as well as cash sales to financial institutions. We also handle bill payments,
credit and debit card processing, international payments, commercial lending and asset
finance.

Looking after the needs of small business customers
Services to small business customers include a full 24-hour service, accessible by
phone or the Internet, together with a choice of low-cost banking accounts to suit
individual circumstances. And, thanks to our close partnership with the Post Office™,
we offer small businesses the opportunity to deposit takings at over 17,000 locations
throughout the UK.

Products and services
With a wide choice of financial products for private and commercial customers,
Alliance & Leicester has created money-saving, simple-to-use services specifically for
small businesses:

- *Free Direct Banking Account,* for businesses that keep a minimum cleared
  balance of £5,000 in their account. The account includes monthly transactions
  of 50 cheques and 25 automated debit transactions. There are no turnover
  restrictions.

- *Low-Cost Cash Account* designed for businesses that bank over £3,000 in cash
  per month. The monthly administration fee is £1.75, with a charge of 65p per
  unlimited cash transaction.

- *Flat Fee Accounts*
  - *£10 Flat Fee Account* - for businesses with turnover under £100,000, the
    monthly fee covers all standard transactions including issuing and
    depositing cheques, depositing cash, standing order and direct debit
    payments.
  - *£25 Flat Fee Banking* – as above, but for businesses with turnover between
    £100,000-£500,000 and depositing less than £3,000 a month in cash.

- *Start-Up Account* includes free banking for the first 12 months and a free advice
  line giving guidance on tax, legal and employment issues.

A Guide to

WORKING FOR YOURSELF

A Guide to

WORKING FOR YOURSELF

TWENTY-SECOND EDITION

GODFREY GOLZEN & JONATHAN REUVID

Alliance
Leicester
Business Banking

**KOGAN
PAGE**

First published in 1975
Twenty-second edition 2003
Reprinted 2003

Kogan Page Limited
120 Pentonville Road
London N1 9JN

© Kogan Page Ltd and individual contributors, 1995, 1997, 1998, 1999, 2000, 2002, 2003

British Library Cataloguing in Publication Data

A CIP record for this book is available from the British Library.

ISBN 0 7494 4029 5

Typeset by Jean Cussons Typesetting, Diss, Norfolk
Printed and bound in Great Britain by Bell & Bain Ltd, Glasgow

Acknowledgements

We should like to thank the many experts who have provided information for this book, in particular Paul Nolan, Head of Strategic Development, Abbey National Business, for his editorial contributions, the Tenon Group who have edited and updated the sections on taxation and National Insurance and to Barclays Bank for the use of content from their recent survey reports on small businesses and start-ups. We also acknowledge the input of the freelance and self-employed people who have contributed to Part 2, particularly those who have supplied case histories and allowed us to reproduce their comments. Finally, our appreciation to Alliance & Leicester Business Banking which has sponsored this twenty-second edition of *A Guide to Working for Yourself*.

We should be grateful for readers' comments and suggestions. There are as many ways of running small businesses as there are proprietors, and any advice on methods other than those we have indicated will be considered for inclusion in future editions of the book.

Comments or suggestions should be sent c/o the publishers.

WHY CHOOSE NEWAYS?
Concerned about your health and wealth?

Neways has something for everyone, whether you want to build a business or simply purchase superior, leading-edge nutritional and personal care products for yourself and family.

Neways International (UK) Ltd, based in Kimbolton, celebrated its 10th anniversary in 2002 and has seen its turnover increase from £1.8 million to £18 million over the last four years. Neways is a long established, debt-free, multi-level marketing company which manufactures powerful nutritional products, superior toxin free cosmetics, dental, hair, skin and personal care preparations, as well as second to none body toning and weight management products, essential oils and environmentally friendly household products. Neways was founded in Utah, in 1987, and is now active in over 40 countries worldwide with a turnover in excess of $450 million.

How do we explain our success?
First and foremost, Neways is a product driven company with no 'middle men'; we rely on people buying, using and recommending the products. There are no retail outlets and, with our Multiplex bonus plan, serious business builders can quickly become very successful.

Climb your own ladder of success...
Enjoy the best of both worlds, buy products at wholesale and receive a commission on your purchases. Depending on your rank and monthly spend, you could earn a few extra pounds or set off on a whole new career! Earn yourself a supplementary income, safe in the knowledge that you are offering people great alternative products free from potentially harmful ingredients. With the Neways opportunity you have the flexibility to choose and work the hours that suit you and your family!

In a society where more and more people are taking responsibility for their own health, and a vitamin, mineral and supplement retail market in the UK valued at £335 million* in 2000 – what better time to climb your own ladder of success and build a business with Neways.

Why Neways products?
'Personal Products with Integrity' – Neways product ranges offer you a comprehensive alternative to leading brands. Each formula is based on the very latest scientific discoveries and is free from harmful, potentially toxic or carcinogenic ingredients. Moreover, our products are environmentally friendly and the ingredients in our products have not been tested on animals. From our highly bioavailable antioxidants to our glamorous cosmetic range there is something for everyone.

For more information on the superb Neways opportunity, visit our website at www.neways.co.uk, send us an email to AandL@neways.co.uk, or alternatively call Neways International (UK) Ltd direct on 01480 861764.

WHY CHOOSE NEWAYS?

A personal care range which includes:

talc-free powder

fluoride-free toothpaste

aluminium-free deodorant

sls-free shampoo and
bubble bath

propylene glycol-free
shampoo and bubble bath

...as well as a leading edge range of effective
nutritional products

For more information
please contact us:

t: 01480 861764
f: 01480 861769
e: info@neways.co.uk
w: www.neways.co.uk

...IS THERE ANY OTHER CHOICE?

Contents

Preface

The recession of the early 1990s showed that businesses which depend heavily on financial support from the banks and which are based on optimistic cash-flow forecasts are very vulnerable. That lesson still holds true and is reinforced as we appear to be entering another difficult phase in the business cycle. Those that do best are either service businesses with low overheads, those that have genuinely spotted a gap in the market (but are flexible about moving into other opportunities the moment they sense their business section going off the boil) or those that manage to plug into an enduring, recession-proof niche.

THE SCOPE OF THE BOOK

Those who become self-employed, whether full-time or part-time, are joining a trend which, whatever the state of the UK economy, remains on an upward curve. The National Labour Force Survey of Sep/Nov 2002 estimated that the total number of self-employed people represented 11.3 per cent of the workforce.

They are, however, a diverse group and not all will flourish equally or consistently. They include: sales and distribution, specialist consultancy, catering and tourism, technology and cleaning services, skilled crafts and techniques (especially where one person can offer more than one skill), and the professions. In this book the last-named group have been excluded because although there are certain sections of it that they would find helpful, there are nevertheless crucial differences between running a professional practice like that of an architect, doctor or lawyer, and an ordinary business. Otherwise we have identified the self-employed as falling into the following broad categories:

☐ People working part-time, often from home, in addition to a main job, perhaps as an interim stage to setting up a full-time business of their own.

☐ Freelances who provide a service and work full-time for several different principals.

☐ Those who provide goods and services as sole traders or partners, usually from premises other than their own home.

☐ Shareholders in small private companies who are also working directors. They are not strictly speaking self-employed, being employees of the companies they control, but in every practical sense the lessons of this book apply to them.

For any enterprise, Parts 1 and 2, which cover the problems of raising capital, making financial projections and understanding commercial and employment law, will be useful. But it is particularly valuable as a crash course in basic business principles for those starting a small business. Yet the person (designer, typist, teacher, etc) who is simply supplementing his or her income by some freelance work will also find something of value in these Parts: how to assess yourself for tax purposes, the importance of proper invoicing, the part played by professional advisers, and the need to plan workload and meet schedules.

Though the reader should be aware of the several 'audiences' at which the book is aimed and should pay closest attention to the section which is of most direct concern, profit may also be gained from the other sections. And, who knows, today's freelance book designer may tomorrow have his or her own art studio, with staff to manage, creditors to satisfy and clients to cultivate. The sections on business management will at least make you aware of the problems and pressures of expanding the scope of any business, and of the pleasures that come with success.

The third Part of this book looks at some specific self-employment opportunities which are divided broadly between those that require capital investment – if on a small scale – and those where the level of investment is minimal or even non-existent. The range of activities described is obviously not comprehensive, but it covers, if briefly, some of the areas in which people thinking of self-employment have been found to be most interested. Certainly the principles that emerge are those that can be applied to any type of enterprise one cares to look at:

☐ Consider the drawbacks.
☐ Be realistic about the risk you are taking.
☐ Be aware of the competition to what you offer.
☐ Be certain that your enterprise is financially sound.
☐ Know and act within the law as it applies to you.
☐ Use professional advice where necessary.
☐ Fulfil commissions accurately and on time.
☐ Commit yourself totally to a project.

These principles apply to the man or woman with a medium-sized business as much as to the retailer or restaurateur, the part-time editor, typist or translator. If a service is required and completion is guaranteed to a satisfactory standard, people are prepared to pay for it – a reputation is established and customers return. An established group of clients provide a basis on which to expand and perhaps diversify, and, if this is achieved without standards falling, the process will be repeated. Whatever your area of interest and size of operation, we hope that our advice aids that process and enables you to avoid the pitfalls and enjoy the profits of self-employment.

Throughout this book, male and female pronouns have been used randomly. This implies no sexual discrimination; in most cases the opposite applies equally, and the reader's good sense will know when this is not so.

The text of this book was correct at the time of going to press. It incorporates the 2002 Budget, but readers should note the tendency to bring in further fiscal measures between Finance Acts.

Part 1

Starting Your Own Business

Section 1

Basic Decisions

1.1 Going it Alone

Between 1979 and 2002 the percentage of self-employed people in the total UK workforce rose from 7.4 to 11.3 per cent. That was a bigger jump than in any other European Union country, though it does no more than bring the UK closer to the European average, which is 15 per cent.

The important place of self-employment in the economy reflects the changing pattern of employment generally. Big employers in all sectors are cutting down their payrolls and buying in services from outside as and when they need them. Increasingly, that may be true for some goods as well. A logical consequence of just-in-time manufacturing is that components as well as raw materials are sourced from the outside.

But the growth in self-employment is being driven by social as well as economic factors. Self-employment is sometimes seen as an alternative to unemployment. Certainly, this is true in some cases, but the evidence is that more people choose self-employment than are forced into it for lack of an alternative. A lot of people simply prefer it to working for someone else, particularly since the concept of a safe job no longer has any place in this age of mergers, acquisitions and rationalisations.

They are being encouraged in this course of action by the government, which has rationalised numerous initiatives to help small businesses by establishing a single initial point of contact, especially in start-up situations: Business Links (called Business Connect in Wales and Business Shop in Scotland).

The Business Link is the first place to go for advice and information and co-ordinates the efforts of the Small Business Service (SBS), Chambers of Commerce, local authorities and Local Enterprise Agencies. Depending on the nature of your request, they will or should direct you to the appropriate body, for example for advice on training, the availability of funding and consultancy services, premises and even business opportunities. For details of your local Business Link, ring 0845 600 906.

WHO ARE THE SELF-EMPLOYED?

Research by the Institute of Employment Studies *(Self-Employment in the United Kingdom* by Nigel Meager) several years ago came up with some interesting conclusions:

☐ Men are more likely to be self-employed than women, though the number of self-employed females has been going up rapidly.

☐ More older people are self-employed, which may be a reflection of the fact that the self-employed do not have to retire.

☐ More married than single people are self-employed, which points to the importance of the spouse (possibly as unpaid help?) in self-employment.

☐ More highly qualified women than men are self-employed, which may be a reflection of the difficulties women continue to experience in getting to senior positions in a great many firms.

☐ Self-employed people work considerably longer hours than their counterparts in the employed sector.

According to the Family Resources Survey 1998/9 and 1999/2000, the age profile of the self-employed nationally was:

Age	All self-employed
16–24	3%
25–44	46%
45–64	46%
65 and over	5%

Average age (years) 45

The proportion of older self-employed people is rising as those whose retirement pensions fall below exepctations need to supplement their income.

WHAT SELF-EMPLOYED PEOPLE DO

As might be expected, self-employment is stronger in the service sector than in manufacturing. The arts, building trades and management services feature prominently. Over the past decade entry into self-employment has been disproportionately high in financial, business and personal services such as catering and cleaning.

This also points to the nature of the market for self-employment. It is mistaken romanticism to think that we can go back to a society of individual craftspeople without an unacceptable drop in our standard of living. But maybe, it has been argued, we should leave to machines what machines do best, and get human beings to cater to the individual taste, the quirky needs, the one-off problems and the sudden emergencies and breakdowns that machines cannot handle.

This is certainly where the opportunities for the self-employed lie, and one of the objects of this preamble is to make an important practical point. The game the giants play has its limitations, but do not take them on direct. If, for instance, you are a skilled cabinet-maker, do not get into mass-produced furniture: you simply will not be able to get your prices down far enough to make a living, nor will you be able to handle distribution on the scale that mass production implies. Do something the giants do not do, such as making things to individual specification. If you have always wanted to own a grocery shop, do not do the same thing as the supermarket round the corner. Bake your own bread or make your delicatessen stay open round the clock – do something you can do better or differently.

HOW WELL PREPARED ARE YOU?

Having a sound idea is only part of the story. How prepared you are to take it further depends on the extent of your experience;

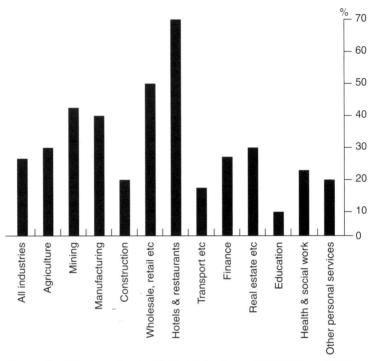

Source: Small Business Service SME statistics for the UK 2000 (June 2001)
(a) Excludes firms with no employees

Figure 1.1.1 *Percentage of firms with 1–249 employees in each sector*[a]

not that it is absolutely essential at the 'thinking about it' stage to have all-round direct experience of the sort of self-employment opportunity you want to exploit. But you have to be aware of what you know and do not know about it. You may be a manager who is also a keen gardener and you want to set up a market gardening business. In that case, you probably have a rather better knowledge of management essentials than that of a hypothetical competitor who is currently employed by a market gardener and wants to set up on his or her own. But on the finer points of growing techniques and hazards, and where to sell the products, your competitor is going to be much better equipped than you.

The first step, therefore, is to make a list of all the aspects you can think of about running the business: show it to someone who is already in the field to make sure nothing of importance has been missed out, and tick off the ones you think you can handle and consider how you are going to deal with the areas where your experience is limited. The best way may well be to gain practical first-hand experience. If you are thinking of buying a shop, for instance, working in one for a few weeks will teach you an amazing amount about the public's tastes – what sells and what does not – and you may save yourself hundreds of pounds in making the right buying decisions later on. As far as management principles are concerned, your library will provide you with lists for further reading.

You should also take advice from your local Business Link (Business Connect in Wales and Business Shop in Scotland) which is the prime source of information and support for local businesses. Information is free and counselling incurs only a modest charge. You should also ask about the business start-up courses that are being offered by business schools such as Cranfield School of Management, by LEAs and many universities (the Scottish Institute for Enterprise runs a course at Edinburgh University, for example). These courses are heavily subsidised by the government and are very good value for the modest fees they charge. By all accounts, attending such a course will dramatically increase your chances of small business success.

Background before starting business	Male %	Female %
In the same line of work	71	41
In a differnt line of work	26	42
A student or in full time education	2	3
Retired	1	2
Unemployed	–	2
Homemaker/housewife/house husband	–	9

Source: Women in Business – the barriers start to fall – Barclays Bank 2000

The Barclays Bank Small Business Survey Report for Quarter Three, 2002 notes that:

> Just over 911,400 new businesses started trading between July and September 2002, an increase of 14 per cent on the same period a year ago during which 80,500 companies opened their doors for the first time. This is the biggest percentage growth since the 17 per cent increase in start-up numbers in the first quarter of 1999, and the first increase in new business numbers for over a year.

The small-business boom is attracting publishers in droves and it is already possible to spend quite a lot of money on books of advice of varying quality. It is worth mentioning, therefore, that several of the clearing banks have got into the act and are producing free books and pamphlets, some of which are very good. Ask your bank for any such material.

THE IMPORTANCE OF PLANNING

If you are going to borrow money to get your firm off the ground, the lender (if he has any sense!) will want to know how you plan to use his money and if the operation you have in mind is going to give him an adequate return on his investment. This means that you must have a clear idea of how your business is going to develop, at least for the next year, where you see work coming from and whether you are going to have the future resources, human and financial, to handle it (see Chapter 2.3 on the importance of cash flow and financial forecasting).

Even if you do not need to borrow money, planning is vital. Landing a big contract or assignment for a new business is a heartening beginning, but well before work on it is completed you should be looking around for the next job. The completion dates you have given should take this into account, unless the amount of money you are going to get from it is so much that you will have plenty of time to look for more work after this first job is done. But that, too, is a matter of planning.

IS SELF-EMPLOYMENT RIGHT FOR YOU?

Let us leave aside Samuel Smiles-like homilies about having to be your own hardest taskmaster. We will take it for granted that you are not considering working for yourself as a soft option. But apart from the question of whether your health can stand the fairly demanding regime that full-time self-employment implies, there are also other questions you have to ask yourself about your aptitude – as opposed to a mere hankering – for going it alone. First of all, there are severely practical considerations: whether you have enough money or the means of raising it. And remember you will need money not only to finance your business or practice, but also for your own personal needs, including sickness and holiday periods.

Self-employment may mean a drop in your standard of living, possibly a permanent one, if things do not go as planned. Are you prepared for that? Is your family going to like it? Have you seriously considered the full price to be paid for independence? Is your wife or husband able and willing to lend a hand?

Insecurity, a necessary condition of self-employment, is not everyone's cup of tea. Neither are some of the implications of being your own boss. One of the most important of them is the ability to make decisions and if you very much dislike doing this, self-employment is probably not the right channel for your abilities. You are constantly going to be called on to make decisions, some of them rather trivial, where it does not matter greatly what you do decide so long as you decide *something*; but some of them will be fundamental policy decisions that could make or break your business.

You are also going to be called on to make decisions about people, and these are often the hardest of all. It is extremely difficult to sack someone with whom you have worked in the intimacy of a small office, but sooner or later that kind of situation will land in your lap. So another quality that is called for is toughness. This does not mean overbearing nastiness, but it does mean the readiness, for instance, to part company with a supplier, even if she is a personal friend, if her service starts to fall consistently below standard.

We have touched on the question of your aptitude for self-

11

employment as such, but there remains the matter of your aptitude for the sphere of activity you have chosen. A management consultant friend of mine uses a basic precept in advising companies on personnel problems: staff are best employed doing what they are best at. The same applies to self-employment and most people go into it with that in mind. The problem with self-employment, however, is that at least at the outset you cannot absolutely avoid all the aspects of the work, such as bookkeeping, that in a bigger organisation you might have delegated or passed on to another department because you yourself do not much enjoy doing them. What you have to do is to maximise the number of tasks you are good at and minimise the others. This may mean taking a partner to complement your skills or employing an outside agency to handle some things for you: selling, for instance, if you are good at making things but not so good at negotiating or dealing with people. That means less money for you, but at the risk of sounding moralistic, you are unlikely to succeed if making money is the only thing you have in mind and overrides considerations such as job satisfaction.

At the same time, the costs of doing anything in business must always be taken into account. For example, if you take a partner, is there going to be enough money coming in to make a living for both of you? Unless you constantly quantify your business decisions in this way, you are unlikely to stay in business very long. In fact, you should not even start on your career as a self-employed person without investigating very carefully whether there is a big and lasting enough demand for the product or service you are proposing to offer, and whether it can be sold at a competitive price that will enable you to earn a living after meeting all the expenses of running a business.

Another survey commissioned by Barclays Bank asked start-ups about the realities of running a small business and found that:

- ☐ 63 per cent of new-business owners agree that running a new business is stressful;
- ☐ 90 per cent do not regret setting up their business;
- ☐ new-small-business owners work an average of 51.5 hours a week and only take five days holiday in their first year.

_____

It is said, of course, that business is a gamble and that there comes the point where you must take the plunge. However, there are certain times when the odds are better than at others. For instance, the closing down of a factory with heavy lay-offs would affect local business conditions, though it may also create opportunities if the demand for what the factory has been producing still continues. You have to weigh up such factors in arriving at the conclusion that your chances of success are better than 50:50. Unless you are reasonably sure you can beat those odds with whatever it is you are setting out to do, you ought to think again or get further advice on how you can either improve your chances or minimise your financial risk.

CHANCES OF SUCCESS

If you have faced the issues we have touched on in the last paragraphs and feel confident about dealing with them, your chances of success in self-employment, whether full-time or part-time, are good. As for the opportunities, they are legion and later we examine what is involved in some areas. The list obviously cannot be comprehensive (though it should serve as a stimulus to looking in other directions as well) and neither can the coverage of basic management techniques in Part 2, Section 5. But one of the essentials of effective management is to pick out no more from any topic than you need to know to accomplish the task in hand. We hope that these chapters give you the kind of technical information that you will be concerned with at this early stage of your career as a self-employed person.

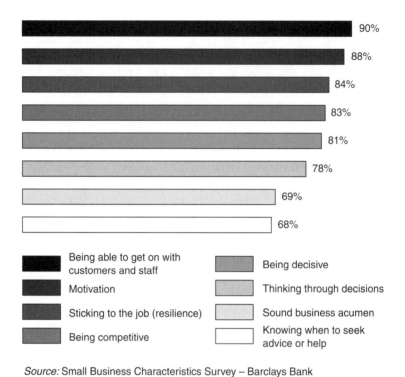

Source: Small Business Characteristics Survey – Barclays Bank

Figure 1.1.2 *What do you consider to be the main strengths in helping you run your business?*

Checklist: going it alone

1. Can you measure the demand for your product or service in terms of money?
2. Who are your competitors and what can you offer that they cannot?
3. Is the market local or national and how can you reach it? Can you measure the cost of doing so in financial terms?
4. How much capital do you have and how easy is it to realise?
5. How much money do you need for start-up costs and if it is more than your capital, how can you make up the difference?
6. How long is it likely to be before your income meets your outgoings and how do you propose to manage until then?
7. Do you have any established contacts who can give you business?
8. Is your proposed activity a one-off opportunity or a line for which there is a continuing demand?
9. What aspects of your proposed activity do you have first-hand experience in and how do you propose to fill the gaps?
10. How good is your health?
11. What are you best at/worst at in your present job and how does this relate to your area of self-employment?
12. Is there any way you can combine your present job with self-employment for an experimental period while you see how it goes?
13. Have you made a realistic appraisal of your aptitude for going it alone, both generally and in the context of the line of work you have chosen?
14. Should you join up with someone else and, if so, is the net income you anticipate going to provide a livelihood for all the people involved?
15. Can you work from home or do you have to be in an office or other rented premises?

1.2 Starting a Business

Before you start talking to bank managers, solicitors, accountants or tax inspectors, you will have to start thinking about what sort of legal entity the business you are going to operate is to be. The kind of advice you seek from them will depend on this decision, and you have three choices. You can operate as a sole trader (ie a one-person business – it does not necessarily have to be a 'trade'), a partnership, or as a private limited company. Let us see what each of these options implies.

SOLE TRADER

There is nothing – or at least very little – to stop you from starting a business under your own name, operating from a back room of your own house.* But if the place you live in is owned by someone else, you should get the landlord's permission. If the business you are starting in your home is one that involves a change of use of the premises, you will have to get planning permission from the local authority's planning officer. In that case you may also find that you are re-rated on a commercial basis. If you own your house, you should also check that there are no restrictive covenants in the deeds governing its use. On the whole, a business conducted unobtrusively from a private residence is unlikely to attract attention from the local authority but, to be perfectly safe, it is as well to have a word with the authority's planning

---

*If your business is likely to disturb neighbours or cause a nuisance (noise, smells, clients taking up parking space) or if it necessitates your building an extension, converting an attic, etc, you must apply for planning permission. Your property may then be given a higher, commercial rateable value.

department since any change of use, even of part of your residence, requires planning permission.

The next step is to inform your local tax inspector or to get your accountant to do so (see Chapter 1.4 on choosing professional advisers). This is always advisable if the nature of your earnings is changing and imperative if you are moving from employee to full-time self-employed status, because it changes the basis on which you pay tax. The inspector will give you some indication of allowable business expenses to be set off against your earnings for tax purposes. These will not include entertainment of potential customers but will cover items 'wholly and exclusively incurred for the purposes of business'. These are spelt out in more detail in Chapter 3.4. Some things, of course, are used partly for private and partly for business purposes – your car or your telephone, for instance. In these cases only that proportion of expenditure that can definitely be attributed to business use is chargeable against tax. Careful records of such use must, therefore, be kept, and its extent must also be credible. If you are not exporting anything in the way of a product or service, you may be unable to convince the inspector that a weekend in Paris was in the course of business! But if you are, he is unlikely to quibble about a modest hotel bill.

The principal cautionary point to bear in mind about operating as a sole trader is that you are personally liable for the debts of your business. If you go bankrupt your creditors are entitled to seize and sell your *personal* possessions, not just equipment, cars and other items directly related to your business.

PARTNERSHIPS

Most of the above points are also true if you are setting up in partnership with other people. Once again, there are very few restrictions against setting up in partnership with someone to carry on a business, but because all the members of a partnership are personally liable for its debts, even if these are incurred by a piece of mismanagement by one partner which was not known to his colleagues, the choice of partners is a step that requires very careful thought. So should you have a partner at all? Certainly it is not advisable to do so just for the sake of having company, because unless the partner can really contribute something to the business, you are giving away a part of what could in time be a very valuable asset to little purpose. A partner should be able to make an important contribution to running the business in an area which you are unable to take care of. He may have some range of specialised expertise that is vital to the business; or he may have a range of contacts to bring in work; or the work may be of such a nature that the executive tasks and decisions cannot be handled by one person. He may even be a 'sleeping partner' who is doing little else apart from putting up some money in return for a share of the eventual profits.

But whatever the reason may be for establishing a partnership as opposed to going it alone and owning the whole business, you should be sure that your partner (of course, there may be more than one, but for the sake of simplicity we will assume that only one person is involved) is someone you know well in a business, not just a social, capacity. Because of this, before formally establishing a partnership it may be advisable to tackle, as an informal joint venture, one or two jobs with the person you are thinking of setting up with, carrying at the end of the day an agreed share of the costs and profits. That way you will learn about each other's strengths and weaknesses, and indeed whether you can work together harmoniously at all. It may turn out, for instance, that your prospective partner's expertise or contacts, while useful, do not justify giving him a share of the business and that in fact a consultancy fee is the right way of remunerating him.

Even if all goes well and you find that you can cooperate, it is vital that a formal partnership agreement should be drawn up by a solicitor. This is true even of husband-and-wife partnerships. The agreement should cover such points as the following:

1. Who is responsible for what aspects of the operation (eg production, marketing)?
2. What constitutes a policy decision (eg whether or not to take on a contract) and how is it taken? By a majority vote, if there is an uneven number of partners? By the partner

concerned with that aspect of things? Only if all partners agree?

3. How are the profits to be divided? According to the amount of capital put in? According to the amount of work done by each partner? Over the whole business done by the partnership over a year? On a job-by-job basis? How much money can be drawn, on what basis, and how often in the way of remuneration?

4. What items, such as cars, not exclusively used for business can be charged to the partnership? And is there any limitation to the amount of money involved?

5. If one of the partners retires or withdraws, how is his share of the business to be valued?

6. If work is done in office hours, outside the framework of the partnership, to whom does the income accrue?

7. What arbitration arrangements are there, in case of irreconcilable differences?

8. If one of the partners dies, what provisions should the other make for his dependants?

There are obviously many kinds of eventualities that have to be provided for, depending on the kind of business that is going to be carried on. Some professional partnerships, for instance, may consist of little more than an agreement to pool office expenses such as the services of typists and telephonists, with partners drawing their own fees quite independently of each other. The best way to prepare the ground for a solicitor to draw up an agreement is for each partner to make a list of possible points of dispute and to leave it to the legal adviser to produce a form of words to cover these and any other points he may come up with.

PRIVATE LIMITED COMPANIES

Legislation over the years before the appointment of Gordon Brown as Chancellor of the Exchequer has made it less attractive to start out trading as a limited company unless you are in a form of business that might leave you at risk as a debtor – as might be the case, for instance, if you were a graphic designer commissioning processing on behalf of a client. The reason for this is that, in law, a limited company has an identity distinct from that of the shareholders who are its owners. Consequently, if a limited company goes bankrupt, the claims of the creditors are limited to the assets of the company. This includes any capital issued to shareholders which they have *either paid for in full or in part*. We shall return to the question of share capital in a moment, but the principle at work here is that when shares are issued, the shareholders need not necessarily pay for them in full, though they have a legal obligation to do so if the company goes bankrupt. Shareholders are not, however, liable as individuals, and their private assets outside the company may not be touched unless their company has been trading fraudulently. On the other hand, if creditors ask for personal guarantees, directors of limited companies are not protected and *personal* assets to the amount of the guarantee as well as business assets are at risk in the event of bankruptcy.

There is also another important area where the principle of limited liability does not apply. Company directors are liable, in law, for employees' National Insurance contributions. This is a personal liability which is being enforced by the Department for Work and Pensions in the same way as bank guarantees. There have even been cases of non-executive directors of insolvent companies being pursued for non-payment of NI contributions by companies with which they were involved, though the Social Security Act of 1975 states that the directors are only responsible in such circumstances if they 'knew or reasonably could have known' that these were not being paid.

Company directors can also be held guilty of 'wrongful trading', which essentially means trading while they know their company is insolvent. In that case they may be obliged to contribute personally to the compensating of creditors.

Under EU legislation, a limited company can be formed by a single shareholder who must be a director. It must also have a company secretary, who can be an outside person such as your solicitor or accountant. Apart from this, the main requirements relate to documentation. Like sole traders or partnerships, a limited company must prepare a set of accounts annually for the inspector of taxes and it must make an annual return to the Registrar of Companies, showing all the shareholders and directors, any changes of ownership that have taken place, a profit and loss account over the year and a balance sheet.

Apart from the more exacting requirements regarding documentation, a significant disadvantage of setting up a limited company as compared to a partnership or sole trader is that sole traders and partnerships can set off any losses they incur in the first four years' trading retrospectively against the owners' income tax on earnings in the three preceding years. This may enable you to recover tax already paid in earlier years of ordinary employment. This concession does not, however, apply to investment in your own limited company, or to investments made in such a company by those closely connected with the shareholders. If it makes losses, those losses can only be set off against the *company's* corporation tax in other years when it makes a profit. If it fails altogether, then the loss of your investment is a *capital* loss which can only be set off against other capital gains you make – not against other earned income. Therefore, if the nature of your business is a service which does not involve exposure to liabilities that you need to protect – for instance, if you are a consultant, rather than a shopkeeper or a manufacturer incurring liabilities to suppliers – there may be a distinct advantage in opting for partnership or sole trader status rather than establishing a limited company; but see the recommendation to seek professional advice below. There may, for instance, be factors other than trading risks which need to be protected by limited liability. Highly profitable ventures can also benefit from limited company status because their profits are taxed at corporation tax rates rather than the much higher personal income tax ones. As your start-up business prospers you should review the alternative taxation status of a limited company to self-employment at regular intervals.

The cost of forming a company, including the capital duty which is based on the issued capital (we shall come to the distinction between this and nominal capital shortly), is likely to be around £250, depending on what method you use to go about it. The cheapest way is to buy a ready-made ('off the shelf') company from one of the registration agents who advertise their services in specialist financial journals. Such a company will not actually have been trading, but will be properly registered by the agents. All that has to be done is for the existing 'shareholders' (who are probably the agent's nominees) to resign and for the purchasers to become the new shareholders and to appoint directors. Full details of the procedures are available from Companies House.

Alternatively you can start your own company from scratch, but whichever course you choose, professional advice is vital at this stage. The technicalities are trickier than they sound, though simple enough to those versed in such transactions.

Ultimately, the decision on whether or not to form a limited company depends on your long-term objectives. If you are planning to become an entrepreneur, and to build a business for significant capital growth, a limited company structure and the creation of shares has to be considered at an early stage. It will, for instance, be essential if you want to raise serious amounts of money from outside investors, as we will show in Chapter 2.1. But if you are thinking about what is essentially a salaried income replacement venture, a sole trader or partnership structure would usually be the better and simpler option.

REGISTRATION OF BUSINESS NAMES

One problem you may encounter with an 'off the shelf' company is when it has a name that does not relate meaningfully to the activity you are proposing to carry on. In that case you can change the company name by contacting the Companies Registrations Office on 029 2038 0801 and they will guide you through the procedure, which is straightforward and costs around £50. You can also contact the new companies section on the same number, and register a new company. This again is a straightforward procedure and costs £10. You can also write to the Registrar of Companies for information (The Registrar of Companies, Companies House, Crown Way, Cardiff CF14 3UZ). If your inquiry is about registering a new company, address it to The Registrar of Companies – New Companies Section.

The other option is to trade under a name which is different from the company's official one; for instance, your company may be called 'Period Investments Ltd', but you trade as 'Regency Antiques'. Until 1982 you had to register your business name with the Registrar of Business Names, but that office has since been abolished. Instead, if you trade under any name other than your own – in the case of a sole trader or partnership – or that of the name of the company carrying on the business in the case of a company, you have to disclose the name of the owner or owners and, for each owner, a business or other address within the UK.

The rules of disclosure are quite far-reaching and failure to comply with them is a criminal offence. You must show the information about owners and their addresses on all business letters, written orders for the supply of goods or services, invoices and receipts issued in the course of business and written demands for payment of business debts. Furthermore, you have to display this information prominently and readably in any premises where the business is carried on and to which customers and suppliers have access.

It is worth giving a good deal of thought to the choice of a business name. Clever names are all very well, but if they do not clearly establish the nature of the business you are in, prospective customers leafing through a telephone or business directory may have trouble in finding you; or, if they do find you, they may not readily match your name to their needs. For instance, if you are a furniture repairer, it is far better to describe yourself as such in your business name than to call yourself something like 'Chippendale Restorations'. However, if your name already has a big reputation in some specialised sector, stick with it.

Legislation makes it possible to protect a trading name by registering it with the Trade Marks Registry at the Patent Office. The advantage of that is that you can prevent other traders from using your name – or something very similar – and cashing in on your goodwill. You can also register a trade mark – the sign or logo that identifies your business on letterheads, packaging and so forth. The activities for which marks can be registered include service industries as well as manufacturing ones.

The rules governing the use of business names are like those for company names, except that the Registrar is less concerned about the fact that a similar trading name may already be in existence. Obviously, however, it is advisable in both cases to wait until the name you have put forward is accepted before having any stationery printed. There are, it should be said, certain words that the Registrar of Companies has proved likely to object to: those that could mislead the public by suggesting that an enterprise is larger or has a more prestigious status than circumstances indicate. Cases in point are the use of words such as Trust, University and Group. National adjectives ('British') are also unpopular. When you get to this stage the names of the proprietors (or, in the case of a limited company, the directors) have to be shown not only on letterheads, but also on catalogues and trade literature.

Limited companies, in addition, have to show their registration number and the address of their registered office on such stationery. This address may not necessarily be the same as the one at which business is normally transacted. Some firms use their accountant's or solicitor's premises as their registered office. You will probably see quite a number of registration certificates hanging in their office (they are required by law to be so displayed) when you go there. This is because it is to that address that all legal and official documents are sent. If you have placed complete responsibility for dealing with such matters in the hands of professional advisers, it is obviously convenient that the related correspondence should also be directed there. Bear in mind, though, that this does involve a certain loss of control on your part. Unless you see these documents yourself, you will have no idea, for instance, whether the important ones are being handled with due despatch.

LIMITED COMPANY DOCUMENTS

When you set up a limited company, your solicitor or accountant will be involved in drafting certain papers and documents which govern its structure and the way it is to be run. When this process has been completed you will receive copies of the company's Memorandum and Articles of Association, some share transfer

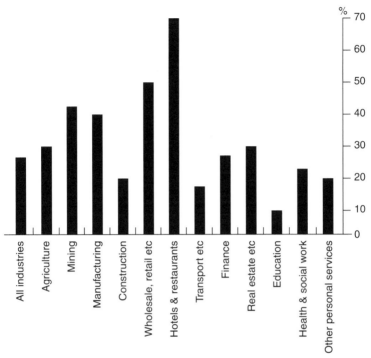

Source: Small Business Service SME statistics for the UK 2000 (June 2001)
(a) Excludes firms with no employees

Figure 1.1.1 *Percentage of firms with 1–249 employees in each sector*[a]

not that it is absolutely essential at the 'thinking about it' stage to have all-round direct experience of the sort of self-employment opportunity you want to exploit. But you have to be aware of what you know and do not know about it. You may be a manager who is also a keen gardener and you want to set up a market gardening business. In that case, you probably have a rather better knowledge of management essentials than that of a hypothetical competitor who is currently employed by a market gardener and wants to set up on his or her own. But on the finer points of growing techniques and hazards, and where to sell the shareholders have put into the company or are prepared to accept liability for. Therefore, in raising money from a bank or finance house, the manager there will look closely at the issued share capital. To the extent that he is not satisfied that the liability for the amount he is being asked to put up is adequately backed by issued share capital, he is likely to ask the shareholders to guarantee a loan or overdraft with their own personal assets – for instance, by depositing shares they privately hold in a public quoted company or unit trust – as security. In the case of a new company without a track record this would, in fact, be the usual procedure.

The nominal share capital of a new small-scale business is usually £100. It can be increased later, as business grows, on application to the Registrar of Companies. The point of such a move would be to increase the *issued* share capital, for instance if a new shareholder were to put money into the company. But, once again, it should be borne in mind that if the issued share capital was increased from £100 to £1,000, and a backer were to buy £900-worth of shares at par value, the original shareholders would only own one-tenth of the business; the fact that they got the whole thing going is quite beside the point.

One last question about issued share capital which sometimes puzzles people: must you actually hand over money for the shares when you start your own company, as is the case when you buy shares on the stock market, and what happens to it? The answer is yes. You pay it into the company's bank account because, remember, it has a separate legal identity from the shareholders who own it. However, you need not pay for your shares in full. You can, for instance, pay 50p per share for a hundred £1 shares. The balance of £50 represents your liability if the company goes bankrupt, and you actually have to hand over the money only if that happens or if a majority at a shareholders' meeting requires you to do so. The fact that you have not paid in full for shares issued to you does not, however, diminish your entitlement to share in the profits, these being distributed as dividends according to the proportion of share capital issued. The same applies to outside shareholders, so if you are raising money by selling shares to people outside the firm, you should normally ensure that they pay in full for any capital that is issued to them.

_____

The Articles of Association

These are coupled together with the Memorandum, and set out the rules under which the company is run. They govern matters such as issue of the share capital, appointment and powers of directors and proceedings at general meetings. As in the case of the Memorandum, the clauses are largely standard ones, but those relating to the issue of shares should be read carefully. It is most important that there should be a proviso under which any new shares that are issued should be offered first of all to the existing shareholders in the proportion in which they already hold shares. This is particularly so when three or more shareholders are involved, or when you are buying into a company; otherwise the other shareholders can vote to water down your holding in the company whenever they see fit by issuing further shares. For the same reason, there should be a clause under which any shareholder who wants to transfer shares should offer them first of all to the existing shareholders. The Articles of Association also state how the value of the shares is to be determined, the point here being that if the company is successful and makes large profits, the true value of the shares will be much greater than their par value of £1, 50p or whatever. It should be noted, though, that the market valuation of the shares does not increase the liability of shareholders accordingly. In other words, if your £1 par shares are actually valued at, say, £50, your liability still remains at £1.

Table A of the Companies Act of 1948, which can be purchased at any Stationery Office branch, sets out a specimen Memorandum and Articles.

The minute book

Company law requires that a record be kept of the proceedings at both shareholders' and directors' meetings. These proceedings are recorded in the minute book, which is held at the company's registered office. Decisions made at company meetings are signed by the Chair and are legally binding on the directors if they are agreed by a majority. Therefore, any points of procedure that are not covered by the Memorandum and Articles of Association can be written into the minutes and have the force of law, provided that they do not conflict with the former two documents. Thus, the various responsibilities of the directors can be defined and minuted at the first company meeting; so can important matters such as who signs the cheques. It is generally a good idea for these to carry two signatures to be valid.

The common seal

This used to be a stamp affixed with the authority of the directors, but nowadays documents can be executed by the signatures of two directors. That has the same legal effect as the seal used to have, but it may still be used in some special circumstances.

The Certificate of Incorporation

When the wording of the Memorandum and Articles of Association has been agreed and the names of the directors and the size of the nominal capital have been settled, your professional adviser will send the documents concerned to the Registrar of Companies. He will issue a Certificate of Incorporation which is, as it were, the birth certificate of your company.

COMPANY DIRECTORS

When your Certificate of Incorporation arrives, you and your fellow shareholders are the owners of a fully fledged private limited company. You will almost certainly also be the directors. This title in fact means very little. A director is merely an employee of the company, who is entrusted by the shareholders with the running of it. He need not himself be a shareholder at all, and he can be removed by a vote of the shareholders which, since each share normally carries one vote, is a good reason for not losing control of your company by issuing a majority shareholding to outsiders.

Another good reason is that since the ownership of the company is in proportion to the issued share capital, so also is the allocation of profits, when you come to make them. If you let control pass to an outsider for the sake of raising a few hundred pounds now – there are other means of raising capital than the sale of shares, as we shall show in Chapter 2.1 – you will have had all the problems of getting things going, while only receiving a small part of the rewards. Remember, furthermore, that without control you are only an employee, even if you are called 'managing director'.

Checklist: setting up in business

Sole trader
1. Do you need planning permission to operate from your own home?
2. Does your lease allow you to carry on a trade from the premises you intend to use?
3. If you own the premises, whether or not they are your home as well, are there any restrictive covenants which might prevent you from using them for the purpose intended?
4. Have you notified your tax inspector that the nature of your earnings is changing?
5. Are you aware of the implications of being a sole trader if your business fails?
6. Have you taken steps to register a business name?

Partnerships
1. Points 1 to 6 above also apply to partnerships. Have you taken care of them?
2. How well do you know your partners – personally and as people to work with?
3. If you do not know them well, what evidence do you have of their personal and business qualities?
4. What skills, contacts or other assets (such as capital) can they bring into the business?
5. Have you asked your solicitor to draw up a deed of partnership and does it cover all the eventualities you can think of?
6. Have you talked to anybody who is in, or has tried, partnership in the same line of business, to see what the snags are?

Private limited companies
 1. Do you have the requisite shareholders?
 2. Do you have a competent company secretary, who can carry out the legal duties required under the Companies Acts?
 3. Are you yourself reasonably conversant with those duties?
 4. Have you registered, if this is required, a company name and a business name?
 5. Has permission been granted to use the names chosen?
 6. Have the necessary documents been deposited with the Registrar of Companies? (Memorandum and Articles of Association, a statutory declaration of compliance with registration requirements, a statement of nominal share capital.)
 7. Have you read and understood the Memorandum and Articles? Do they enable you to carry out all present and any possible future objects for which the company is formed?
 8. Do your stationery, catalogues, letterheads, etc show all the details required by the Companies Acts?
 9. Is the Registration Certificate displayed in the company's registered office, as required by law?
 10. Do you understand the wide range of benefits – company cars, other business expenses, limited liability, self-administered pension schemes, etc – enjoyed by limited companies?
 11. Clauses 1 to 3 of the 'Sole trader' checklist may also apply to you. If so, have you taken care of them?

1.3 Self-employment Alternatives

Self-employment has traditionally taken the form of running a full-time business as either a limited company, partnership or sole trader as described in the last chapter. However, recent years have witnessed the rise in alternative forms of work. Not only can the number of hours that you work be a question of choice, but also who you supply and what form that relationship takes has become more flexible. For example, the rise in contract work has also opened up opportunities for the self-employed to work in a freelance capacity and this is the choice of a growing number of people. At the other end of the spectrum, taking up a franchise or participating in a management buy-out can provide opportunities for self-employment in national organisations with high turnovers. This chapter will examine the pros and cons of each of these opportunities.

PART-TIME WORK

Part-time work has become a significant part of the UK economy. Official figures show that one-third of the workforce is employed on this basis.

The range of ways in which people work part-time is also wide.

☐ 'Portfolio' part-time work – doing part-time jobs for several different employers on a regular basis.

In business for yourself, not by yourself!

If you own a camera and regularly invest in films and developing, yet still have photos in drawers and envelopes, or fading and yellowing in unsafe albums, read on! And if you've already discovered the joy of making memory albums, you'll love teaching others to do the same!

Creative Memories is a member of the Direct Selling Association. Founded in 1987, we manufacture and sell photo-safe albums and album-making supplies, and there are now more than 75,000 Creative Memories Consultants worldwide. As a self-employed Consultant, you'd be helping people to protect, preserve and present their photos and memories in a meaningful way: holding Classes and Workshops, and teaching the importance of, and techniques for, organising, documenting and preserving photographs and memorabilia in photo-safe safe, scrapbook-style photo albums.

It's the perfect business for everyone who wishes to work from home; choose the hours they work; be their own boss; and of course, be affiliated with a reputable, established company. It's also a worthwhile occupation with a very large potential market – most UK households have a camera, and you'll be helping people to secure their photographic investment. You'll earn money through sales (30%) and bonus schemes; win incentive prizes and trips; and you can also significantly increase your income if you choose to build and manage a local team.

You don't need to be a qualified teacher or creative genius – just someone who likes people and enjoys sharing something positive. You bring the enthusiasm, we'll provide the training! Call Creative Memories on **(01635) 294700** for more information on starting your own Creative Memories business.

□ Working part-time for a single employer – for instance, the human resource strategy director for the employment agency, Reed Executive, works there only three days a week.

□ Doing a part-time job as a spare-time activity, usually to earn extra money. Sometimes this takes the form of extending the job you do for your employer into private work in your spare time – a matter we will cover in a little more detail shortly.

□ Casual work – occasionally taking on work to help out a friend or to augment one's income.

The Inland Revenue suspects that a significant part of the black economy, through which some £40 billion a year is lost to the Exchequer, flourishes through casual and spare-time work. Anecdotal evidence suggests they are probably right. A great many tradespeople express a strong preference to be paid in cash by private customers. Such payments are extremely difficult for tax inspectors to trace.

It is likely, however, that people who fail to declare their income from part-time work are more concerned to conceal their activities from the Department for Work and Pensions than from the Inland Revenue. It is very easy to cease to be eligible for unemployment benefit by earning income of more than the basic unemployment benefit for any given six-day period. If this source of earned income does not continue and you wish to sign on again, there can be considerable delays before you receive unemployment benefit. There is a strong temptation, therefore, if you do something that brings in a few pounds a week while you are unemployed, not to declare it.

The government recognises the fact that income from a new business is usually less than the dole and the Business Start-Up scheme helps to bridge the gap.

TAX ADVANTAGES OF PART-TIME EMPLOYMENT

If you are married with another source of income, not declaring your earnings from part-time work might be a very unwise move – apart from being illegal. In the first place it is usually unlikely that you would have to pay tax on it at all because of the single person's earned income allowance of £4,615. This means that the first £4,535 of everyone's earnings is free of tax; so if you can arrange for your spouse to earn that amount of money from your source of extra income, you will not pay any tax on it – assuming he or she does not already have a job. Remember, it is the profit that is taxed, not the total earnings. If you cannot get that figure close to £4,385 by setting off against gross earnings all the allowances described in Chapter 3.4, then you are either doing so well as to make it worth considering turning your spare-time occupation into a full-time activity, or you should get an accountant, or you should change the accountant you have. However, you do have to prove, to the satisfaction of the tax inspector, that your spouse really is working in the business – taking messages, typing invoices, bookkeeping, or whatever. Holding the fort by looking after the kids and doing the shopping so that you can get on with it does not count.

All this is reinforced by the fact that even if you do not pay tax on them, there are definite advantages in earnings that are taxed under Schedule D. You will be able to claim allowances on services (gas, electricity and water) for the use of part of your house, plus a proportion of your bill for the telephone, stamps and stationery – whatever, in fact, can be shown to be reasonably related to the nature of the activity you are carrying on. Small is beautiful, provided you declare it.

PLANNING AND OTHER PERMISSIONS; INSURANCE

Strictly speaking, if you carry on a business from home you have to apply for planning permission, as indicated in Chapter 1.2. In practice, very few people bother when it comes to part-time work, though if what you are intending to do creates a noise, a nuisance or a smell (and some crafts and home repair activities do some or all of these things even when carried on in quite a small way) you should inform the local authority of your intentions. Complaints

Thinking of earning extra cash?
We're looking for new consultants

The Body Shop at Home is one of the most innovative and fastest-growing home shopping enterprises in the UK with over 3,000 consultants working on a self-employed basis. For many of them, joining **The Body Shop at Home** has been a turning point in their lives. Over 90% of consultants are women returning to work part-time, fitting in around families or full time work. Whether returning to work, enjoying a rewarding second job, or simply having fun, consultants find **The Body Shop at Home** offers an empowering business opportunity and a chance to enhance their self-esteem.

Joining **The Body Shop at Home**, you'll be surprised at how much you can earn with our fantastic team of consultants. With full support from business leaders, a well-known reputable company, an attractive career plan offering real opportunity for substantial incomes and a free training programme, the world is your oyster! Our most successful consultants run local teams of up to 220 and earn around £40,000 annually.

In the last three years, over 2,532,038 customers have shared the fun of a The Body Shop at Home party, putting their feet up and being pampered with some of the best-loved hair and body products in the UK. Our new **Host Reward programme** offers more choice when selecting rewards. Hosts receive a free makeover (or other treatment), choice of free products to the value of £16 and a selection of products at half price depending on party sales.

Find out more about becoming a **The Body Shop at Home** Consultant, or experience a **The Body Shop** party; simply telephone **08459 05 06 07** or visit our web-site **www.the-body-shop.com**

Go on pick up the phone you have nothing to lose and who knows what you could gain!

JOIN US

THERE'S ALWAYS ROOM FOR ONE MORE

ANYONE CAN BE A THE BODY SHOP AT HOME CONSULTANT
GREAT FOR MEETING PEOPLE AND HAVING FUN
FANTASTIC OPPORTUNITY TO EARN EXTRA MONEY
FULL OR PART TIME OPPORTUNITIES
CALL NOW FOR DETAILS: 08459 05 06 07

from neighbours not only cause embarrassment but can also result in your being required to find proper premises, the cost of which may invalidate your whole idea. Applying for planning permission will highlight such potential problems, and forewarned is forearmed. By the same token, if planning permission has been granted you will be able to face most complaints with equanimity.

If you are doing anything with food – making pâtés for your local delicatessen, for instance – you should inform the environmental health inspector. Here again, very few people bother and, in fact, the health officials are more concerned with commercial kitchens than domestic ones, which are generally cleaner; on the other hand, you could be liable for prosecution if it turns out, for instance, that the cause of someone being made ill by your pâté was a breach of the health regulations.

One important precaution you should not neglect if you are planning to work from home, whatever that work is, is to tell your insurance company. This is because your normal house and contents policy covers domestic use only and if you change the circumstances without telling the insurers they could fail to pay you in the event of a claim – and would probably do so if the loss was caused by the undeclared activity. Additional insurance cover will not normally cost you much, which is often more than could be said for any loss that occurs.

ASSESSING THE MARKET

From the point of view of anyone contemplating full-time self-employment, the principal advantage of part-time work is not really that it is a source of extra income, however valuable an incidental that may be, but that it serves as a trial run for the real thing. Opinions may differ as to what the prime factors here are in order of priority, but few would disagree that the most important thing is to assess whether there is a market for the goods or services you are proposing to offer, at a price that will bring you a worthwhile profit. Working part-time at something will give you an idea whether the demand and the competition will enable you to do that.

For instance, if working 12 hours a week, evenings and weekends, produces a gross £100 a week – £4,800 a year, allowing for four weeks' holiday – and your present income is, say, £22,000, there is a marginal case for considering full-time self-employment. By working 48 hours a week you could, on that evidence, gross about £19,000 in a 48-week year. Of course, it would depend on what your costs were, but some of the fixed ones – tools, for instance – would not change if you expanded your activities. If there was evidence of a very strong demand, you might even consider raising your prices, especially if the experience you have gained about the market indicates that you are appreciably cheaper than the competition. Alternatively, you might discover that by making one or two modifications you could either charge more than the competition or create a stronger demand for your original concept. It is much easier to make these adaptations to market conditions while still operating at a modest level and with a main income from another source.

OBJECTIVES

Whether the person in a £22,000-a-year secure job throws her hand in for £19,000-worth of insecurity depends not only on financial factors but on personal objectives. Here again, working part-time before making the commitment to full-time self-employment will help you to shape your thinking about what those objectives are and what they are worth to you. If independence is the overriding factor, you might feel that even a sizeable financial sacrifice is worth making. On the other hand, if money is the main objective and you are secure in your main job, then clearly, in the instance we have given you, you are much better off earning an extra £4,800 a year from your part-time job, plus £22,000 a year from your main one, than giving up the latter altogether – unless you could see a way of doing better than £4,800 _pro rata_ over a 48-hour week.

Another objective that could be tried out is whether you can work with an intended partner. Some very successful businesses are run by people who have little in common except a respect for each other's abilities, but it is usually difficult to test such

39

You can make a difference...

"I believe that individuals can make a difference in society"
(Dalai Lama, 1992)

Did you know that about one fifth of adults in the UK are obese?[1] Even more worrying than this startling statistic is the fact that the proportion is much worse than previous estimates from 1980, despite government advice to eat more healthily and to take more exercise. A person is considered to be obese when their weight seriously endangers their health and the same report estimates that treating the effects of obesity costs over half a billion pounds, whilst overall economic costs could be well in excess of £2 billion – every year.

Whilst the conventional advice of 'moderate, healthy eating and more exercise' helps to prevent people from becoming more at risk, the evidence is that these measures alone will not have any significant impact on those who are already overweight or obese.

But there is another method of weight control which is already available – a formula food that has a number of advantages over other approaches. Each meal or serving is quality regulated and formulated to a specific calorie level, making it very convenient to use whilst offering complete nutritional assurance. Moreover, dieters chances of long-term success are much improved thanks to the support and advice from their individual weight management Counsellor.

One such option is the Cambridge Diet – a tried, tested and trusted range of programmes at various calorie levels that have worked consistently well since 1984. The provision of individual advice and support through a trained and accredited Counsellor gives Cambridge a unique advantage, and has certainly made a difference to millions of people.

Those who are currently overweight need someone to make a difference for them.

Wouldn't you like to make a difference?
Wouldn't you like to be a Cambridge Counsellor?

Call Freephone 0800 161412

---

[1] The National Audit Office Report 'Tackling Obesity in England' (Feb 2001), states that in 1998, one in five adults was obese, and that nearly two-thirds of men and half of women were overweight or obese.

Self-employed Opportunities with

Cambridge
HEALTH *plan*

A division of
Cambridge Manufacturing Co Ltd

The Cambridge Diet is a tried ... tested ... and trusted solution to weight loss

Within the United Kingdom, Cambridge is only available through independent Counsellors. These Counsellors receive training and support from the Company and are supported by literature and sales aids, medical information and regular product and news updates.

Cambridge Health Plan is now looking for suitable people to lead its expansion into new areas of the UK, including Scotland, Wales, Northern Ireland as well as many parts of England.

Features of the scheme include:
❖ training and support from Cambridge Health Plan
❖ flexible working hours
❖ earnings related to the hours and commitment YOU give

The role would ideally suit anyone who:
❖ is interested in people
❖ has a friendly and out-going manner
❖ is well-organised

Current Counsellors come from all walks of life: from teachers to nurses; lorry drivers to office managers; from 20 to 70-year olds; men and women

For further details and an Information Pack
Call FREEPHONE 0800 161412

Cambridge Health Plan is a division of Cambridge Manufacturing Co Ltd qualities unless you have actually worked closely with someone. Trying out a partnership arrangement on a part-time basis is a good way of doing this.

ASSESSING YOURSELF

There is also the question of assessing your own suitability because there is a big gap between pipe dreams of independence and the reality, even when it comes to working full-time at something you have previously enjoyed doing as a hobby. Apart from the fact that what is fun as a hobby can sometimes be quite another proposition done hour after hour and day after day, there is often a huge difference between amateur and professional standards. For instance, it may take you all day to turn out a widget – that mythical, all-purpose British unit of manufacture – whereas a professional can do it in a couple of hours. That is fine when you are doing it more or less for fun, but fatal if you are trying to earn a living, unless you are confident you can get to professional standards fairly quickly.

Whether you can actually do so usually depends on how good you are at working for very long hours, initially for not much money and spending a great deal of your 'spare time' on administration: keeping records, writing letters and preparing quotes. You will not know your capacities in this respect until you try, but working part-time will give you an inkling.

It will also give you some indication of your family's attitudes to your work. If you are working part-time on top of a full-time job, you are probably reasonably close to putting in the sort of hours that are needed to make a success of self-employment at least for an initial – and usually prolonged – period of time. In other words, your family will not see a great deal of you unless they are able and willing to pitch in as well. They may view this prospect with equanimity; on the other hand, workaholism can be as great a source of family tension as alcoholism. When working part-time, it is quite easy to cut down the hours you are putting in, or even to stop altogether. If your living depends on it, the case is altered completely.

FINANCIAL COMMITMENT

One of the advantages of part-time work is that you are keeping your overheads, or fixed costs, low. You can work from home instead of renting premises or offices. You can hire equipment instead of buying it. You may even be able to use facilities available at your place of work – photocopying, for instance – though to what extent that is a wise move depends on the attitude of your employer. Some take it as a sign of initiative, provided that it does not interfere with your regular job. Others hate it, in which case you will have to be very careful how you go about it, and at least account for everything you use. The point is, though, that for part-time work you will not have to 'tool up' expensively and, indeed, you should avoid irreversible financial commitments as much as possible. Do not, for instance, buy a van until you are sure you are going to get profitable use out of it, or unless you want one anyway. Do not, to take another case, buy a knitting machine – hire it and see whether you really can make knitting pay.

The principle can be extended to any given activity. You should never buy anything unless you have to and until you have established an ongoing need for it. This is so with full-time activities, and it is even more the case with part-time work, because by definition the number of hours you have in which to amortise the cost – to make a profit and get your money back – are far fewer.

OPPORTUNITIES

Extension of full-time employment

In the previous section we referred to the situation where someone is carrying on into evenings and weekends private work normally done for an employer in the daytime: typical examples might be repair and building work, some forms of design, and teaching extended into exam coaching. The great advantage of this type of work is that it can give you a direct access to the market. Everybody who walks through the door at your place of employment is a potential private customer, whereas in other forms of part-time work, finding the market is an important but difficult part of the total concept. Furthermore, private, part-time

In business for yourself, not by yourself!

If you own a camera and regularly invest in films and developing, yet still have photos in drawers and envelopes, or fading and yellowing in unsafe albums, read on! And if you've already discovered the joy of making memory albums, you'll love teaching others to do the same!

Creative Memories is a member of the Direct Selling Association. Founded in 1987, we manufacture and sell photo-safe albums and album-making supplies, and there are now more than 75,000 Creative Memories Consultants worldwide. As a self-employed Consultant, you'd be helping people to protect, preserve and present their photos and memories in a meaningful way: holding Classes and Workshops, and teaching the importance of, and techniques for, organising, documenting and preserving photographs and memorabilia in photo-safe safe, scrapbook-style photo albums.

It's the perfect business for everyone who wishes to work from home; choose the hours they work; be their own boss; and of course, be affiliated with a reputable, established company. It's also a worthwhile occupation with a very large potential market – most UK households have a camera, and you'll be helping people to secure their photographic investment. You'll earn money through sales (30%) and bonus schemes; win incentive prizes and trips; and you can also significantly increase your income if you choose to build and manage a local team.

You don't need to be a qualified teacher or creative genius – just someone who likes people and enjoys sharing something positive. You bring the enthusiasm, we'll provide the training! Call Creative Memories on **(01635) 294700** for more information on starting your own Creative Memories business.

Power Lunch

Let us show you how Creative Memories can provide you with a challenging career, excellent income and plenty of time for "power lunches".

With Creative Memories you can develop a financially rewarding, meaningful career by teaching others how to preserve their photos and their memories.

Creative Memories provides the finest in album-making products and professional training.

For more information, call Creative Memories on (01635) 294700 or log onto www.creativememories.co.uk

clients can later be turned into sources of work on a larger scale, either directly or as leads to other work. Even suppliers can be useful people to get to know, both in terms of establishing your credibility when it comes to asking for credit and in the matter of sorting out good and reliable suppliers from the many other varieties.

The principal disadvantage of this type of work is that it can lead to a conflict of interests. The temptation to steer work your way rather than towards your employer can be very strong. It need not be anything as blatant as buttonholing your employer's customers at the door. There are subtler ways of bending the rules. The best way to avoid such temptations is to develop your own clients and contacts as soon as possible.

Turning a hobby into a source of income

This is usually the most satisfying form of part-time work because people generally perform best at what they most enjoy doing. Furthermore, many people, especially the over-30s, find that they have gone or been pushed into careers that do not reflect their real interests or skills, or that they have simply developed new ones that they find more satisfying than what they do for a living. Practising crafts of various kinds is a case in point.

The trap here is the one that we have referred to earlier – that there is a world of difference between doing something for fun and working at it full-time. Professional craftspeople have years of experience which enable them to turn out work quickly and economically. They also know the market: who buys what, at which price; what sells and what does not. In the case of photography, to take another instance, the good amateur turned professional is competing in a field where contacts are all-important and where high standards of work depend not only on individual skill, but on having the latest equipment.

Learning a new skill

Sometimes people learn a new skill, perhaps at an evening class, which is capable of being turned to commercial use – particularly these days when the range of services available from shops and manufacturers has become increasingly scarce and expensive. Popular examples are picture framing and upholstery.

There are also non-manual skills which can be turned to good account, such as selling; quite a number of people are engaged in party plan or catalogue selling. The problem there, however, is that it is difficult to go into a higher, full-time gear to make a living from that type of work, because commissions are fixed percentages and, in the case of catalogue selling, quite small ones.

Reviving an unused skill

This is also very popular, especially with women thinking of returning to work. The most frequently cited example is typing, but, as it happens, this one neatly illustrates the importance of observing the laws of supply and demand in choosing even a part-time source of income. Because there are many women available for such work, the rates are not particularly good. The only way you can lift yourself into a higher bracket is by identifying a service which few other typists offer and for which there is also a demand: in a university town, for instance, there might be a call for someone who can type theses quickly and accurately. An exporter, to take another example, might have a demand for someone who can type accurately in another language.

The same supply-and-demand principle also applies to translating. There are many graduates around who can translate from one of the main European languages into English, but rather fewer who can do the more difficult, reverse kind of translation: from English into idiomatic French, German or Spanish. Even rarer, and therefore more marketable, is fluency in another language _plus_ a qualification in a specialist subject such as law or science.

USING AN EXISTING ASSET AS A SOURCE OF INCOME: ACCOMMODATION

By far the biggest asset that most people own is their house. When there is a need for more money, or as members of the family grow

With **Demarle**, cooking is a *pleasure!*

With Demarle you can develop a profitable hobby or a substantial income in a rewarding career.

The recent launch of Demarle Ltd in the UK creates an exciting new network marketing opportunity with a company boasting 25 years of success, including seven years of impressive growth in direct selling.

Demarle's product range has been built on two inventions by Guy Demarle that revolutionised bread and pastry making in France – the Silpat baking sheet and the Flexipan.

Unique

The finest professional cooks all around the world have used Flexipans for over 10 years, but it was only seven years ago that Demarle SA decided to sell its unique product into the domestic market. The unique features and benefits of these unusual looking, flexible, non-stick baking moulds and trays make them ideal products for direct selling. More quality cookware products have been added to the range, which now contains over 100 items.

The success of Demarle's direct selling business in France (currently 3,800 consultants generating a turnover of £11.7 million) led to its launch in Belgium in 2000, Germany in 2001, the UK in 2002 and the Netherlands in 2003. A powerful network marketing business plan has been developed, which enables anyone with a love of cookery and fine cuisine to develop a profitable hobby or a substantial income in a rewarding career.

Popular

Preparing and enjoying fine cuisine at home has become a popular pastime and a large part of home entertaining. It is also a growing industry where people are spending many pounds a year on kitchenware to indulge this passion.

In a Demarle cookery workshop the company's mission is to take the difficulty and the mystery out of gourmet cooking. By combining state-of-the-art cooking technology with the concepts and traditions of fine French cuisine, Demarle allows amateurs to cook like professionals.

up or move away, that asset can be a source of income: rooms can be let, the house can be subdivided into flats or even – ultimately – the whole place can be turned into a guest house. The advantage of these courses of action is that little skill or training is required to turn them into money-making activities. The disadvantage is that they are full of legal pitfalls which deter a great many people. The common option is to circumvent the law by moving into a cash only, black economy relationship with tenants, but by that token you also lose much legal protection that would be available if there was a dispute. By getting a tenancy agreement drawn up you can protect yourself to a large degree, especially if you are also the kind of student of human nature who can spot a potential troublemaker before she crosses your threshold.

The best kind of asset to have is a country house grand enough to attract paying sightseers rather than tenants. But in that case you would have an army of legal and financial advisers at your elbow and perhaps would not be reading a book like this!

Letting rooms

In recent years, and especially since the 1980 Housing Act, there have been many horror stories about the difficulty of getting rid of unwanted tenants, even, on occasion, when they have been well behind with the rent. For this reason it is very unwise to let rooms without having an agreement drawn up by a solicitor; even the Citizens' Advice Bureau staffed, in general, by people whose natural sympathies lie with the tenant, recommend this. It is usually unwise, incidentally, to have a room-letting agreement which runs much longer than on a month-to-month basis because, except in extreme circumstances, the courts are likely to take the view that an agreement will have to run its full course before being terminated.

The other piece of legislation to beware of is the Rent Act of 1977 which gives the tenant the right to go to a tribunal and ask for a 'reasonable' rent to be applied if he thinks you are asking too much. A register of reasonable rents is kept at your local authority's Rent Assessment Panel office, if you want to check what these are, but you will often find that these do not allow for subtle shades of amenity – the social difference between nearby streets, for instance.

The best way to get good tenants is to select them – not by race or sex, which is illegal – but by asking for references from their previous landlord.

If you let a room or part of your house and you have a mortgage, you should contact the mortgage lender to make sure you are not breaching your contract with them. Most lenders will not have a problem if your letting income falls within the 'rent a room' scheme. Under this scheme, you may be able to claim tax relief (£4,250) against the income from your tenant.

FREELANCING

There are obviously overlaps between working part-time and working as a freelance. A person contributing regular articles to journals and newspapers could be doing so part-time and still be described as a freelance. In general, though, a freelance is regarded as someone who is self-employed full-time, providing a service to a range of different principals as the demand occurs, or as she can persuade them to buy the service that is being offered.

Some occupations have a very high freelance content because of the unpredictability of the flow of work. The prime example is the world of films and television. Over a third of the members of BECTU (Broadcasting, Entertainment, Cinematograph and Theatre Union), the principal trade union in this sphere, are freelancers, employed by a variety of different companies for anything from a day to six months, according to the duration of a particular project. Performing artists, too, tend almost exclusively to be freelancers, even though they may have spells when they are attached to a particular orchestra or a repertory company.

In the media and even in certain parts of industry, the tendency to put work out to freelancers and other suppliers of _ad hoc_ labour is growing rapidly. When trading conditions are uncertain, employers are reluctant to commit themselves to taking on people full-time. It makes more sense to bring them in as and when they are needed or to commission them – even to the point of subcontracting whole jobs to them.

51

A personal message from Mr Motivator

"The decision you make today is the force that can change your life forever"

'All of us, no matter what our age, no matter what our financial situation, will have to make a life changing decision at some time. What you decide today will have a profound effect on your tomorrows.

Ask yourself the following questions:-

Would you like to be financially independent?

Would you like to spend more quality time with your family?

Would you like to achieve a better or improved state of health and wellbeing?

All of the above is achievable, I will show you how.

A few years ago I came across a company called Nature's Sunshine Products that offered me the chance to have another occupation that would enable me and my family to enjoy more of what life had to offer, without costing me anything more than my time.

I was promised greater security, more money coming in per month and some fun at the same time, together with a long term business that would continue, even though I may be retired to some remote Island. I had to say 'tell me more'.

I have now been with this company a number of years and all that was promised is coming to fruition. Now I'm giving you the chance to join my team and enjoy the same benefits. I will be able to offer you my personal guidance and I will be only a phone call away.'

Remember

'Don't wait for your ship to come in, swim out to it'.

For your information pack about this opportunity or to find out more about our products please call Mr Motivator's Team on
01952 671615

There are also many tasks in many firms which need to be done but where the in-house demand is neither large nor constant enough to justify the employment of a full-time member of staff. It is people in such occupations, which can range from manual jobs like that of the firm's carpenter to services like public relations, who often find themselves at risk when times get hard. Yet, operating as freelancers for their own firm, plus other clients, they often have a highly profitable new lease of working life.

HOW FREELANCERS FIND WORK

The circumstances just described bring out a number of points about freelance work. It is often very difficult, for instance, simply to decide to 'go freelance', as many redundant executives have found to their cost when they wanted to set up as consultants. You need to have contacts, reliable sources of work and a known track record in your chosen area. Many freelancers report, in fact, that their first client was their previous employer or someone whom they got to know through their former workplace.

Even so, freelance work is patchy and unpredictable. The elements of self-marketing and constant self-motivation are vital. Freelance management consultants, for instance, reckon to spend at least 40 per cent of their time hunting for work: identifying opportunities from reports in the business, trade or professional press, and following them up with letters, phone calls or proposals. The same pattern can be seen in other freelance occupations: photographers and entertainers check in with their agents; writers prepare material 'on spec' for book and magazine publishers. It is a fairly insecure life until you get established and clients start ringing you, rather than the other way round. Indeed, many freelancers are of the opinion that to make a success of it, you need at least one reliable source of regular work – someone who brings you in for one day a week, for instance.

CHARACTERISTICS OF FREELANCE WORK

The reason why a lot of practising freelancers recommend getting this kind of underlay is not purely financial. There are also psychological factors involved, especially for those who have previously worked alongside others. Freelancing is a lonely way to earn a living. With some kinds of job – writing for instance – you can spend weeks on end without seeing anyone.

It is also unpredictable. There can be long periods, particularly when you first start, when little or no work comes in and your bank balance sinks as low as your spirits. As a self-employed person, you cannot claim unemployment benefit either, even though no work is coming through. On the other hand, you still have to pay your National Insurance stamp.

Periods of inactivity may be broken up by spells when the workload is almost too much. Very few freelancers ever turn work away, though. Once you lose a potential customer – even though you may not need him at that juncture – he is very difficult to get back when circumstances change. If, however, you can't do the job because it coincides with something else, it is essential to say so rather than to make promises that cannot be kept. This applies to delivery dates as well.

COSTING AND PRICING

Broadly, the rules set out in Chapter 5.2 apply, but there are additional factors to consider. As we have said, you often have to spend a considerable amount of time just looking for work; it varies, obviously, according to your status and occupation. On the other hand, whether you can reflect this fact in full in your scale of charges depends on our old friends – supply and demand. As against that, you have the advantage, in the case of many types of freelance work, that you are working from home. Usually your equipment costs are low too, though that would not be true of photography. The employer, in engaging you, should consider that it is generally reckoned that the cost of having a person on the staff full-time is twice their annual salary, taking into account NI contributions, holidays, pensions and so forth.

INCOME TAX AND FREELANCE WORK

Freelancers are normally taxed under Schedule D. However, as we will point out at the end of Chapter 3.4, the Inland Revenue is challenging Schedule D status where a substantial amount of work is done for one particular employer, as that in effect constitutes a master-and-servant relationship. This is a particular danger when people work through an agency and are paid by the agency, not by the client.

FRANCHISING

The risky nature of freelancing might not be suitable for everyone. However, another form of self-employment that *is* regarded as providing reasonable security is running a franchise. The best-known UK franchises are Body Shop and McDonald's, though in fact quite a number of familiar high street shops, restaurant chains and a great many kinds of home and business services are operated as franchises. This means that the person operating the franchise – the franchisee – has bought from the franchisor the right to trade under an established name, rather than establishing his or her credentials from scratch.

That in itself can be a great advantage, but taking up a franchise goes further than that. The franchisee is buying a working business blueprint that has previously been tried, tested and debugged by the franchise owner – the franchisor – and by his other franchisees. With it he buys training, start-up support, an operating manual and a helpdesk for day-to-day problems, at least in the early stages. He also buys the exclusive right to operate that franchise in a given territory.

The format for operating the business is laid down very precisely, down to the stationery headings, the uniform you wear when on duty, the layout of your premises and how much you charge your customer for goods or services. The idea is that if you follow the format, you cannot fail because it has been tested and found to work. If you put in the hours, you will generate a predicted level of turnover and predicted net profit margins. These will enable you to recoup your initial investment – the start-up costs and the upfront fee you pay for the right to operate the franchise and to be trained in running it as a business – within two to three years.

The net margin is calculated to allow not only the usual over-heads, but also a royalty to the franchisor. That varies between 5 and 10 per cent, depending on whether or not the franchisee involved is buying goods from the franchisor on which the franchisor himself makes a profit as a supplier or wholesaler.

It sounds like a wonderful idea. Where's the catch? First of all let us say that franchising has proved itself to be a very good way of starting a business of your own. Failure rates are low and because of this the banks have been more ready to lend money to franchisees than for many other forms of small business, especially in the start-up phase. In fact the franchising depart-ment of your bank is the best place to start investigating a franchise proposition, because there are quite a number of snags to watch out for.

CHOOSING A FRANCHISE

One unscrupulous operator confessed to me in an expansive post-lunch mood, 'There's two born every minute – in case one of them dies.' There is very little legislation in the franchising field and there have been plenty of instances where franchisees have been induced into parting with their upfront fee and have seen very little in return for their money. The bank may not say outright that this or that franchise proposition should not be touched with a bargepole, but if several banks refuse to lend you money on it, don't go further. Either you are wrong for the business or the busi-ness is wrong for you. Or it is just plain wrong, full stop, probably because the pilot stage when the format is tested has not been carried out properly, or not at all, or because the upfront fee and/or royalties are regarded as too high or because the thing is simply known to be badly run.

Direct selling and network marketing are two ways of developing business opportunities from the comfort of your own home. Put simply, direct selling is the sale of a consumer product or service, person-to-person, away from a fixed retail location. It accounts for sales in excess of £1.6 billion every year in the UK[1]. Products are sold primarily through in-home product demonstrations, parties and one-on-one selling.

Network marketing extends this idea by inviting more direct salespeople to join a 'network' to build the business. In this case, income is generated at more than one level (also referred to as multi-level marketing or referral marketing).

Direct selling and network marketing provide a unique opportunity to effectively start and run your own company, while benefiting from the support of an established business. The product or service is already developed, and the company infrastructure and support systems are in place.

There are a number of reputable and successful businesses that have flourished using these techniques – from traditional favourites such as Tupperware and Avon through to newer alternative telecoms companies such as Telco Global and Telecom Plus.

The key to success for both these opportunities lies in your attitude to the products and services, company and opportunity you are representing. Don't consider backing a product you would not be proud to own or use yourself – it's all about believing in what you're selling. The most successful salespeople are very familiar with the products and services they are offering, and what the real world benefits are.

Here are a few hints and tips for making the most of direct selling or network marketing:

- Go with a reputable company – consider speaking to the company's existing agents
- Check the terms and conditions – is there a minimum you need to sell before you can reap the benefits?
- Find out about support – how much training does the company offer?
- Consider selling services – there's no initial outlay to build a portfolio of stock samples
- Meet new people – the more people you come into contact with, the quicker you will build a solid customer base and the more money you will make
- Set goals for yourself – when you're in sales you must be self-motivated

[1] Direct Selling Association UK

Are you earning
£4,000
a month?

Have you ever recommended a restaurant or film to someone? We all do it naturally.

"Well, by recommending a way of saving money on phone calls, you could be earning thousands each month. Teach others to do the same and you'll be earning even more! Some of our agents have earned £4,000 a month in just 6 months - and you can too!"

Earn full or part-time
No sales experience needed
Full training and ongoing support
Run your own business with Telco's backing
No stock to buy or catalogues to distribute

Angela Huntriss

Angela Huntriss
Telco Independent Agent

Start earning like Angela - call us FREE on
0800 594 5554

Saving people money has never been so rewarding!

telco | agent

There are also businesses that call themselves franchises but are really variants of pyramid selling, where you get paid for recruiting other members to a chain of people, each one selling stuff, often of very little intrinsic value, to the next link down. Strictly speaking, this form of trading is illegal, but there are ways around it which sail very close to the borders of the law without actually breaking it.

Even if you don't actually need the money, a check with the bank is worth making. It will cost you nothing and it could save you a great deal of money. Indeed, if the franchisor tries to pressurise you out of taking sensible precautions, walk away immediately.

In addition to the bank check, you should always ask to talk to existing franchisees, even of a reputable franchise, chosen by you at random, not ones nominated by the franchisor. Things can change. Ask whether they are achieving the income levels and profit margins forecast and how many hours a week it takes to do that; whether, given the chance, they would make the decision to take up that franchise again; and if there is anything they would like to change. That could be a negotiating point if and when you come to signing a contract.

A final check is to ask whether the franchisor is a member of the British Franchise Association (BFA). Not all of them are, but many of the good ones have membership. The BFA is a franchisor body but it lays down standards and conditions which also protect franchisees.

One of the problems in franchising is that not all good ideas work well everywhere. That is certainly true of franchises that have been a great success in other countries, notably the United States, but it is also true within the UK. In the 1980s there was a household-name health food franchise which did extremely well in the south-east of England, but turned out to be a terrible flop in the meat and two veg belt north of the Wash. A tremendous amount depends on the area, even within the same town.

Franchisors make great play with the notion of an 'exclusive territory' but it doesn't mean all that much. There is nothing to stop a franchisee from a different franchisor opening up a similar business in your exclusive territory, or indeed a similar, nonfranchised business doing this. Think how many fast-print shops and fast-food outlets there are around, for instance.

At the same time, there is no doubt that those who get into a good franchise at an early stage, before all the plum territories are assigned, can make a lot of money. Some of the early Body Shop franchisees are now very wealthy. It shows that franchising, format though it is, still calls for the exercise of some commercial judgement.

The average length of a franchise agreement is seven to ten years, but these days very few products or services hold their competitive advantage for as long as that. You need to be sure that the franchisor is sufficiently resourceful to keep coming up with new ideas and sufficiently resourced to develop them. In the recession of the 1990s it was noticed that some franchisees got into difficulties because the franchisors were themselves under pressure. They could not give the franchisees enough support.

Not everyone is temperamentally suited to being a franchisee. Though to a large extent it is your own business, you are still tied to the franchisor in regard to what you can and cannot do – for instance, you may be limited as to the range of services you can offer or the goods you stock. That condition may become very irksome if you think you see business opportunities that your contract prevents you from exploiting.

The franchise agreement is a long and complicated document which sets out what your obligations are to the franchisor, and vice versa, during the term of the contract. Only sign it after making sure that you understand it fully and that it neither omits nor adds anything different from that which you agreed or assumed verbally. In fact, you should also show it to a lawyer who knows about franchising. That may not necessarily be your usual lawyer. If he is not confident of his knowledge in this field ask him, or the bank, to recommend someone who is.

A fuller account of this topic is given in _Taking Up a Franchise: the Daily Telegraph Guide_ by Colin Barrow and Godfrey Golzen, also published annually by Kogan Page.

MANAGEMENT BUY-OUTS

Management buy-outs are at the more expensive end of the spectrum of self-employment opportunities discussed in this book, but they have become more common and, at the lower end of the cost range, are comparable to setting-up costs of franchises in the medium to upper price field: £100,000 to £250,000.

The opportunity for a buy-out occurs when the owners of a business decide to dispose of all or a part of it. That may give the existing management the chance to become bidders for it them-selves. Indeed, there have been cases where the entire workforce became bidders, with the existing management becoming their spearhead. A notable example some years ago was the manage-ment buy-out of the National Freight Corporation, which received a great deal of publicity when, on a subsequent flotation, large capital gains were made by those members of the workforce who had participated in the buy-out.

The NFC buy-out was a large one which occurred in conse-quence of a privatisation measure. More commonly, buy-out opportunities occur because the owners:

☐ want to sell out to raise cash;
☐ decide that the business is not a core activity;
☐ feel the business is not sufficiently profitable;
☐ feel the business needs investment which they are unable or unwilling to make.

Another cause can be the business going into receivership.

In recent years finance for buy-outs that look as though they stand a chance has been readily available from sources of venture capital, though the bidders are expected to shoulder a consider-able part of the risk. As with other kinds of business loan, the providers of finance expect to see a business plan. Where larger sums are required, it has to go into a lot of detail. Among the points to be covered are:

☐ descriptions of the assets and liabilities of the company;
☐ the nature and value of work in progress;
☐ detailed cash-flow projections;
☐ the background and qualifications of the buy-out team, which must include a good finance director.

However, there is another equally important set of conditions that have to be fulfilled. By law the owners have to satisfy their shareholders that the buy-out represents the best deal for them, though that need not necessarily mean that they are the ones that have come up with the best offer financially. But if that is not the case, they do have to demonstrate that a sale to them is the best solution, either because it is the quickest or because, if the buy-out participants left the company, its saleability would be diminished. The latter is often particularly true of service-based companies with few tangible assets.

Buy-out negotiations are complex and can be fairly protracted: four to six months is about the minimum. Good (and therefore expensive) legal and financial advice is essential and should be costed into the total financial requirements.

The question is, though, whether the owners should be approached with an offer or be asked to name a price. Some financial institutions like to have a clear idea from the start about how much money they are being asked to put up – in other words, they prefer the owners to name a price. On the other hand, a cash bid can sometimes surprise the owners into parting with the business for a modest price. This is where commercial judgement about how to structure the bid is called for.

It also requires a lot of preparation in assessing the value of what the buy-out team is acquiring. That should be clearly specified in the bid document; otherwise you may find that the owners are excluding a particularly promising development or valuable asset. However, the advice given by the experts is that having fixed a maximum price for the buy-out related to a sum that will enable you to repay the loan and its interest charges (and also make a living) within a reasonable period of time, you should not go beyond that figure.

Checklist: further self-employment opportunities

Part-time work

1. Have you informed your local authority if your employment creates a noise, nuisance or a smell and you intend to use your home for part-time work?
2 If you are involved in preparing food, have you informed the environmental health inspector?
3. If you are planning to work from home, have you informed your insurance company to arrange additional cover?
4. Have you assessed whether there is a market for your goods or services at a price that will bring you a worthwhile profit?
5. Have you identified your objective for working part-time and, if it is to reduce the hours worked, is the financial sacrifice worth making?
6. Are you able to fulfil the administrative demands as well as your core product/service?
7. Can you hire equipment instead of buying it?
8. If you are developing a hobby as part-time work, are you able to upgrade your work, to meet professional standards and to produce it quickly and economically?

Freelancing

1. Have you a good source of contacts? Could your current employer provide you with freelance work?
2. Are you self-motivated and have you identified further areas and media where you can investigate future freelance opportunities?
3. Are you able to work by yourself?
4. Have you identified the going rate for your work and, after taking into account periods without work, are you able to survive financially?

Franchising

1. Have you approached your bank to see if they support your franchise application?
2. Have you talked to other franchisees to see their financial outlook and hours of work?

3. Have you contacted the British Franchise Association for good guidelines and advice?
4. Does your location suit the franchise product?
5. Is the franchisor well enough established to support you through economic downturns?
6. Are you prepared to follow a business structure prepared by someone else?
7. Ask your bank to recommend a lawyer who specialises in franchising.

Management buy-outs
1. Have you prepared a business plan including the assets and liability of the company, the nature and value of the work in progress, detailed cash-flow projections and the qualifications and skills of the buy-out team?
2. Check the bid document to see that important assets are included.

1.4 Choosing Professional and Other Outside Advisers

We have already touched on the importance of the role that professional advisers, particularly accountants and solicitors, are going to play in the formation of your business, whether it is to be a limited company or some other form of entity. You are going to be using their advice quite frequently, not only at the beginning but also later, in matters such as acquiring premises, suing a customer for payment, preparing a set of accounts or finding out what items are allowable against you or your company's tax bill. Obviously, therefore, how you choose and use these advisers is a matter for careful thought.

MAKING THE RIGHT CHOICE

Many people think that there is some kind of special mystique attached to membership of a profession and that any lawyer or accountant is going to do a good job for them. The fact is, though, that while they do have useful specialist knowledge, the competence with which they apply it can be very variable. A high proportion of people who have bought a house, for instance, can tell you of errors and delays in the conveyancing process, and some accountants entrusted with their clients' tax affairs have been known to send in large bills for their services while over-looking claims for legitimate expenses that were the object of employing them in the first place.

So do not just go to the solicitor or accountant who happens to be nearest; nor should you go to someone you only know in a social capacity. Ask friends who are already in business on a similar scale and, if possible, of a similar nature to your own, for recommendations. (If you already have a bank manager you know well, he may also be able to offer useful advice.) The kind of professional adviser you should be looking for at this stage is not in a big office in a central location. They will have bigger fish to fry and after the initial interview you may well be fobbed off with an articled clerk. Apart from that they will be expensive, for they have big office overheads to meet. On the other hand, a solo operation can create a problem if that person is ill or on holiday. The ideal office will be a suburban one, preferably close to where you intend to set up business, because knowledge of local conditions and personalities can be invaluable, with two or three partners. Apart from that, personal impressions do count. You will probably not want to take on an adviser who immedi-ately exudes gloomy caution, or one who appears to be a wide boy, or somebody with whom you have no rapport. Some people recommend that you should make a shortlist of two or three possibles and go and talk to them before making your choice.

Professional associations will also have details of members in your area. The Law Society runs a scheme, Lawyers for Your Business (LFYB), to help small companies assess their legal needs by offering a free consultation with a local member. The LFYB telephone hotline is 020 7405 9075 and free guides are avail-able at 020 7316 5521. Details can also be found on the Law Society's Web site at www.lawsoc.org.uk. The Institute of Chartered Accountants in England and Wales (ICAEW) also provides details of local practitioners to members of the public. Its Practitioner Bureau can be contacted direct on 01908 248090 and its Web site address is www.icaew.co.uk/. The Institute of Chartered Accountants Scotland also publishes a list of members and can be ordered on 0131 347 4883, with details shown on the Web site www.icas.org.uk.

CRONER
www.smallbusiness-centre.net

Four Steps to Improving Your Business

1 – Analysis
Before undertaking any business venture research is important. Finding that gap in the market, researching your routes to market and looking at yourself and your company are vital first steps. SWOT analysis is a useful tool, by conducting an internal appraisal you can ascertain your strengths and weaknesses. And by looking at the external environment you can gauge any opportunities or threats to your plans.

2 – Planning
Great business plans are the key to any successful business; they help you focus your ideas into coherent strategies. Whether you're applying for finance, launching a new product/service or just looking to grow your existing business, business plans will help you achieve your personal, business and financial goals.

3 – Implementation
Planning maybe the key to successful businesses but unless plans are fully implemented they will not reach their revenue potential. Before starting you need a plan of action and tasks to make that plan happen need to be allocated, ensuring that all legislation is complied with. Regulations such as health & safety, employment law and data protection, are often over looked, but this could lead to damaging penalties for non-compliance. When a great business plan is implemented well, you can see your business and financial dreams become reality.

4 – Control
Once a project has commenced it is imperative cost and deadlines are controlled to ensure sufficient cash flow and to maximise its potential. Gantt charts can be used to track deadlines, actual spend should be closely monitored against budget to ensure that there is no divergence from either delivery dates or budget.

Croner can help your company grow and succeed!
Too often brilliant business ideas are not seen through to their full potential. As the day-to-day running of your business takes over you find yourself firefighting, dealing with 'red tape', instead of driving your business forward.

For over 50 years thousands of people have used Croner to help cut through legislative red tape, keep their business driving forward and improve their profitability and efficiency.

Our services include business planning and project management software detailed information services helping you cut through red tape and telephone advisory helpline. We also have a website dedicated to the smaller business. Register free at **www.smallbusiness-centre.net**

Speak to us today on **020 8247 1630** or visit **www.smallbusiness-centre.net** and see how we can help you.

WHAT QUESTIONS DO YOU ASK?

Obviously, later on you will be approaching your adviser about specific problems, but at the outset you and he will be exploring potential help he can give you. Begin by outlining the kind of business or service you intend to set up, how much money you have available, what you think your financial needs are going to be over the first year of operation, how many people are going to be involved as partners or shareholders and what your plans are for the future. An accountant will want to know the range of your experience in handling accounting problems and how much help you are going to need in writing up the books, and he will advise you on the basic records you should set up. Remember to ask his advice on your year end/year start; this does not have to be 6 April to 5 April, and there may be sound tax reasons for choosing other dates. He may even be able to recommend the services of a part-time bookkeeper to handle the mechanics but, as we shall show in Chapter 3.1, this does not absolve you from keeping a close watch on what money is coming in and going out. It should be stressed at this point that, certainly in the case of a private limited company, the accountant you are talking to should be qualified, either through membership of the Institute of Chartered Accountants or the Chartered Association of Certified Accountants. Someone who advertises his services as a bookkeeper or merely as an 'accountant' is not qualified to give professional advice in the true meaning of that term, though someone good if unqualified can do a very adequate job in preparing tax returns for something like a small freelance business.

A solicitor will also want to know the kind of business you are in and your plans for the future. But she will concentrate, obviously, on legal rather than financial aspects (so do not go on about money – she is a busy person and this is only an exploratory visit). She is interested in what structure the operation is going to have and, in the case of a partnership or limited company, whether you and your colleagues have made any tentative agreements between yourselves regarding the running of the firm and the division of profits. She will want to get some idea of what kind of property you want to buy or lease and whether any planning permissions have to be sought.

___

HOW MUCH ARE ADVISERS GOING TO CHARGE?

This is rather like asking how long is a piece of string. It depends on how often you have to consult your advisers, so it is no use asking them to quote a price at the outset, though if you are lucky enough to have a very clear idea of what you want done – say, in the case of an accountant, a monthly or weekly supervision of your books, plus the preparation and auditing of your accounts – they may give you a rough idea of what the charges will be. Alternatively, they may suggest an annual retainer for these services and any advice directly concerned with them, plus extra charges for anything that falls outside them such as a complicated wrangle with the inspector of taxes about allowable items. When calculating the likely cost of using an accountant remember that his fees are tax-deductible.

An annual retainer is a less suitable way of dealing with your solicitor because your problems are likely to be less predictable than those connected with accounting and bookkeeping. A lot of your queries may be raised, and settled, on the telephone: the 'Can I do this?' type. Explaining that kind of problem on the telephone is usually quicker and points can be more readily clarified than by writing a letter setting out the facts of the case (though you should ask for confirmation in writing in matters where you could be legally liable in acting on the advice you have been given!). However, asking advice on the telephone can be embarrassing for both parties. You will be wondering whether your solicitor is charging you for it and either way it could inhibit you from discussing the matter fully. You should therefore check at the outset what the procedure is for telephone inquiries and how these are accounted for on your bill.

A GUIDE – NOT A CRUTCH

For someone starting in business on their own, facing for the first time 'the loneliness of thought and the agony of decision', there is a temptation to lean on professional advisers too much. Apart from the fact that this can be very expensive, it is a bad way to run a business. Before you lift the telephone or write a letter, think. Is this clause in a contract something you could figure out for yourself if you sat down and concentrated on reading it carefully? Would it not be better to check through the ledger yourself to find out where to put some item of expenditure that is not immediately classifiable? Only get in touch with your advisers when you are genuinely stumped for an answer, not just because you cannot be bothered to think it out for yourself. Remember, too, that nobody can make up your mind for you on matters of policy. If you feel, for example, that you cannot work with your partner, the only thing your solicitor can or should do for you is to tell you how to dissolve the partnership, not whether it should be done at all.

YOUR BANK MANAGER

Traditionally, the other person with whom you might make contact when starting up your business was your bank manager. The importance of picking a banking service of the right quality, which we have mentioned in connection with professional advice, holds true with your choice of bank. However, the first question to consider is whether you actually need face-to-face contact with a bank manager rather than organisation which can answer your questions promptly when they arise.

The direct banking revolution and electronic communication have made the distance management of bank accounts a time-saving and cost-effective alternative for the small business. Possibly you will want to consider the bank that holds your personal account, or your accountant may offer to introduce you to the local branch of another high street bank. However, if you are trying to arrange a sizeable overdraft or business loan, any bank, whether it is a high street branch or a direct bank such as Abbey National, will want to examine your track record when considering an application. Choosing your bank and account management are discussed in greater detail in Chapters 1.6 and 2.4.

If you do decide to offer your business to your personal bank, you must inform your bank manager of your intention to set up in business, providing her with much the same information as you gave to your accountant. Indeed, it is quite a good idea to ask your accountant to come along to this first meeting, so that he can explain any technicalities.

You may be operating a small-scale freelance business that does not call for bank finance. It is very important, in that case, to keep your personal and business accounts separate, with separate cheque and paying-in books for each one. Mixing up private and business transactions can only lead to confusion, for you as well as your accountant. Even if you are simply, say, a one-person freelance consultancy, it is worth keeping your bank well informed about your business. Your cashflow as a freelance might well be highly erratic and unless your bank knows you and your business well it will be firing off letters about your unauthorised overdraft.

INSURANCE

If you are setting up a photographic studio and an electrical fault on the first day destroys some of your equipment, you are in trouble before you have really begun. If you are a decorator and a pot of paint falling from a window sill causes injury to someone passing below you could face a suit for damages that will clean you out of the funds you have accumulated to start your business. Insurance coverage is, therefore, essential from the start for almost all kinds of business.

Insurance companies vary a good deal in the premiums they charge for different kinds of cover, and in the promptness with which they pay out on claims. The best plan is not to go direct to a company, even if you already transact your car or life insurance with them, but to an insurance broker. Brokers receive their income from commissions from the insurance companies they represent, but they are generally independent of individual companies and thus reasonably impartial. Here again, your accountant or solicitor can advise you of a suitable choice, which would be a firm that is big enough to have contacts in all the fields for which you need cover (and big enough to exert pressure on your behalf when it comes to making a claim), but not so big that the relatively modest amounts of commission they will earn from you initially are not worth their while taking too much trouble over, for instance when it comes to reminding you about renewals. Apart from these general points you will have to consider what kinds of cover you need and this will vary some-what with the kind of business you are in. The main kinds are:

1. Insurance of your premises.
2. Insurance of the contents of your premises.
3. Insurance of your stock.
   (The above three kinds of cover should also extend to 'consequential loss'. For instance, you may lose in a fire a list of all your customers. This list has no value in itself but the 'consequent' loss of business could be disastrous. The same is true of stock losses. If a publisher loses all his books in a fire it is not only their value that affects him, but also the consequent loss of business while they are being reprinted, by which time the demand for them may have diminished.)
4. Employer's liability is compulsory if you employ staff on the premises, even on a part-time basis.
5. Public liability in case you cause injury to a member of the public or their premises in the course of business. You will also need third-party public liability if you employ staff or work with partners.
6. Legal insurance policies, which cover you against prose-cution under Acts of Parliament which relate to your busi-ness (eg those covering unfair dismissal and fair trading).
7. Insurance against losing your driving licence – important if your business depends on your being able to drive.
8. Insurance of machinery, especially mechanical failure of computers, the consequences of which can be disastrous for most kinds of business.
9. Professional indemnity insurance. If you are offering a service, such as consultancy, many clients will demand that you are covered for loss that they might incur as a result of your advice.

> 10. Product liability insurance. The same principle as the above applies if you are manufacturing or supplying goods. Your customers will expect you to be covered against claims from faulty products.

Your broker will advise you on other items of cover you will need. You should check, for instance, that your existing policies, such as home and vehicle insurance, cover commercial use if that is what you envisage, but do not leave the whole business of insurance in his hands. Read your policies carefully when you get them and make sure that the small print does not exclude any essential item.

Insurance is expensive (though the premiums are allowable against tax inasmuch as they are incurred wholly in respect of your business), and you may find that in the course of time you have paid out thousands of pounds without ever making a claim. However, it is a vital precaution, because one fire or legal action against you can wipe out the work of years if you are not insured. For this reason you must check each year that items like contents insurance represent current replacement values and that your premiums are paid on the due date. Your broker should remind you about this, but if he overlooks it, it is you who carries the can.

Membership of the Federation of Small Businesses (see Appendix 1) includes automatic free legal insurance which covers legal and professional insurance of up to £1,000,000 to protect your business against various legal actions including: Inland Revenue investigations, VAT Tribunals, employment disputes, Health and Safety at Work prosecutions, Consumer Protection Act prosecutions and claims against your business for personal injury. This service also includes a free legal help line open 24 hours a day, 365 days of the year.

Another interesting scheme is Allianz Legal Protection. Its Lawplan enables policyholders to pursue business-to-business debts. It also covers a wide variety of legal costs related to business activities, such as contract disputes. Obviously the need to get cover for such eventualities would depend on the kind of enterprise in which you are engaged.

OTHER ADVISERS AND SUPPLIERS

In the course of transacting your business, you will probably need the services of other types of people: builders, to maintain and perhaps refurbish your premises; printers, to produce letterheads, advertising material, etc; surveyors and valuers to assess your property; and so on. You should apply the same criteria to these as to your professional advisers. The services should be reasonably priced, and the service performed to the required standard. If the service is of a professional nature, the consultant should be a member of the relevant professional body. If this does not apply, it may be worth asking for recommendations from the local Chamber of Commerce, or via your nearest Business Link (Business Connect in Wales, Business Shop in Scotland).

Local Enterprise Agencies

There are LEAs throughout the country – a complete list is available from Business in the Community (see address in Appendix 1). LEAs are sponsored by local firms or local branches of national companies, banks, accountancy practices and various public sector bodies. Apart from underwriting the running costs, sponsors often second members of their staff to them. Sometimes these are experienced managers on the eve of retirement, but quite often they are young high-flyers on the way up, being exposed, as part of a career development plan, to a wider variety of business problems than they would get in their own offices.

The quality of advice and their general helpfulness is high – for instance, they will help you to prepare a business plan and advise you on methods of obtaining finance. LEAs also run courses on basic topics like marketing and finance. They are less able to advise on the conduct of specific types of business activity, unless it is one that a seconded member of the LEA's staff happens to know about. Many do, however, operate 'marriage bureaux', putting small businesses in touch with potential customers or investors. Some also maintain registers of suitable properties for small businesses.

Calling in to your Local Enterprise Agency in the early stages of setting up business increasingly ranks with visiting your bank manager as one of the vital first steps of working for yourself.

The Department of Trade and Industry

The Department of Trade and Industry runs a number of programmes, many at regional level, to help small businesses. They fall into three main groups:

1. Consultancy help, ranging from initial advice on the telephone to troubleshooting visits by approved independent consultants.
2. Information and technology transfer, which covers issues like specialised advice on how to protect intellectual property.
3. Grants for research and development.

The Small Business Service has also been set up to help start-ups. The SBS offers guidance on compliance with regulations and provides a new automated payroll service to all new small employers.

The initial contact in all these cases is the DTI itself (1 Victoria Street, London SW1H 0ET; 020 7215 5000) but it is as well to be able to describe, before you ring them, exactly what the nature of your problem or request is. Useful information is also available on the DTI Web site with information fact-sheets on employment and other issues; see www.dti.gov.uk.

Checklist: professional advisers

Solicitors
1. How well do you know the firm concerned?
2. What do you know of their ability to handle the kind of transactions you have in mind?
3. Is their office convenient to the place of work you intend to establish?
4. Do they know local conditions and personalities?
5. Are they the right size to handle your business affairs over the foreseeable future?

---

6. Have you prepared an exhaustive list of the points on which you want legal advice at the setting-up stage?

Accountants

1. Have they been recommended by someone whose judgement you trust and who has actually used their services?
2. Are the partners members of one of the official accountants' bodies? If not, are you satisfied that they can handle business on the scale envisaged?
3. Is their office reasonably close by?
4. Does it create a good and organised impression?
5. Can they guarantee that a member of the firm will give you personal and reasonably prompt attention when required?
6. Have you thought out what sort of help you are going to need?
7. Have you prepared an outline of your present financial position and future needs?
8. Have you considered, in consultation with your solicitor, whether you want to set up as a sole trader, a partnership or a limited company?

Bank manager

1. Is your present bank likely to be the right one for you to deal with in this context?
2. Have you informed your bank manager of your intention to set up a business?
3. Have you established a separate bank account for your business?
4. Have you discussed with your bank manager the possibility of switching your account to a local, smaller branch?

Insurance

1. Do you have a reliable reference on the broker you intend to use?
2. Is he efficient, according to the reports you receive, about reminding you when policies come up for renewal?
3. Has he any track record of paying promptly on claims?

4. Have you prepared a list of the aspects of your proposed business which require insurance cover?
5. Are you fully insured for replacement value and consequential loss?
6. Have you read the small print on your policies or checked them out with your solicitors?

1.5 Business Planning

Whatever kind of business you are planning to start, from a self-employed service provider to retailer or manufacturer, it is important that you begin by undertaking a disciplined planning process. You ought to do this even if you are funding the start-up from your own resources, and certainly if you aim to raise capital externally. Whichever route you are taking, the first step is to prove to yourself that your business concept is sound and that the start-up you contemplate is financially sensible.

It is unwise to rely on your instinct or perception of a business 'opportunity' without carrying out the basic research to support the case. Formal business planning forces you to do just that, applying the same logic and critical judgement that you would in any normal business situation. Below, in sequence, are the recommended steps in your business planning process.

STEP 1: THE BUSINESS SECTOR AND YOUR MARKET

Describe the business sector and the market in which you intend to operate:

☐ What is the current size of the market you will be entering?
☐ Who are the major participants: your competitors, market leaders, and suppliers?
☐ What are the critical success factors in the sector?
☐ What do published forecasts say about the profile and future growth of the business sector?
☐ What fashions, legislation or environmental trends affect the sector?

As an example, if you intend to open a private limousine service for business people and their families travelling to the local airport or for evening social engagements, you will need to evaluate the niche market for that service within your catchment area, the market shares of local taxi firms and other freelance operators. You will need to clarify the key ingredients of the service (eg reliability, timeliness, safety, comfort and so on) and the likely growth in demand. You must also take a view on what changes are likely in licensing and insurance legislation, and whether business travel by air is likely to increase or families will decide to drive themselves more often to social events in the evening.

STEP 2: YOUR PRODUCT OR SERVICE

Write down a full description of the product or service you intend to provide and compare it with the products or service offerings of competitors. It may be helpful to open a file of photographs or drawings to illustrate the differences between your product and the competition. In the case of a service, it may clarify your mind and will certainly help third parties reading your plan to understand how your service is provided if you illustrate this section of your plan with diagrams:

- ☐ Fully describe the product or service. What need does it fulfil? What features will make it unique?
- ☐ Discuss the development of your product or service. Are there opportunities to expand the product line or service range? Is it patented or otherwise protected by copyright?
- ☐ How will your product or service compare in quality, features and price with competitors' products?
- ☐ Discuss the influence of new technology on your business and the technical risks (if any). What will be the next generation of derivative products or services?

Do not overestimate your strengths or underestimate your weaknesses, or undervalue your competitors' abilities. There will be no room for self-delusion in evaluating whether you can reach your sales goals in the face of competition.

STEP 3: MARKETING AND SALES

This is the point where you have to identify how you will get your business off the ground, translating a bright idea into reality and generating the revenue that will provide you and your family with a sufficient income and support the development of the business:

☐ Describe your prospective customers. Who are they and where are they located geographically? How sensitive are they to price, quality or service? Who has expressed an interest in your product or service?

☐ Is your product or service a substitute for other products or services? Conversely, what existing products or services are substitutes for yours?

☐ Describe your target market. Identify unusual market characteristics such as barriers to entry. Are you aiming for particular market segments or a quantifiable market share?

☐ Explain how you will achieve your sales goals and what your marketing strategy will be. How will you identify potential customers? What customers will be the target in your initial marketing effort and how will you attract them away from the competition? How will you be using advertising or direct mail?

STEP 4: RUNNING THE BUSINESS

It is now time to consider how you will run your business on a day-to-day basis. If you are self-employed, you will certainly be doing most of the income generating as well as the administrative work yourself. As the owner of a small business your role is also sure to be multi-functional:

☐ Define the production and delivery processes simply, without technical jargon. ('Production' includes the artwork if you are a graphic designer, or the client contact and report writing if you are a management consultant). To what extent will you be dependent on key factors: suppliers, materials, and skilled labour? What will be your relationship with suppliers? What will be the capacity of your business? How will you increase it as the business grows?

☐ Personnel requirements. If you do not plan to be a self-employed sole trader, what are your employee needs in terms of skills and functions? What will be your employee costs, including benefits, and are there suitably qualified people available? Include a skills audit in your analysis.

☐ Premises. Will you be able to operate from home? If not, describe the premises you will need. How much will they cost to rent and maintain?

STEP 5: MANAGEMENT

The hardest part of your realistic planning process, unless you are determined to be a one man or woman business, is to assess your own management capabilities and what additional management support you will need to be successful. Perhaps you have all the necessary creative or organisation skills, but have poor personal sales skills. The solution may be to bring in an effective sales agent whom you can pay on commission without adding to the overhead costs of your business.

Alternatively, bookkeeping and accountancy may be functions that you have difficulty in performing efficiently and in a timely fashion and, in any case, feel they would be a poor use of your time. Often these are part-time tasks and, if you are lucky, a family member can be enlisted. If not, you should plan for part-time assistance. In either case, what is important is that you should recognise your own shortcomings and plan accordingly.

STEP 6: TIMING

Set down a timetable for starting your business, scheduling all key events from identifying sources of finance, setting up your place of business, launching your product or service and through to the receipt of revenue from your first month of sales. This simple exercise will give you the time-frame for your financial planning.

STEP 7: FINANCIAL ASPECTS

Your initial business plan for your own use will be incomplete unless you include the initial financial plan for the start-up and how you and your business will survive for the first 12 months. At this stage all that you need is a cash-flow forecast; the key elements of how to forecast your cash requirements are detailed in Chapter 2.3.

Accurate cash-flow forecasting is far more important to you in starting and running your business, at least in the early years, than profit planning. The cash flow is based on when you expect to actually receive payment from your customers and when you have to pay your suppliers, and tells you what finance you need to survive. There are plenty of businesses with high profit margins that have gone bust simply because they were unable to balance revenue and expenditure timing. If you are looking to borrow working capital, the first detailed information requirement of whatever external financial source you approach will be your cash-flow forecast.

The cash-flow forecast that you prepare now should be on a month-by-month basis for the start-up period from the time when expenditure is first required and for at least 12 months. It will show clearly what are the cash demands on your personal finances to get started and what funding you need from a bank or other source.

If you are unhappy with the result, either because the cash generated is inadequate to support you or because the assumptions on which the plan is based seem over-optimistic, you have an early opportunity to rethink before 'going public' with your plan. Of course, you should be mindful of the hazards of massaging the variables to achieve a more satisfactory result at the expense of reality.

STEP 8: SUMMARY

The final step in your business planning exercise is a concise summary, which should be repositioned as the introduction to the plan. This summary, which is sometimes given the rather grandiose title of 'Executive Overview', should express succinctly the uniqueness and viability of your venture. If possible, limit its length to two pages – certainly less than four. It is the most important section in that it may determine how much consideration any proposal you may make for financial support will receive.

You may find it useful to attach to the summary a one-page analysis of strengths, weaknesses, opportunities and threats, known as a 'SWOT' analysis. Be honest about your weaknesses and the threats you face, spelling out any mitigating circumstances and the defensive action you will take to address them.

Now that you have a business plan, and assuming that you are comfortable with it, it is a good idea to expose it to friendly criticism. You will certainly want your family's opinion – and they will probably give it anyway! However, it is a good idea to ask one or more of your business acquaintances whose opinion you respect to read your business plan and pass objective comment. They may well perceive weaknesses (or strengths) in the plan that you did not appreciate and help you produce a more compelling case later to third parties for whom you are an 'unknown quantity'.

Checklist: business planning

1. The purpose of the business plan is to set out the strategy and action plan for the next one to three years.
2. Base your plan on reality. Write it as if an outsider was the reader, and keep it short.
3. Define the market in which you plan to sell. Focus on the segments in which you will compete. Include photographs or diagrams to identify the product or service.
4. Identify barriers to entry and competition.
5. Describe what your marketing strategy will be and how you will achieve your sales goals.

6. Detail how you will run the business with reference to the production and delivery processes, key skills and personnel, and premises.
7. Identify your bookkeeping and management systems, financial controls and use of IT.
8. Set down the timing for starting your business.
9. Produce financial projections concentrated on cash-flow forecasts for at least 12 months from actual start-up and add on the planning and preparation period.
10. Include a two-page summary as the introduction to the plan and a one-page SWOT analysis as an attachment. Present the plan professionally with a contents page and section numbering and put a cover on it.

1.6 Choosing Your Bank

In some cases, the choice of bank when starting your own business is almost automatic. To a degree, this depends on whether you are becoming self-employed and intend to operate a small-scale freelance business, or whether you are setting up a company and are also taking professional advice from an accountancy and/or legal professional.

Most advisers would recommend strongly that you keep your personal and business bank accounts separate, with separate cheque and paying-in books for each one, even if you are simply, say, a one person freelance consultancy. Indeed, with increasing Inland Revenue demands that businesses keep adequate records for tax purposes, all but the simplest businesses may find a separate business account essential.

In the past, that advice has been tempered by the higher costs of business account banking and the generally reduced personal element in banking relationships. If your one person business is very simple, confusion between private and business transactions can be avoided by maintaining a standard value-added tax (VAT) account book in which details of your business debit and credit invoices only are logged. Currently, a number of high street banks are offering 'free' banking for the first two years of new business accounts, and one or two are offering permanent relief from bank charges.

Your local Business Link is a good source of advice on available banking arrangements and may help to point you in the right direction for your kind of business. Many new business owners may choose to meet their financial adviser (bank manager or accountant) before putting the business plan into action.

In the case of self-employment as the sole proprietor of your business, if you already have a long-standing banking relation-

CURRENT ACCOUNTS

'Now one small fee covers all my banking, and the service is outstanding'

Phil Collins, Surveyor

If you deal in cash and cheques like Phil, the Alliance & Leicester Monthly Flat Fee Account is the one for you.

Just one simple, single fee covers all your everyday transactions, including making standing order and Direct Debit payments, issuing and depositing cheques and paying in cash.*

You have a choice of two tariffs:

■ Our £10 Monthly Flat Fee Account is designed for businesses with an annual turnover of up to £100,000

■ Our £25 Monthly Flat Fee Account is designed for businesses with an annual turnover between £100,000 and £500,000 and deposit less than £3,000 per month in cash

Find out more today

☎ **0800 587 0800**

Quote ref. AD0147

 Visit your local branch

 www.mybusinessbank.co.uk/self

Alliance Leicester
Business Banking

BIG BENEFITS FOR SMALL BUSINESSES

Alliance & Leicester Business Banking helps out small businesses with a range money-saving accounts

There can't be many of us who haven't dreamed of swapping the daily grind of 9-5 employment for the freedom of running their own small business. In reality, of course, running your own business is no easy option. As well as generating the business, you've got to send out the bills, collect the money, bank it and work out your own finances – never mind look after staff, keep the office clean – and prevent the fridge from clogging up with half-empty milk cartons!

Life for small businesses – the facts

According to recent research by Alliance & Leicester Business Banking, almost a third of small business owners won't be taking a holiday this summer because they're too busy – or because they can't find anyone to look after their business whilst they're away. What's more, the research indicates that nearly half of all small business owners do their own cleaning to cut costs – whilst, over the last six months, 22% of business owners have taken a pay cut or foregone a holiday in order to conserve their company's hard-earned cash.

Practical help for the small businessman

So what can be done to help Britain's hard-pressed owner-managed companies? As one of the UK's leaders in small business banking, Alliance & Leicester has taken tangible, practical steps to make life easier for the small business community by introducing a range of easy-access financial products and services designed to ease the pressure on their time and money.

Addressing Competition Commission report issues

"All our accounts are directly aimed at relieving the financial and time pressures that small businesses so often experience," says Alliance & Leicester Business

Banking Director of Business Development, Stewart Fraser. "It also addresses the issues raised by the survey we undertook into whether small firms feel significantly better off as a result of the recent changes instituted by the Big Four banks, following the Competition Commission report."

Only 1 in 10 firms feel the benefit

The Alliance & Leicester survey also revealed that only one in ten small firms felt that their financial circumstances had improved after the Competition Commission Report changes. One in three said that they'd benefited slightly, whilst a similar number had seen no difference at all. Four per cent reported that they were worse off, whilst ten per cent said that changes were confusing.

Free Direct Banking

Directly addressing the Competition Commission findings is the Alliance & Leicester Free Direct Banking Account, paying interest and wiping out bank charges for those who keep a minimum cleared balance in their account of at least £5,000 and operate their account within certain usage parameters. It also taps into the 17,000 Post Office™ branches nationwide, making it easy for customers to bank at a convenient location. And to make banking even easier, the account also includes a LINK card, which gives access to over 35,000 ATMs all over the UK – so those operating their own businesses are never far from a source of ready cash when – and where – they want it.

The Low-Cost Cash Account – with interest on credit balances

In support of the benefits delivered by the Free Direct Banking Account, Alliance & Leicester Business Banking has also introduced a Low-Cost Cash Account for businesses with a turnover of between £100,000 and £500,000, and which bank high levels of cash (in excess of £3,000 deposits per month). The monthly administration fee is only £1.75, with a charge of just 65p per transaction. "We believe this account offers substantial savings for businesses with a high cash turnover," says Andrew Cucksey, Senior Marketing Manager of Alliance & Leicester

Business Banking. "Interest is also paid on credit balances, allowing the customer to earn interest on everyday business funds, so the whole account adds up to a very beneficial package for small business owners," he adds.

The Flat Fee Account – for better cash flow planning

Another money-saving account from Alliance & Leicester Business Banking is the £10 Flat Fee Account, for businesses with an annual turnover of under £100,000. "For just £10 a month, customers are covered for cheque issuance, cash and cheque deposits, standing orders and direct debits', says Andrew Cucksey. "Moreover, a flat fee provides certainty and transparency of charges that provide better cash flow planning."

Business Moneyfacts award–winners!

All the Alliance & Leicester Business Banking accounts attracted a good deal of interest within the finance industry – helping them win the 'Best Business Current Account Provider' award at the *Business Moneyfacts* Awards 2003. To win this accolade they came top in a survey of current accounts offered by almost thirty banks – no small achievement in a very competitive market.

Judges impressed by Alliance & Leicester's commitment

"The judges were impressed by the commitment Alliance & Leicester Business Banking has shown the SME market, with a range of easily understood, good value current account products", said Nikki Cann, Editor of *Business Moneyfacts*. "Alliance & Leicester Business Banking has performed consistently well in our surveys of bank charges – reflecting the fact that it has accounts to meet a wide variety of small firms' needs."

Small businesses face enough challenges, Alliance & Leicester aim to ensure that business banking is not one of them. Business owners can take comfort in the fact that Alliance & Leicester is on their side – and has the money-saving, award-winning business accounts to prove it!

ship with the local branch of a high street bank it would be normal to maintain your present personal current account and maybe open a second business account for your firm. If you are running an overdraft or a loan account with your personal bank, this does not preclude you from opening a business account with another bank that will look at your business as a separate issue. However, the new bank may ask you to transfer your personal accounts, and you may be reluctant to do this at a time when you are planning to make a leap into the financial unknown.

Although most business start-ups are self-funded from the internal financial resources of the owners and their families, you may need an overdraft facility at the outset unless you are fortunate enough to have advances or retainers from your first customers. In any case, it is a good idea to talk through your preliminary business plan and your cash-flow forecast with your financial adviser. As a cash management professional, he or she will spot any errors and will question any assumptions you have made that seem unrealistic.

BANKING FOR THE SMALL BUSINESS

If working for yourself means starting up a small business in the form of a limited liability company or partnership, and possibly employing staff, there is a legal requirement to 'appoint bankers' and open a bank account in the name of the company or partnership. Therefore, the issue of choosing your bank arises before you begin to trade.

Company law no longer requires every company to appoint auditors, but you may engage the services of an accountancy firm to form the company for you or, more likely, to purchase an 'off the shelf' company and adapt it to your use as described in Chapter 1.2. Most local firms of chartered accountants have good relationships with the local branches of leading banks, building societies and other financial institutions in your nearest business centre and, if asked, the partner who is advising you will introduce you to the bank he or she considers to be most appropriate for you and your kind of business. Such introductions are helpful because they will encourage confidence in the bank that your affairs will be subject to professional accounting disciplines, and may make the difference between the bank granting you the overdraft or business loan that you need to get started and turning down your proposal – commonly, the fate of about two in three applications.

If your start-up company requires more than working capital that can be provided by basic bank borrowing, you will need to prepare for the more formal process of raising finance described in Chapter 2.2, which will involve approaching several financial institutions, possibly venture capitalists as well as banks. For the present, we will assume that your funding requirements are modest and that a local bank will be able to accommodate you.

FACTORS AFFECTING THE SELECTION

It is important to understand what you can expect from your bank in terms of personal attention and service. The IT revolution has changed forever the way in which banks conduct their business. Not only can the bank monitor your account continually but it can impose controls electronically so that payments that would take your account into debit or over the limit where an overdraft has been agreed can be rejected automatically when your cheque or a direct debit is presented.

Gone are the days when your Bank Manager would use his discretion and either sanction the debit before writing or calling you, or call you first. The computerised system will simply follow its instructions and return the cheque to your payee.

The computerised instructions can be overridden but this requires an intervention prior to the event, which means that you must be aware of what might happen and call the bank yourself. Fortunately, electronic banking also gives you immediate access to the position of your bank account, either by telephone or the Internet from your PC or via your TV, so that you can track the arrival of credits and debits. Of course, the system cannot register the cheques outstanding that you have drawn but that have not yet been presented. On the one hand, the need to control your bank account has heightened; on the other hand, it is now possible to do so on a daily basis.

Checklist: choosing your bank

With the new banking environment in mind, the following is a checklist of the factors that you should consider when choosing your bank:

1. Do you want access to branch counter services to make transactions on your account?
2. If not, consider direct banking with a bank that does not have a local branch office.
3. Does the bank provide the level of service online or by telephone that you want for your business?
4. Will you want regular face to face contact with your bank manager?
5. If so, do you think that the manager you have met understands the business you are starting and is likely to be helpful? Does he have a sufficient level of authority for the demand of your business as it grows?
6. Compare the tariff of bank charges with the competition.
7. Does the bank offer the level of overdraft and business loan facilities that you may need?
8. How do the bank's interest and repayment terms compare to the competition?
9. How responsive do you think the bank would be to an emergency such as the unexpected loss or insolvency of a major customer?
10. If there is little or no difference between the services offered, and you need some face-to-face contact, choose the bank that your accountant advises or business friends recommend rather than the manager who seems most sympathetic.

Section 2
Raising capital

2.1 Different Sources of Capital

Starting your own full-time business usually requires the provision of working capital, if only to cover the gap between your previous income ceasing and a positive cash-flow from your self-employed activities, or your ability to make drawings from the partnership or to take a salary if you set up a company. Most people setting out in business on their own account provide the initial funding from their own financial resources, using personal savings, cashing in on a pension or insurance policy, borrowing against the surrender value of an endowment insurance policy or borrowing from family and friends. Even personal credit cards are a common source of finance to support initial cash flow. If you do need to turn to external sources, a variety are available depending on the size and nature of your business and its requirements.

DEBT FINANCE

Bank borrowing

The banks form the most important source of external finance for the self-employed and small businesses in the United Kingdom and their dominance of business funding seems sure to continue. Bank lending takes the form of term loans and overdrafts, and banks rely heavily on taking security for lending any significant sum. The owners of small businesses should expect to provide security over personal assets when negotiating bank funding for start-up or early stage development.

In recent years there has been an increase in other bank products, such as factored debt and asset-based finance. Factoring is, effectively, the discounting of trade debtors whereby you receive a proportion of the face value of your invoices to credit acceptable customers and the bank or factoring company takes on the financial risk and the responsibility of collection. Plainly, this means of raising cash applies to your operation only when you have built up a sufficient level of business; it is not normally available within the first 18 months of trading until you can produce your first 12 months accounts and show a satisfactory level of business and a sound debtor payment record.

Asset finance is applied particularly to the acquisition of office or manufacturing equipment and motor vehicles; it can take the form of hire purchase, finance leasing or operating leasing. Before choosing which route to take, you should consult with your accountant regarding the real cost of each alternative and the implications for tax allowances and ownership of the asset.

If you do borrow from the bank in the name of the company you have set up for your business, it is likely that the bank will require your personal guarantee. Likewise, 'joint and several liability' will probably be a pre-requisite of borrowing in the name of a partnership, which means that each partner will have liability to the bank in respect of the total partnership debt.

If things go wrong, the bank calls in the partnership debt and, if some partners are unable to pay or have given security that is inadequate or not easily realisable, will look to those whom they identify as being most able swiftly to repay the partnership's borrowings in full. Those who pay up more than their share of the total amount will have recourse against those who do not, but pursuit will be extended and may be fruitless. The same problem can arise for the directors of a private limited company who provided their guarantees jointly for the company's borrowings or a debt.

Commonly, if the sum you wish to borrow is substantial and the only significant asset you hold is the equity interest in your house, the bank may ask for a second charge on the house (after the mortgage provider). This involves you and your family in an unwelcome decision that you should not take without seeking advice from a solicitor who will explain the full implications, nor without ensuring that there is family unanimity.

Private loans

You may have friends or relatives who are prepared to lend you money, but private loans are a rich source of misunderstanding and so you should be clear about all the implications of such an arrangement. The best plan is to get a solicitor to draw up the terms of the loan, covering the rate of interest, the period over which the loan is repayable and the circumstances under which it can be withdrawn. It must also be made clear to what extent, if any, the lender has any say in the running of the business and what the nature of this control is. Normally, however, lenders should not be entitled to participation in management matters; nor does the existence of the loan entitle them to a share of the profits, no matter how strong a moral claim they think they might have once your business starts making real money.

In the case of a limited company, you must explain to the lender that a loan is not the same thing as a shareholding, although, of course, the offer of a loan might be conditional on acquiring shares or the option to acquire them. You should be clear that a shareholding entitles the shareholder to a percentage of the profits in proportion to his holding and, though loans can be repaid, it is virtually impossible to dismantle issued share capital in this way.

Often private loans are not offered directly but in the form of guaranteeing an overdraft, on the basis that if the recipient of the overdraft is unable to repay it, the guarantor is liable for that amount. Losses incurred by the guarantor of a capital loan can be treated as a capital loss, to be set off against capital gains.

The Small Firms Loan Guarantee Scheme

There is one third-party source of relief for small firms located in England with viable business proposals that are unable to secure conventional finance because they and their owners lack collateral security to offer against a loan. The Small Firms Loan Guarantee Scheme (SLGS), administered by the Small Business

Service (SBS), may provide a guarantee against default that encourages lenders who are otherwise satisfied with the business proposal but will not advance funds without adequate security.

Participating banks and other financial institutions that take responsibility for commercial decisions regarding borrowers provide loans over 2 to 10 years. The SBS provides an 85 per cent guarantee on loans of up to £250,000 for established businesses that have been trading for two years or more at the time of application. For other businesses, including start-ups, the SBS may provide a guarantee of up to 70 per cent on loans up to £100,000.

The SBS is a Government Agency under the Department of Trade and Industry (DTI) and was launched in April 2000 as the sole agency responsible for business support in England. It provides business support, advice and access to appropriate expertise through the Business Link network. In return for the guarantee, a borrower pays a premium to the SBS. The premium is 0.5 per cent per year on the outstanding loan amount for loans with a fixed rate of interest, and 1.5 per cent a year on the outstanding amount for loans with a variable rate of interest.

To make an application you should approach one of the approved lenders who will consider whether to lend you money, either by way of a conventional loan or overdraft or the SLGS. The lender will apply to the SBS for a guarantee. With some of the approved lenders there is a fast-track, simplified procedure for loans up to £30,000 that enables the lender to approve applications without first referring them to the SBS.

Of course, not every application for the SLGS succeeds. However, in the first 20 years since the start of the scheme in 1981 over 76,000 loans, valued at more than £2.7 billion, were guaranteed.

Equity finance

Since the mid-1990s the supply of risk capital to enterprises from both formal venture capital funds and from informal investors, known as 'business angels', has grown considerably. Although it still accounts for only a small proportion of total small business financing in the UK, risk capital plays an important role in financing higher growth small firms.

Formal venture capital finance

Formal venture capital finance usually takes the form of a mixture of loan capital and equity (ordinary shares and, perhaps, preference shares). The loan capital is generally combined with conventional bank borrowing to provide most of the funding, while the investment in ordinary share capital is a relatively small proportion of the total, normally representing less than a third of the company's equity. Such a financing structure, which is designed to leave the owners of the business with a majority shareholding and to provide a high rate of return on investors' equity, is described as 'highly geared'. However, formal venture capital is seldom made available for investment propositions involving less than £1 million financing, although deals involving less than £500,000 have become quite common. In 2000 just under half of all deals were in that size band according to the British Venture Capital Association (BVCA). Unless working for yourself involves participation in a management buy-out (MBO) or management buy-in (MBI), your business is unlikely to attract this category of investor. In 2000, when venture capital investment rose by 55 per cent to £2,226 million, only £703 million was invested in 260 early stage enterprises.

One deterrent for small companies and entrepreneurs seeking formal venture capital is the high cost. Specialist advice is required from lawyers and accountants and, perhaps, from a professional corporate finance adviser, unless that role is provided by the accountancy firm with which you work. Overall cost can rise to as much as 10 per cent of the finance raised, and 4 or 5 per cent is commonplace.

Nevertheless, the government has augmented the supply of risk capital for small- and medium-sized enterprises (SMEs) by setting up Regional Venture Capital Funds (RVCF) in each of the nine English regions. The first to launch were in the North East and East Midlands in January 2002.

Business angel investment

Raising equity capital in the amounts required by smaller businesses can be especially difficult, not only because of the high risks but also because of the high costs of making such investments. However, business angels provide smaller amounts of risk capital to businesses with growth potential, particularly start-up and early stage businesses. Currently, the supply of UK business angel investment is estimated at between £500 million to £1 billion per year, from some 20,000 to 40,000 actual and potential business angels, spread over some 3,000 to 6,000 companies.

If your business concept is innovative and your business plan indicates that high profitability and a rapid rate of growth can be achieved, you may be able to attract a business angel. The same kind of 'gearing' between loan capital and equity may be appropriate as for formal venture capital, and you will certainly have to make available up to 30 per cent of the ordinary share capital of your company to the investors. Before setting out to attract an investor, you should be aware that:

- ☐ Business angels are very often successful business people who have built up their own businesses from scratch, as you intend to do.
- ☐ Their preferences for the kind of business in which they want to invest are conditioned by experience, and may seem quite idiosyncratic.
- ☐ They will expect a sufficient personal investment from you to ensure your commitment (but not to cripple you financially).
- ☐ They will require the return of their investment and profit within three to five years, or a shorter time, if you need to go for secondary funding to grow the business.
- ☐ They may want to play an active part in the business (whether or not this is a good thing from your point of view depends on personal chemistry, whether they can make a genuine contribution and whether the terms of participation have been clearly set out).

There is a National Business Angels Network (NBAN), supported by the SBS, a number of clearing banks and other sponsoring organisations. NBAN works with the local Business Angel Networks (BANs), to which many groups and individual investors belong, and with local banks, accountants and solicitors who help to operate this informal market. If you decide to seek investment from this sector, contact the NBAN or your local BAN to be put in touch with investors.

Potential business angel investors are also identified in a directory published by the British Venture Capital Association (Essex House, 12–13 Essex Street, London WC2R 3AA; 020 7240 3846). As a further alternative, you can take a proactive approach by registering with a Business Introduction Service, which sets out to help firms looking for finance present their case in a way that is likely to attract investors. Venture Capital Report (tel. 020 7907 2900) is the market leader in this field and produces a monthly summary of opportunities that it mails to 750 subscribers, ranging from wealthy individuals to financial institutions. The Local Investor Network on 020 7332 0877 also publishes a monthly list of companies looking for investors that is mailed to 350 subscribers.

SBS Equity Initiatives

The SBS is playing an active role in promoting an increased supply of equity finance to SMEs through the RVCFs, the creation of a UK High Technology Fund and proposals for Early Growth Funding. The last of these initiatives targets businesses seeking to raise up to £50,000 for innovative and knowledge intensive businesses, as well as smaller manufacturers needing fresh investment for new opportunities.

Checklist: different sources of capital

1. Most people starting to work for themselves provide initial funding from their personal resources.
2. If you do need to turn to external sources, such as a bank, be prepared to provide security over personal assets for start-up or early stage development. Ensure that you understand the full implications and that there is complete family unanimity.
3. Decide on appropriate types of finance; an overdraft is for working capital.
4. Consider if additional capital is needed. If so, look for a private loan or equity finance.
5. Factoring may be an alternative to overdraft borrowing, particularly if you have a good debtor book, strong credit controls and a track record of two years or more.

---

6. The Small Firms Loan Guarantee Scheme (SLGS) may be available to viable businesses located in England where the banks' requirement for security cannot be met.

7. The Small Business Service (SBS) promotes equity finance through Regional Venture Capital Funds, a UK High Technology Fund and Early Growth Funding. Your local Business Link office is the first source of information on all SBS schemes.

8. 'Business angel' capital can be attracted for smaller amounts of capital for early stage businesses, even start-ups, provided that you can demonstrate innovation and that high growth and profitability are achievable.

9. Formal venture capital finance is often not available for financing requirements of less than £1 million, and is costly for small companies.

10. All venture capitalists will expect the return of their investment and profit within three to five years, and most will require representation on the board of your company.

Note: If you are planning an MBI or MBO or require substantial funding for your business a more comprehensive overview of financing is provided by Reuvid, J M (2002) *Corporate Finance Handbook*, Kogan Page, London.

2.2 Presenting Your Case for Raising Capital

Banks make money by lending out the funds deposited with them at rates of interest which vary according to government policy. During periods of economic expansion that rate will be lower – and money easier to get – than during the 'stop' parts of the 'stop and go cycle' that seems to be endemic in the British economy since the war. But banks, like everybody else, have to continue to trade even through less prosperous times. You will find, therefore, that the bank manager will be willing to discuss making money available to you, because potentially you are a source of income to him. How much that will be depends somewhat on the size of the branch you are approaching. This is an argument in favour of going to a large branch if you need a sizeable sum; on the other hand, in a smaller community, where personal contacts still matter, your professional adviser may well have a shrewd idea of what the bank manager's lending limits are.

EXISTING BUSINESS

Whether you can convince the bank manager your business is a good risk depends on how well you have thought out your approach. To some extent he will go on personal impressions and on what he can gather of your previous business experience. If you have already been running your own firm for a year or two he will have some hard evidence to go on in the shape of your profit and loss account and your balance sheet. He will look at the financial position of your firm, particularly the relationship of current assets to current liabilities of debtors to creditors (see Chapter 3.1). He will want to be satisfied that you are valuing your stock realistically and he will want to know how much money you (and your partners, if you have any) have put into the business from your own resources. In the case of a limited company he will want to know what the issued share capital is.

If a business has been operating for three years, a bank will want to look at its historic cash flow in order to see if it has been able to meet the repayments of future loans. Michael Brand in *A Guide to Sources of Finance for SMEs* (Kogan Page) describes this approach as 'driving by looking in the rear view mirror'. However, this does have the advantage over start-ups in providing hard facts for banks to base their decisions on, rather than projections of future earnings.

NEW BUSINESS

While businesses that are able to show evidence of previous trading are advantaged, the banks do still lend to start-ups even though the amount tends to be less and a number of other factors will need to be taken into account. Proposals for lending to a new business will need to be fully worked out and have realistic and thorough cash-flow projections.

The bank will be looking to see whether your business satisfies three criteria:

1. That its money is secure, and in the case of a new business it will probably ask for security to be in the shape of tangible items like fixed assets within the business, or shares and other assets belonging to the owners in their private capacity in a ratio which may be as high as 1:1.
2. That your firm is likely to have inflow of enough liquid assets to enable the bank to recall its money, if necessary.
3. That you will be able to make profitable use of the business and pay the interest without difficulty.

There is a saying that banks will only lend you money if you do not need it, and reading these requirements you may be coming to the conclusion that there is an element of truth in this. But what it really means is that there is no use going to a bank to bail you out of trouble. A business in trouble generally requires assistance on the management side at the very least and banks are just not in a position to provide such assistance, no matter how glowing the prospects might be if the firm could be brought back on track. So the bank manager is only going to be looking at present and quantifiable situations. He will not be very interested in often vague assets such as goodwill and will be even less interested in your hopes for the future.

If you have only just set up in business you may not have much more than hopes for the future to offer; the bank manager will obviously be cautious in such cases. But can these hopes be quantified and have you outlined a thorough cash-flow budget? If you are opening, say, a new restaurant, facts such as that you and your spouse are excellent cooks, have attended courses in catering and have established that there would be a demand for a good place to eat in a particular locality, are relevant. But what the bank also wants to know is:

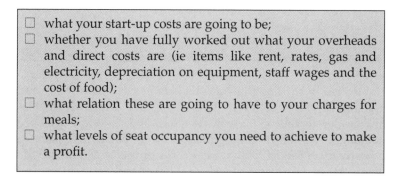

- ☐ what your start-up costs are going to be;
- ☐ whether you have fully worked out what your overheads and direct costs are (ie items like rent, rates, gas and electricity, depreciation on equipment, staff wages and the cost of food);
- ☐ what relation these are going to have to your charges for meals;
- ☐ what levels of seat occupancy you need to achieve to make a profit.

This might take quite a lot of working out and it is advisable that you consult closely with your accountant in preparing your case for the bank. Indeed it may be a good idea to take your accountant along with you when you are approaching the bank for financial help.

It is, however, not impossible to do this by yourself. What you need is a 'business plan' and all the banks actually have kits which show you how to prepare them. Even if you do not need finance, it is a good idea to prepare a business plan because it will focus your mind on the main issues that are likely to determine the success of your venture. The salient points are as follows:

□ your business experience;
□ your existing assets and liabilities;
□ the product or service you are proposing to offer, the geographical market for it and how you propose to reach it;
□ the likely demand for it – ie whether it is continuing and to what extent it is seasonal or susceptible to technological obsolescence;
□ competition: where it is and how you propose to counter it by means of price, service, etc;
□ requirements for and likely costs of premises and/or equipment;
□ how much of your own money you are proposing to put in;
□ the amount of finance required and what it is going to be used for;
□ what security you are able to offer;
□ cash flow and profit and loss forecasts for the first 12 months.

A business plan should always be kept as clear as possible and the information should be structured in a way that enables the reader to follow it easily. Lenders and investors who are looking for hard facts and figures need to be included to back up your case. A lender will want to see projections that include the worst-case scenario as well as the best and you will need to show that you have anticipated some of the pitfalls that might occur, and that you have an idea of how you might deal with them.

It is always worth bearing in mind that you might not be present when your business plan is being read and will not have the luxury of being able to explain complex details. There is also the likelihood that the reader's attention will wander off after four pages. It is perhaps wise then to follow a simple structure which allows the reader to find their way around the proposal and which follows a logical sequence.

Edward Blackwell in *How to Prepare a Business Plan* (Kogan Page) has produced a useful guide to this structure:

1. A brief statement of your objectives.
2. Your assessment of the market you plan to enter.
3. The skill, experience and finance you will bring to it.
4. The particular benefits of the product or service to your customers.
5. How you will set up the business.
6. The longer term view.
7. Your financial targets.
8. The money you are asking for and how it will be used.
9. Appendices to back up previous statements, including, especially, the cash flow and other financial projects.
10. History of the business (where applicable).

You need to be able to demonstrate that you have a good grasp of your business and understand the nature of the industry into which you are proposing to enter. Your professional adviser should be able to provide an objective view before submitting the business plan to the bank and should help point out any areas where the detail is unclear. On the basis of this information the bank manager will decide what form of help he is able to offer.

Checklist: presenting your case

1. Have you prepared a written description of your firm?
2. Have you described what skills the key people in your firm have to offer?
3. Have you identified your objectives?
4. Have you described how your product or service compares with the competition's?

5. Have you included what firm orders you have secured?
6. Have you identified what your realistic expectations, opportunities and goals are?
7. Do you have supporting evidence on orders you have obtained or are likely to obtain?
8. Have you (and your associates if any) made as full a commitment to your enterprise in terms of time and money as can reasonably be expected of you?
9. Have you previously obtained financial help for this or any other business? Have you repaid it within the period due?
10. If you have any loans outstanding on the business, how much are they for, for what purpose and how are they secured?
11. Can you produce an up-to-date balance sheet showing the present financial state of your company?
12. Do you have a detailed cash-flow projection, monthly over the first two years and quarterly thereafter, showing cash flow over the period of the loan?

2.3 Budgeting and Cash-flow Forecasting

One principle that it is vital to grasp is the importance of liquid cash in running a business. This should not be confused with profitability. Because of the way the profit figure is arrived at on the trading account (see Chapter 3.1), it is perfectly possible for a business to be trading profitably and yet be quite unable to pay the tax bill or the rent because its resources are tied up in stock or, even worse, in equipment.

Failure to understand the distinction between profit and cash flow is not uncommon and it can be disastrous. For example, you may be offered very persuasive financial inducements to carry or manufacture additional stock. If it is a good product and one for which there is a consistent demand, you may say to yourself that you are going to need more anyway in six months' time, so why not stock up for a whole year at a bargain price? This can be a valid argument, but before you accept it consider that when the bills come in they have to be paid with money, not with stock. Profitability means very little unless cash is there when it is needed.

This is true even for businesses that do not carry stocks, like a photographic studio producing goods only to order, or a design consultancy selling more or less intangible skills. You are still going to have outgoings on travel or materials; and even if your premises are a back room in your own house there are still bills to be met, apart from the matter of needing money to live on.

PLANNING YOUR CASH REQUIREMENTS

Planning your cash requirements is crucial from the outset of your career as a self-employed person. It will determine much of your policy towards what kinds of work you take on. It is far better, if you are short of liquid capital, to take on a number of small jobs which will keep money coming in than one big, tempting, potentially profitable one where you might run out of cash three-quarters of the way through. For, unless you make provision to receive progress payments from your customer, backed up possibly by a bank overdraft, your suppliers are going to be pressing you for payment before you are in a position to send your bills to the customer.

Even at best, in most businesses which are not taking cash across the counter there is going to be a lag between the time you are being asked for payment and when your customer pays you.

In order to estimate what your needs for cash are going to be, you should set up and revise, at three- or six-monthly intervals, a cash-flow budget; and in order to refine it, you should also check it back against what actually happened. Indeed, before you begin you should have (and the bank manager will want to see) a fully worked out cash-flow projection for the first 12 to 18 months.

The words 'cash-flow budget' sound intimidatingly technical, but mean simply that you should make a realistic forecast of money coming in and going out over the period. Again, how accurate you can be depends somewhat on the circumstances and the type of business you are in. If you have bought a going concern there may be regular contracts that you hope to maintain, or in the case of a retail business or a restaurant some kind of predictable pattern of trade which can be established from the cash book or general ledger. If you have started a new business of your own, on the other hand, you may not have much to go on in the way of facts on cash coming in. You might only have enough certain information on the next two or three months, though if you have asked yourself the questions we outlined in Chapter 1.1 you will have ensured, as far as possible, that there is a continuing demand for your product so that orders will go on arriving while you are completing the work you have already lined up. But even in cases where you do not know where the penny after next is coming from, at the very least the cash-flow budget will tell you what commitments you have to meet and, therefore, what volume of sales should be your target to this end. You can include this sales target in your budget, but do not forget that, in order to achieve it, costs of materials and additional overheads will also be involved. Moreover, both in cases where income is firmly expected and where it is only a forecast of expectations, the cost of materials and wages will have to be met before you actually get paid.

Let us take a hypothetical case here to illustrate a cash-flow budget in operation over the first four months of the year, for a small offset printing business with two partners and one employee. Over these months they have a contract to print the spring catalogue from a local firm of nursery men, a monthly list from a firm selling militaria by mail order and a booklet on the town for the Chamber of Commerce. They also have some orders for what is known as 'jobbing' – small jobs such as wedding invitations, brochures, printed labels and the like – with the prospect that a regular flow of such work can be picked up. Against this, they have to meet wages, PAYE, VAT, telephone, the running of a van, the purchase of materials, rates, electricity, National Insurance contributions, etc.

As you will see from the forecast (see Table 2.3.1), the partners budgeted for a deficit in the first two months, but they were not worried because they knew that in March and April they could expect a couple of big payments from Rosebud Nurseries and from the Chamber of Commerce. However, in order to keep solvent they had to borrow £2,000 from the bank, interest payments on which had to be paid at intervals. They also had to plan the purchase of their most costly item, paper, as close as possible to the month in which they would actually be using it for their two big jobs. There is no point in holding expensive stock which cannot be used at an early date. Even though, with inflation, it might actually have been cheaper for them to have ordered all their paper for the first four months back in January, their bank overdraft would not have been sufficient to meet the bill.

In March they had to allow for three quarterly items, electricity, telephone and their VAT return, and as the year progresses they

Table 2.3.1 An example of a cash-flow budget

Income (£)

January

From December Statement	
Militaria Ltd	500
Other work	400
	900

February

From January Statement	
Militaria Ltd	500
Other work	250
	750

March

From February Statement	
Rosebud Nurseries Ltd	5,300
Militaria Ltd	500
Other work	500
	6,300

April

From March Statement	
Chamber of Commerce	2,000
Militaria Ltd	500
Other work	500
	3,000

Expenditure (£)

January

Wages, salaries, PAYE, National Insurance	750
Rent	100
Maintenance contract	20
Petrol	40
Postage	20
Travel and Entertainment	40
Paper	1,500
Other materials	200
	2,670

February

Wages, etc	750
Rent	100
Maintenance	20
Petrol	40
Postage	20
Travel, etc	40
Materials	100
Bank Interest	60
	1,130

March

Wages, etc	750
Rent	100
Maintenance	20
Petrol	40
Postage	20
Travel, etc	40
Materials	150
Electricity	70
Telephone	40
VAT	300
Paper	1,000
	2,530

April

Wages, etc	750
Rent	100
Maintenance	20
Petrol	40
Postage	20
Travel, etc	40
Materials	100
Paper	1,500
	2,570

Cash surplus (deficit)

January	February	March	April
(1,770)	(380)	3,770	430

will have to make plans to meet such major items as rates and taxes. Note also that expenditure which is central to the activities of the business, in this case paper, has to be forecast more carefully than incidentals such as postage where a monthly average has been extended. If postage was a more crucial factor, as might be the case with a mail-order firm, this part of the cash-flow budget would have to be worked out in more detail.

Regarding the revenue part of the forecast, the partners had enough orders for jobbing work to budget fairly accurately for the first two months. For March and April they guessed a figure, hoping spring weddings and a general upturn of business after the winter would lead to a modest growth in incoming funds after that point.

The overall March and April figures look quite rosy, but after that it was clear that they would have to turn up some more jobs like Rosebud Nurseries and the Chamber of Commerce booklet because the overheads – wages, rent, the maintenance contract on their machines, bank interest – plus the cost of paper and materials needed to fill forecast work were running slightly above the expected income. So even though they are running well ahead of the game at the end of April, they would be unwise to start reducing that bank overdraft just yet.

There are many other lessons to be learnt from your cash-flow budget. They vary from business to business, but the essential points are that it is an indispensable indicator in making your buying decisions both of stock and materials, that it helps you decide your priorities between getting work (and what sort of work) and devoting all your energies to executing it, and points to the importance of getting the maximum credit and allowing the minimum!

2.4 Making the Most of Your Bank Accounts

The following may be stated as golden rules from the point of view of the smaller business: never borrow more than you have to; never buy until you need to. And when you need to, consider whether hire purchase or even leasing might not make more sense for you than committing cash to an outright purchase. There have been periods of recent history, such as the early 1970s, when the value of assets, particularly property, increased much faster than the value of the money borrowed to acquire them, but in a period when interest rates rise sharply borrowing can be so costly as to swallow up the entire profits of a business that is over reliant on borrowed money.

EFFECTIVE CASH MANAGEMENT

A surprising amount of borrowing can be avoided by effective cash management. The following are the key elements of revenue and expenditure which can be managed to your advantage.

Giving credit

Decide a credit policy. It is your choice whether to provide credit to any customer or not; however much your business needs new customers or clients, you will inevitably damage your cash flow –

even your own creditworthiness – by accepting orders on credit from known late payers and companies of doubtful solvency.

Before giving credit, ask each new customer to complete a credit application and, if in any doubt, check creditworthiness by:

- [ ] paying a credit reference agency for an online credit rating;
- [ ] taking up credit references from trade suppliers;
- [ ] writing to the Registry of County Court Judgments at 173–175 Cleveland Street, London WIP 5PE (tel: 020 7380 0133) for details of all County Court Judgements (CCJs) registered in the last six years. (The service currently costs £4.50, payable in advance, for each name at a specified address);
- [ ] ask for a bank reference, but be aware that these are notoriously vague and may be slow to arrive.

Credit control

In any case, when advances or progress payments are not negotiable, always agree your credit terms at the order stage, including:

- [ ] the credit period allowed (eg 30 days from the date of invoice);
- [ ] details of any discounts or rebates you offer (eg for prompt payment or bulk purchases);
- [ ] whether your prices exclude carriage charges ('ex works');
- [ ] whether you charge interest on overdue accounts – and, if so, how much;
- [ ] a 'retention of title' clause (specifying that the goods remain your property until paid for) where appropriate.

Be sure to have these terms printed on the back of your invoices and other relevant business documents – such as credit application forms.

Since November 2000 small businesses benefit from the new late payment legislation giving them a legal right to claim interest from late-paying customers in both large and small companies.

Managing debtors: progress payments

In the case of work done on contract – say, a design or consultancy job involving sizeable sums of money over a longer period of time such as three or four months – try to persuade your customer to make an advance and/or progress payments. After all, you are going to be involved in considerable expenditure of time, at least, before the final sum becomes due. Whether you can make such an approach depends, of course, on how well you know the customer and whether you think he or she needs your services as much as or more than you need the work. In the case of assignments that run over an extended period, subject to periodic review, where the final amount of work or time charged is uncertain, your client will probably accept the case for a regular monthly or quarterly retainer to be set against the final bill.

Facilitating prompt payment

There are a number of steps you can take to make sure that your customers/clients have no cause to delay payment and to position your invoices and statements for prompt attention:

- ☐ Establish how each customer pays invoices (eg payment only if there is an order number or if the invoice is passed to the accounts department by the date of each monthly cheque run).
- ☐ Get the order details right in written form (eg for a consultancy service, the order should specify the work to be undertaken, perhaps by referring to an agreement).
- ☐ Obtain proof of delivery for goods.
- ☐ Ensure the customer/client is satisfied. Sort out any problems immediately.
- ☐ Ensure that your invoices are easy to understand, with the correct order references and the agreed payment date; provide details of your address, VAT number and full bank details.
- ☐ Send your invoice out to the right person on the day the goods are sent or the service performed.
- ☐ Send statements out every month, as early as you can.

☐ Start chasing for payment by telephone as soon as the account becomes overdue.

☐ Use stop lists, where appropriate, for customers to whom you do not wish to give more credit, and make sure that your staff are aware of it. Inform customers/clients that they are 'on stop' and do not supply goods or services until they have brought their accounts up to date.

Managing your creditors

It is not dishonest to take the maximum period of payment allowed by your suppliers within the parameters of your agreement with them and late payment legislation. Although you do not want to get the reputation of being a slow payer, once you have established yourself as a reliable account your suppliers may give you considerable leeway before they start pressing you for payment even on an overdue sum. Nor is it dishonest to take note that some suppliers press for payment quickly whereas others are more lax, and to pay the former first.

In order to smooth out the demands on your cash flow, it may make sense to spread payments to certain core creditors (notably your telephone services and utilities providers who bill you quarterly) into regular monthly payments, normally by direct debit against your current account. However, be careful to ensure that the total of the direct debits you set up and their timing is covered amply by regular assured revenue. Direct debits returned unpaid will damage your credit health seriously.

Managing your VAT payments and receipts

Assuming that you have registered your business for VAT and that your VAT quarter is January to March, you have to complete your VAT return for that quarter and submit payment of the VAT you have billed to your customers minus the VAT you have been billed by your suppliers by the end of April. Therefore, if you can send out a lot of invoices to customers on 1 January and collect the money quickly, you will have the benefit of your VAT, either in your current account or in a special deposit account, for nearly four months. Equally, if you are planning to buy a large piece of equipment (say, a van) on which there are many hundreds of pounds in VAT for you to claim back, juggling with the precise date on which you make the purchase to the end of your VAT quarter, can minimise the damage to your cash flow.

OVERDRAFT VS BUSINESS LOANS

Many businesses will require some form of bank finance when they are starting up, either an overdraft or a business loan. The purpose of an overdraft is to fund short-term (less than 12 months) cash-flow requirements. A business loan should be chosen when the funding is required for fixed assets (not other-wise funded), start-up capital or other longer-term requirements. A key difference between the terms of an overdraft and a term loan is that the overdraft is usually repayable to the bank on demand, whereas the loan is normally repayable only on default (if the borrower is in breach of its terms).

However, from your point of view, an overdraft may be the more acceptable alternative. Unless there is a commitment to reduce the overdraft incrementally, your monthly revenue is not impacted by repayment instalments. Moreover, you will be paying interest only on the day-to-day amount of your indebtedness in a single current account.

Some banks charge a commitment or arrangement fee for setting up a loan account and the interest charges and repayments of principal are debited automatically to your business's current account. However, there is a marked preference by most banks for granting a business loan and sometimes insisting that you main-tain your current account in credit. Fixed-rate loans are becoming more popular, setting the interest rate at the outset so that the cost is known when the loan is taken out. In the case of an overdraft, interest is charged on the daily balance outstanding; while this may save you money, the interest rate will fluctuate.

ADDITIONAL BANK ACCOUNTS

Remember that you can be penalised heavily for late payments of

VAT and income tax or corporation tax falling due. We have referred above to the possible opening of a separate account for VAT received and payable. Unless you are a very diligent book-keeper and cash-flow planner, you may be wise to make such a provision rather than using your VAT collections to minimise temporarily the use of the overdraft on your current account.

There are two other types of payment that you may be prudent to provide for with additional bank accounts.

Taxation reserve account

The payment of self-assessed income tax on self-employed earnings or corporation tax in the case of companies is inescapable, even though there may be considerable time lags between the end of your accounting period and the due payment dates.

Accumulating your estimated taxation liabilities in a tax reserve deposit account is sensible once your business is established. In addition to smoothing your cash flow, it will have the additional value of demonstrating to your bank manager that there will be no unexpected demand for tax on your main business account.

Payroll account

If you employ staff, probably on a monthly salaried basis, it is essential that you pay them promptly at the month end and that employer's PAYE payments are made on time. You can administer salaries most conveniently through a computerised payroll system and a separate bank account from which your bank will make direct transfers of net salaries to your employees' bank accounts on the last working day of each month, provided of course that you have previously transferred from your main account the total sum to be disbursed.

Indeed, payroll is a crucial part of your operations. You are required by law to collect tax and National Insurance (NI) under the PAYE system and penalties are imposed for failure to do so. Tax and NI contributions must be paid to the Inland Revenue Accounts office by the 19th of each month. (Employers who expect to collect less than £1,500 a month in PAYE, NI and student loan repayments may pay quarterly in January, April, July and October.)

As an employer, in addition to making prompt PAYE payments you are required to:

- [ ] register with your PAYE tax office;
- [ ] keep basic payroll information for each employee;
- [ ] keep a list of all wage payments on form P11 or the equivalent;
- [ ] make additional deductions from your employees' pay (subject to individual employee's written consent) for any contributions to occupational pension schemes, holiday pay schemes, union subscriptions, loan repayments, student loan repayments, attachment or earnings orders or corrections to previous payslips.

MANAGING THE UNEXPECTED

In the normal course of events, unexpected crises will arise as a result of failure or success. On the one hand, your cash-flow projections may be blown apart by the sudden loss of a major customer or the decision of a regular client not to renew a long-standing contract. When that happens, it will probably not be possible to replace the business or to cut expenditure to compensate for the loss of revenue immediately. A worse case, because it would probably occur without warning, would be the sudden default of a major debtor through insolvency.

But your business can also 'suffer from the problems of success', a phrase coined by Edward Heath when he was Prime Minister to describe the dire state of the British economy. Many a businessperson is caught unprepared on a tide of expansion. The symptoms may emerge as problems with people, when the staff who were in at the beginning find it difficult to handle a larger-scale operation, or when mistakes are made in interviewing and selecting people for new jobs in an expanding company, or simply when the owners are stretched in too many different directions to look at individual trouble spots in sufficient detail.

Most frequently these trouble spots turn out to be connected, directly or indirectly, with finance. You are producing something for which there is a demand; the world starts beating a path to your door; you appear to be selling your product or service profitably, and, suddenly, in the midst of apparent plenty, you start running out of cash. What has probably happened is that you have forgotten that in general you do not get paid until you have delivered the goods or performed the service, but your suppliers and the additional staff you have taken on have to be paid out of cash flow generated by the previous and smaller scale of operation.

If your business is in manufacturing or in the wholesaling or retailing trades, a common problem arising from expansion is inadequate stock control. A better stock control system could release substantial sums of money. You should aim to maintain just enough of each type of stock to serve your customers at the required service level on an ongoing basis after taking into account seasonal fluctuations. It follows that there is an advantage in choosing suppliers who can deliver promptly, as this will help to minimise your stock levels. You should set a target stock-turn (eg six times a year) for each category of stock and monitor your performance. Sell off any old or obsolete stock, even if the best price you can get is below book value.

In Chapter 5.5 we address the general question of funding growth, but for now the main point is that you must find the time to check and revise your cash-flow projections, preferably weekly, on the basis of the prior month's experience and the changes which you can predict for the business. Develop red light systems which will warn you automatically if something needs querying and, having identified any problems, take immediate action.

Above all, when the storm clouds gather, either as a result of failure or success, be sure to keep your bank manager informed. If you want to maintain the support of your bank you should always signal any unfavourable impact of the unexpected on your forward cash flow together with your plans for tackling the problem.

Checklist: bank accounts

1. Much borrowing can be avoided by effective cash management.
2. Decide a credit policy and enforce it.
3. Beware of the unexpected problems of success as well as disasters. Develop red light systems which will warn you automatically. Check and revise your cash-flow projections regularly, even weekly.
4. Always agree credit terms at the order stage. Have your standard credit terms printed on the back of your invoices and other business documents.
5. If you provide services, you may be able to negotiate retainers or progress payments with major clients.
6. Spread payments to your core creditors and essential suppliers on a regular monthly basis. Otherwise, take the maximum period of payment allowed by suppliers.
7. Consider opening separate bank accounts for VAT and payroll transactions and a deposit account for income or corporation tax.
8. Never borrow more than you have to. Consider using hire purchase or leasing instead of committing cash to outright purchase.
9. Always signal any unfavourable impact of the unexpected on your cash flow to your bank manager in advance, together with your plans for tackling the problem.
10. Make sure that you choose carefully between an overdraft and a loan, taking account of the length of time for which the funds will be needed and that repayment can be afforded.

Part 2

Running Your Own Business

Section 3

Accountancy and Taxation

3.1 Simple Accounting Systems and Their Uses

Any bank manager will tell you that at least 80 per cent of all business failures are caused by inadequate record keeping. Unfortunately, this fault is by no means uncommon in small businesses because the entrepreneurial person who tends to set up on their own is often temperamentally different from the patient administrative type who enjoys paperwork and charting information in the form of business records. He or she is apt to feel that what really keeps the show on the road is obtaining and doing the work, or being in the shop to look after customers. However, unless you record money coming in and going out, owed and owing, you will never have more than the haziest idea of how much to charge for your products or services, where your most profitable areas of activity are (and indeed whether you are making a profit at all), how much you can afford to pay yourself and whether there is enough coming in to cover immediate commitments in the way of wages, trade debts, tax or professional fees, rent, rates, etc.

It used to be the case that only a limited company was obliged to keep proper books of account: the definition is that they have to do so 'with respect to all receipts and expenses, sales and purchases, assets and liabilities and they must be sufficient to give

Considering computerising your accounts?

Congratulations! You've taken a big step and started your own business. Running your own business is exciting and rewarding but, as you'll already know, also very hard work. The administrative side alone can take up a lot of your precious time, when you'd much rather be concentrating on growing your business. There is a solution to this problem – business software. Computerising many aspects of your business can take the pain out of managing the more boring administrative tasks such as your accounts and payroll.

But where do you start when considering computerising your business processes?

Don't

Walk into a shop and buy the cheapest product on offer – make sure you buy a system which is suited to your business and this will save time and money in the future.

Do

Think about the type of software package most suitable for your business. For example, do you need to automate purchase and sales ledgers, do you need to be able to handle invoicing or is managing your stock an issue? You may want to be able to link your accounting software to your website or be able to take advantage of ebanking. Whatever your needs, it's important that you establish your software requirements before you go shopping.

Collect information on accounting software and PCs – read some reviews in leading PC magazines.

Talk to your accountant who will be able to advise you on the best software for your business. You could also visit your nearest IT dealer or retailer such as PC World or Staples where you'll find a good selection.

You could also start by talking to us. Sage has been providing software and support to businesses like yours for more than 20 years and with over 400,000 customers in the UK we like to think that we understand your software needs.

a true and fair picture of the state of the company's affairs and to explain its transactions'. Under the 1994 Finance Act this provision has effectively been extended to apply to all kinds of business. You are now required to:

□ Set up adequate records of all business transactions, including personal drawings and personal money put into the business. Retailers will have to keep separate records of goods taken for personal use.
□ Maintain those records throughout the year and keep them up to date.
□ Retain the documentation for a recommended six years.

As a rule of thumb, if your scale of operations is big enough to come within the orbit of VAT (that is, if your turnover is, or is likely to be, over £55,000 a year) we suggest you get qualified help with the bookkeeping that will be required. But first of all, let us look at the very basic records you ought to keep if you are in business for yourself at all, even as a part-time freelance.

TWO STARTING POINTS

At the small-scale sole trader end, one reason why you need to keep records is to justify your expenditure claims to the tax inspector. For this purpose you may find that your most useful investment is a spike on which incoming receipts, invoices, statements and delivery notes can be placed. This ensures that essential documentary evidence of expenditure is retained and kept together, not used to put cups on or carried around in your wallet for making odd notes on the back. As your business grows you may find that the spike should be supplemented by a spring-loaded box file in which all such items should be placed in date order.

However, not all expenditure can be accounted for in this way. Fares, for instance, are not generally receipted, nor is postage, or you may be buying items for personal use at the same time as others that are directly connected with your business. Thus it is a good idea to carry a notebook around with you and enter up any expenses that you have incurred that are not documented. You will find that the tax office will accept a certain level of claims of this kind provided they bear a credible relationship to the business you are in. For example, if you are earning income from travelling round the country giving lectures, they will accept a fairly high level of claims for fares, but not if the nature of your business is carrying out a local building repair service.

For larger outlays you may find credit cards a useful record-keeping aid. Apart from the fact that when card companies render their account for payment they provide a breakdown of where, when and how items were purchased, they also, in effect, give you six weeks' credit.

KEEPING A CASH BOOK

The next stage is to keep a cash book. It does not have to be anything elaborate. The object of the exercise is to provide a record from which an accountant or bookkeeper can write up a proper set of books and to save their time and trouble (which you have to pay for) in slogging through dozens or possibly hundreds of pieces of paper in order to do this. Since your professional adviser will have to work from your records it is a good idea to ask him what is the most convenient way of setting them out. He may suggest that you buy one of the ready-made books of account, though such books are not suitable for every kind of self-employment. If you find it difficult to follow his instructions, or you are using a ready-made book and are having trouble with it, here is something very simple you can do (see Table 3.1.1).

Buy a large (A4) ruled notebook and open it up at the first double page. Allocate the left-hand page to sales and the right-hand page to expenditure. If sales and expenditure fall into further categories which you want to keep track of, say, if you want to keep travel costs separate from the cost of materials, or if you are registered for VAT, divide up the page accordingly. You should also rule up columns for the date, the invoice number and

Table 3.1.1 Sample entries from the cash book of a cabinet-maker

	INCOME						EXPENDITURE				
Date	Invoice No	Date paid	Details	Amount (£)	VAT (£)	Date	Invoice No	Cheque/Credit card	Details	Amount (£)	VAT (£)
2.5.03	8061		Six tables	224.00	39.20	3.5.03	–	911112	Wooden Top timber yard	850.00	148.75
6.5.03	cash		Desk	400.00	70.00	4.5.03	Petty cash voucher 23	cash	Stamps	6.00	–
10.5.03	8062		Dining table	300.00	52.50	5.5.03	Petty cash voucher 24	cash	Expenses: trip to Harwich to inspect timber	40.00	7.00
12.5.03	cash		Repair of wooden chest	160.00	28.00	13.5.03	–	911113	Electricity bill	80.00	14.00

the details of the invoice. Enter up these details at the end of each day's trading and you will find that it works both as a discipline in checking that all your sales and purchases are logged and that you now have a further record in addition to the documents on your spike or in your box file.

MORE ELABORATE SYSTEMS

This sort of record is fine as far as it goes and in a small business engaged mainly in cash transactions your accountant may not need very much more than this to produce a set of accounts. In a larger concern, or one that operates extensively on taking and giving credit, it has some obvious limitations. For example, keeping track of when payments are made or received can become rather messy and difficult, and you will need to have a separate record, called a ledger, of the customers and suppliers with whom you do business so that you can see at a glance how much you owe or are owed in the case of individual accounts. Such details will be taken from further books – purchases and sales daybooks and a more elaborate kind of cash book than the simplified one we have described above. Though we have recommended that you leave the details of this kind of book-keeping to a qualified person, let us look briefly at what is involved:

1. *Cash book.* Shows all payments received and made, with separate columns for cash transactions and those made through the bank (ie payments by cheque). Amounts received from customers are credited to their account in the ledger (see below). Payments made to suppliers are debited to their account in the ledger.
2. *Petty cash book.* Shows expenditure on minor items – postage, fares, entertainment and so forth, with a column for VAT.
3. *Sales daybook.* Records invoices sent out to customers in date order, with some analysis of the goods or service supplied and a column for VAT.
4. *Purchases daybook.* Records similar information about purchases.

5. *Ledger.* Sets out details, taken from sales and purchases daybooks, of individual customers' and suppliers' accounts and serves as a record of amounts owed and owing. Details from the analysis columns of the sales and purchases daybooks are also transcribed, usually monthly, under corresponding headings in the ledger. This enables you to see at a glance where your sales are coming from and where your money is going.

6. *Capital goods ledger.* If you own expensive capital equipment – cars, lorries, machine tools, high-class film or photographic equipment, etc – you should have separate accounts for them in the ledger because the method of accounting for them is somewhat different. Capital items depreciate over a period of time (as you will know if you have ever sold a car) and this fact must be reflected both in your balance sheet and profit and loss account, and in the way you price your goods and services.

Writing down capital goods affects your tax liability. With some items you can write down the full advantage of this concession. How you deal with depreciation is very much an area where you are dependent on your accountant's expert advice.

ELECTRONIC BOOKKEEPING

There are many different reasons for putting your accounts system on to a computer. Routine tasks become much quicker, statements and other regular correspondence can be mail-merged and personalised and up-to-date balances included. Correcting any mistakes can be done at the touch of a button and if your business is growing, a computerised accounting system will make life much easier when you take on new staff, increase your spending or have more invoices to chase.

Perhaps the most useful aspect of a computerised accounts system is the fact that once the information is recorded, it can be used to give you a snapshot of the business performance at any time, which is ideal when preparing your end-of-year accounts.

The following are a few points to bear in mind when looking to purchase a bookkeeping package:

☐ Don't walk into a shop or dealership and buy the cheapest thing on offer. Remember, it is not the PC that does the real work, it is the software and if you buy a system that is not suited to your business it could cost you a lot of time, effort and money later on.

☐ Define what it is that you need your accounting software package to do. Do you want to run your whole system on it or just do some sales invoicing? Will you need to automate just the main ledgers or would you like to put sales-order processing, purchase-order processing and stock control onto the computer? Do you have any special procedures or requirements specific to your business that you must stick to, whatever the system? It is important that you answer these questions before you start shopping around.

☐ Collect some information on accounting software products and PCs and read some of the reviews published in computer magazines.

☐ Talk to your accountant, who may be able to advise you about some packages. Information may also be available from authorised software dealers, large retail stores such as PC World and professional bodies such as the Institute of Chartered Accountants.

It is also worth remembering that computers do crash and if you have failed to make copies of your accounts on disk on a regular basis you could land yourself in deep water. Back-up stationery, such as invoices, are worth having as well in such a situation so that a technical problem shouldn't turn into an income-threatening crisis.

TRADING AND PROFIT AND LOSS ACCOUNT

From the books described above, your accountant can draw together the information needed to compile the trading and profit and loss account (see Table 3.1.2). The function of the account is to tell you whether you have been making a gross profit and a net profit on your trading. It must be compiled annually and preferably more often than that, quarterly for instance, to enable you to measure your progress and make your VAT return.

To put together the account he begins by identifying the period you want to cover. He then totals up the value of all sales, whether paid for or not. Then he takes your opening stock and adds it to the purchases (but not expenditure such as rent or repayment of interest on loans). From this he takes the value of your stock (based on cost or market value, whichever is lower) at the end of the period you want to cover. Deducting the value of opening stock plus purchases less closing stock from the value of sales will give him your gross trading profit (or loss) over the period.

Table 3.1.2 *Example of a trading and profit and loss account*

Trading and Profit and Loss Account for year ended 31.12.00

	£	£
Sales		65,000
Purchases	30,000	
Opening Stock	5,000	
	35,000	
Less Closing Stock	6,000	29,000
Gross Profit		36,000
Rent and Rates	3,000	
Salaries	9,000	
Heat, Light	600	
Phone	350	
Travel	800	
Repairs	500	
Depreciation	1,800	
Professional Advice	450	
		16,500
Net Profit		19,500

Using this information he can work out the net profit and loss over the same period. The gross profit figure from your trading account appears at the top and against it he sets all the items from the various expenditure accounts in the ledger. He also includes in this figure the depreciation on capital equipment, but not its actual cost (even if you purchased it during the period in question) because that crops up later, in the balance sheet.

Deducting these from the gross profit gives you your profit over the period. If the total expenditure exceeds the gross profit you have obviously incurred a loss.

THE BALANCE SHEET

We have mentioned in the previous section that capital equipment does not figure in the profit and loss account, but goes into the balance sheet. The balance sheet is a picture, taken at a particular point in the year (usually at the end of a company's financial year), of what the firm _owes_ and what it _owns_ (see Table 3.1.3). (This is not the same as a profit and loss account, which covers a period of time.)

In a balance sheet the assets of the firm used to be set out on the right and the liabilities on the left, but it is modern practice to display them as below. However, all the assets and all the liabilities are generally not lumped together, but distinguished qualitatively by the words 'fixed' and 'current'.

'Fixed assets' are items which are permanently necessary for the business to function, such as machinery, cars, fixtures and fittings, your premises or the lease on them. 'Current assets', on the other hand, are things from which cash will be realised in the course of your trading activities. These include the amount owed to you by your debtors (from the customers' accounts in the ledger), and the value of your stock (from the trading account). It also, of course, includes cash at the bank (from the cash book).

With liabilities, the position is reversed. 'Fixed liabilities' are those which you do not have to repay immediately, like a long-term loan from a kindly relative. What you do have to repay promptly, however, is the interest on that loan and this goes under

Table 3.1.3   *An example of a balance sheet*

Balance Sheet as at 31.12.00

	£	£	
Fixed Assets			
Vehicles	3,200		
less depreciation	800	2,400	
Fixtures and fittings	2,000		
less depreciation	500	1,500	
		3,900	
Current Assets			
Stock	6,000		
Debtors	1,800		
Cash	150		
	7,950		
Less Current Liabilities			
Trade Creditors	1,590		
Net Current Assets		6,360	
Total Assets		10,260	
Represented by			
		Authorised	Issued
Capital (2,000 shares at £1 each)		1,000	1,000
Loan repayable 2,000			2,000
Profit			7,260
			10,260

'current liabilities' if it is due, but has not been paid at the time the balance sheet has been prepared. The same is true of any amounts you owe to your suppliers' accounts in the ledger. Another item that goes on the 'liabilities' side is the share capital in the business and the profit from the trading account, because both these amounts are ultimately owed by the company to the shareholders. Where, on the other hand, the company has been making a loss, the amount is deducted either from profits retained from earlier periods or from the shareholders' capital.

WHAT SHOULD YOU BE LOOKING FOR IN YOUR RECORDS?

You will want to know whether you are making or losing money, but there are many other useful bits of information to be gleaned as well. If you are making a profit, what relationship does it bear to the capital employed in the business? You can calculate this by subtracting total liabilities from total assets. If you are making less than a 15 per cent return on capital, you are not, on the face of things, making much progress, though, of course, you could be paying yourself a very handsome salary before the profit figure was arrived at.

The percentage return on capital can be calculated by the following sum:

$$\frac{\text{profit}}{\text{capital employed}} \times 100$$

Another thing you can work out from your balance sheet is whether you are maintaining sufficient working capital to meet your requirements for new stock or materials or to pay for wages and rent. Here you look at current assets and current liabilities. The calculation:

$$\frac{\text{current assets}}{\text{current liabilities}}$$

gives you your *current* ratio. If you have, say, £1,000 of each you are said to have a current ratio of 1:1. Clearly, in that case you would be in trouble if a major debtor were to go bankrupt. So it may be that you should cut back on some item of expenditure you were planning on. Furthermore, the current ratio includes certain items, like stocks, which may not be immediately realisable. If your current ratio is low, and you are still in two minds whether or not to buy that new machine, you might apply what is known as the *acid test ratio*, which shows your ability to meet liabilities quickly if the need arises. Here you simply deduct stock from your figure for current assets to give you a figure for liquid assets, ie debtors and cash. If the ratio of liquid assets to current liabilities is too low, you may have more money tied up in stock than you should have.

Even the acid test ratio assumes that your debtors are going to pay you in a reasonable period of time: most likely within the terms of trade you are allowing. But is this assumption really correct? Look at the annual sum:

$$\frac{\text{debtors}}{\text{sales}} \times 365$$

If your sales are £10,000 and your debtors owe £1,000, they are near enough to meeting net monthly terms for you not to worry about it. But if your debtors, on the same sales turnover, are running to £3,000, there is something wrong with your credit control and you are probably heading for serious trouble.

Another important ratio is profit to sales. What this should be depends on the sort of business you are in. Your accountant should be able to advise you here on the basis of her knowledge of similar traders. If your percentage is on the low side you may be buying badly, failing to pass on cost increases, or possibly incurring losses from pilferage.

There are other ratios to look out for, but we hope that you will now be clear that the balance and trading and profit and loss accounts are not just a financial rigmarole you have to go through, but very valuable indicators of the way your business is going, or the financial state of some other business you are thinking of buying. They are also useful for:

1. assisting the bank manager to determine the terms of an overdraft;
2. selling your business to a proposed purchaser;
3. agreeing tax liabilities with the inspector of taxes.

Checklist: simple accounting systems

1. Do you carry a notebook to record smaller items of business expenditure, such as taxi fares, as soon as they are incurred?
2. Have you considered using credit cards for larger outlays?
3. Do you have a system for filing incoming invoices as soon as they are received?
4. Have you asked your accountant what books and records he/she advises you to keep?
5. Do you know and understand the procedures involved? If not, have you asked your accountant to recommend someone who can help you on a regular basis – at least once a week or once a month, depending on your scale of operations?
6. Do you have any idea of the ratios current in your type of business, so that you can measure your performance against the norm?

3.2 Invoicing and Credit Control

Time is money, as the old saying goes. It ought to be written large in the minds of anyone giving credit, that is, any business that supplies goods and services which are not on a strictly cash-on-the-nail basis.

In these days of tight money there is a tendency for many customers, including large and reputable firms, to delay payment as long as possible because, as noted in Chapter 2.4, taking credit long – and preferably giving it short – is one way to maintain a flow of cash in the business. The supplier who does not demonstrate that he is in a hurry for payment, therefore, is the one who comes last in the queue. However, help to improve the payment culture has come in the form of the Statutory Right to Interest (SRI) which was introduced in November 1998. Under the SRI any business with under 50 employees – including sole traders – can charge interest on late payment. While the DTI hopes that the parties involved can work out a payment time between themselves, the SRI can enforce a payment schedule of 30 days after which interest can be charged. The right will eventually be rolled out to all businesses regardless of size.

SENDING OUT INVOICES AND STATEMENTS

The first step towards ensuring that you are not in this position is to issue an invoice for work done or goods supplied as soon as possible after you deliver. On the invoice you should give the customer's order number. If it was a telephone order and you forgot to get an order number, you should at least give the date of the order. You should also state when you expect to receive payment. The usual period is between seven and 30 days after delivery. Many private individuals, in fact, pay on receipt of an invoice. Business firms, on the other hand, expect to receive a statement of their account at the end of the month, setting out invoices due or sent during this period: their dates, invoice number, the nature of the goods and the amount. You can have statement forms printed, but if you are not a limited company you can use your letterheads for this purpose, simply typing the word STATEMENT at the top. Every customer who has received an invoice and not paid at the end of the month when it is due should get a statement, which should repeat your payment terms.

The particulars of the invoice(s) are drawn from your customer's ledger, though it is essential to keep copies of the actual invoices as well, filed in date order. You are going to need them for VAT purposes, or to check queries. When you receive payment, check that it tallies with the amount due on the customer's ledger entry, mark off the details against each individual item as shown in the previous chapter and enter the amount in the cash book. If the customer requires a receipt, ask her to return the statement (or the invoice if she has paid on that) with her remittance – otherwise you will be involved in time-consuming typing – tick off the items paid, and attach a receipt form or bang on a rubber stamp, 'Paid'. Be uniform about your systems. If you have two different ones for the same part of your operation you are going to waste a lot of time looking in the wrong place when you come to check a document.

Do not neglect the process of checking payments, because any amounts unpaid must go into next month's statement. Some invoices which have appeared on your statement will not be paid because they are not yet due for payment. For example, if your terms are 30 days and you have invoiced an item on the 20th of the month, a business customer is unlikely to pay until the month following. Quite often he only activates payments at the end of the month, unless he is unusually punctilious, efficient or being offered extra discount for quick settlement.

As already mentioned, the Statutory Right to Interest does allow interest to be charged on late payment. At the time of its introduction in November 1998, according to Barclays Small Business Bulletin only 24 per cent of small business owners said that they were planning to use the legislation because they did not want to upset customers and create additional administration. However, there is some indication that the introduction of SRI has already improved the payment culture even when so few people are planning to use it.

Even with the additional threat of being able to add interest, there will still be times when a client can't or won't pay. What, then, happens when the payment becomes overdue? This is extremely annoying, because at best it is going to involve you in extra correspondence. You must be tactful and patient if you want more business from your clients, and remember that some large organisations are slow in paying, not by choice but because they are dictated to by their computer accounting systems. But if your patience is exhausted, there are usually three stages. The first is a polite reminder of the amount due, how long it has been due and of your terms of supply. This should be coupled with asking the customer whether she has any queries on any of the invoices which might explain the delay. If there is no reply by the end of that month, write again, referring to your first reminder and setting a deadline for payment with additional payment. A telephone call to the customer is often opportune at this stage. If that deadline is not met, you will have to write again, referring to your previous reminders and threatening legal action unless a new and final deadline is met. (If you have a large number of credit accounts, it may pay you to have sets of blank letters for each stage prepared in advance.)

In most cases the threat of legal action will do the trick, but how you proceed after that depends on the amount of money involved. Fortunately the Court and Legal Services Act of 1990 has simplified procedures. Debts of any amount can be recovered in the County Court, without involving solicitors – though, of course, their services may ultimately be necessary if the claim is disputed by the debtor.

Then there are three important points to establish before starting legal action:

1. Can the defendant actually pay? Wringing blood from a stone is a notoriously fruitless exercise.
2. Can you prove the claim by producing documentation about what was actually agreed, such as a confirming letter? Bounced cheques, reminders to pay, etc are also relevant.
3. Are you sure you have got hold of the right person? You may have been dealing with an individual acting on behalf of a company. In that case the claim is against the company.

The next stage is to issue a default summons in the County Court. It does not have to be in the area where the defendant lives, which could be in your favour if the case is undefended. If it is defended, the matter will automatically be heard in the defendant's County Court, though here again there is an option to full-scale proceedings. If the amount involved is less than £1,000 the matter automatically goes to arbitration. This means both parties are obliged to accept the arbitrator's judgement.

The default summons involves a certain amount of paperwork. The court officials will brief you if you choose to do this yourself rather than getting your solicitor to do so. Remember, he may charge you anything from £50 to £200 per hour, depending on how high-powered a firm you choose.

In the first place the summons is sent by post. The defendant then has 21 days in which to reply and if he fails to do so or to announce his intention to defend the action, then you as the plaintiff are entitled to judgement, which will include the amount claimed, plus court costs: a maximum of £70 for claims of under £5,000, plus extras which can mount up if the case drags on. The problem is not so much the court costs but the time and trouble that it all takes. However, the good news is that few defendants will let matters go as far as this and the ultimate sanction of having bailiffs called in on them, if they can pay and unless they intend to defend the case.

You can, of course, ask for references before giving credit, though this is a matter which has to be approached with some delicacy; but if you receive a sizeable order out of the blue from some business firm with whom you have not previously dealt, it is advisable to ask for a couple of references in acknowledging the order. Ask the referees to what amount they give credit to this particular customer, how long they have been doing business with her and whether she pays promptly.

If your business consists of making or repairing goods to order – tailoring, for instance – it is not unusual to ask the customer to pay up to 50 per cent on account where an estimate of over £50 or so has been given. This helps cash flow as well as protecting you against possible default. Equally, if goods of resaleable value are left with you for repair you should display a notice reserving the right to dispose of them if the customer does not come to collect them within a reasonable time of completion of the work.

A common delaying tactic, or it may be a perfectly legitimate query, is for the customer to ask for copy invoices on receipt of your statement. Do not part with your file copy. You will have to send a photocopy if you do not keep duplicates for this purpose.

CREDIT CARDS

For larger personal transactions and for items such as the settlement of restaurant bills, credit cards are a popular method of making payment. A business which wants to offer credit card payment facilities to its customers has to make application to the company concerned, which then sets a money limit to the transaction per customer for which the business in question can accept payment on that company's cards. Above that limit, which is based roughly on the applicant's average transaction per customer, the sale has to be referred back to the credit card company. This can be done over the telephone.

Each sale, as it is made, is entered up on a voucher supplied by the credit card company. The voucher is paid into the bank by the seller and the amount is debited to the card holder's account. The advantage of credit cards from the seller's point of view is that he receives guaranteed payment. Against this, he has to pay to the bank a small percentage on every transaction, the amount of this percentage being negotiated at the time he joins the scheme.

Most credit card companies operate on lines very similar to the scheme we have just outlined. Diner's Club vouchers, for instance, though not paid into a bank, are sent to the Club organisation on certain specified dates, whereupon payment is made to the seller.

CHECKING INCOMING INVOICES AND STATEMENTS

Unless you transact your business by paying in cash or by cheque on the spot (which is likely in only a few business spheres), you will also be at the receiving end of invoices and statements from your suppliers. The moment they come in, put them on the spike. Then, daily if possible, enter the details in the suppliers' ledger, as described in Chapter 3.1. File incoming invoices in date order, for you will need them for VAT purposes.

When you receive your statement, make sure it tallies with the amounts and details which you have entered in the suppliers' ledger, mark off all the items paid and write up the amount in the cash book.

If you are paying by cheque there is no need to ask for a receipt (which only adds to the paperwork) since an honoured cheque is itself a receipt. Make sure, though, that you enter up the stubs, unless you write up the cash book at the same time as you draw the cheques.

Checklist: invoicing and credit control

Invoicing
1. Are you invoicing promptly, on or with delivery?
2. Do your invoices clearly state your terms?
3. Do you ensure that the customer's name, address and order number (if any) or date are correctly stated on your invoice?
4. Are your statements sent out promptly at the end of the month? Do they state your payment terms?
5. Are they clear and easy to follow? Would they make sense to you if you were the recipient?

6. Are you checking payments received against ledger entries?

Credit control

1. Does every account have a credit limit?
2. Is it based on first-hand knowledge of the customer as a credit risk or personally, his track record as a payer with you or others in your line of business, on representatives' reports or reliable trade references, or on bankers' references, in that order of decreasing usefulness?
3. Do you exercise special vigilance on new accounts?
4. Do your statements show the age of outstanding balances and do you or your credit controller look at outgoing statements to check on customers whose payments situation seems to be deteriorating?
5. Do you have a system for dealing with customers who exceed their credit limit?
6. Do you have a sequence of reminder procedures for dealing with overdue accounts by telephone calls and/or letters?
7. Do you check orders received against a list of customers who have exceeded their credit limit or who are proving to be reluctant payers or non-payers?
8. Does the person in charge of credit control liaise with those responsible for supplying the account in question to make sure that there are no special reasons for non-payment before sharper warnings are delivered?
9. Do you regularly check on the debtor:sales ratio to make sure you are not heading for a liquidity problem by being too generous about extending credit?
10. Do you have a list of people you can contact in your principal customers' accounts departments if there are payment problems?

3.3 | **VAT**

If the taxable outputs of your business, which for practical purposes means what you charge your customers for any goods or services that are not specifically 'exempt', exceed, or are likely to exceed, £55,000 in a year, you will have to register with the Customs and Excise (not the tax office, in this case) as a taxable trader for VAT purposes. This means that you will have to remit to Customs and Excise, either monthly or quarterly, 17.5 per cent of the ex-VAT price you charge on your 'outputs', this being the current standard rate of VAT. However, you will be able to deduct from these remittances most VAT which you yourself have been charged by your suppliers – your 'inputs'. This item covers not only VAT on materials used in producing the goods or services you supply to your customers, but everything which you have to buy to run your business, including such things as telephone charges. VAT also extends to goods purchased from outside the EU.

Not all goods and services carry 17.5 per cent VAT. Some are 'zero rated' – basic foodstuffs, newspapers and exported goods being notable examples. Full details are contained in VAT Notices 700 and 701, issued by Customs and Excise, New King's Beam House, 22 Upper Ground, London SE1 9PJ, and you should obtain from them these Notices together with any others about VAT which are relevant to your trade or profession. You will find your local office listed in the phone book. The significance of zero rating is that even though you do not charge VAT on goods of this nature that you supply, you can still claim back VAT on all your inputs, excluding the purchase of cars and business entertainment of domestic customers.

Zero rating is not, however, the same as 'exemption'. Zero rating carries a theoretical rate of VAT, which is 0 per cent.

Exemption means that no rate of VAT applies at all and examples of exempt suppliers are bookmakers, persons selling or renting land and buildings, and various types of medical services. The exempt status is not particularly desirable, because if you are exempt you still have to pay VAT on all your inputs but have no outputs to set the tax off against.*

In this sense exempt traders are like private individuals, and the question, therefore, arises as to whether you should, as you are entitled to do, ask to be registered as a taxable trader even though your outputs are less than the mandatory £55,000 a year level. Customs and Excise may, of course, refuse to register you on the grounds that your outputs are too low, though no hard-and-fast minimum figure for this has been fixed. Your accountant should be able to advise you on this point, but the main consideration would be the level of your taxable inputs. Thus if you are a part-time cabinet-maker you would be buying a lot of materials which carry VAT. But, if you were doing something like picture research, the VAT inputs might be quite low and the administrative work involved in being a taxable trader might not be justified by the amount of VAT you could claim back against your outputs.

The point to be realised is that if you register as a taxable trader, voluntarily or otherwise, you are going to be involved in a fair bit of extra administration. At the end of each VAT accounting period (quarterly or monthly, the latter being more usual with traders in zero-rated goods), you will have to make a return of all your outputs, showing their total value and the amount of VAT charged. Against this you set the total of your inputs and the amount of VAT you have paid. The difference between the VAT on your outputs and that on your inputs is the sum payable to Customs and Excise. This obviously causes problems for retailers making a great many small sales and particularly for those supplying a mixture of zero-rated and standard-rated goods (eg a shop supplying sweets, which are taxable, and other items of foods, which are mostly zero rated). It also underlines the vital

---

* The distinction between zero-rated goods and exempt goods is important in determining whether you should be registered for VAT. Exempt goods do not count towards total 'turnover' for this purpose, but zero-rated goods do. Thus, if your turnover is over £55,000 including exempt goods but under that figure without them, you are not liable to pay VAT.

importance of keeping proper records and retaining copy invoices of all sales and purchases, because although your VAT return need only show totals, Customs and Excise inspectors are empowered to check the documents on which your return is based and require you to keep these records for six years. There is obviously, therefore, a link between the records you have to maintain for ordinary accounting purposes and those that are needed to back up your VAT return.

There is also a close connection between VAT and the problem of cash flow. When you receive an invoice bearing VAT, the input element can be set off against the VAT output on your next return, irrespective of whether you yourself have paid the supplier. Therefore, if you are buying an expensive piece of capital equipment it will make sense for you to arrange to be invoiced just before your next return to Customs and Excise is due.

The boot is on the other foot, though, when you yourself are extending credit to a customer. The sale is reckoned to have taken place when the invoice has been rendered, not when you have received payment. Therefore you will be paying VAT on your output before you have actually received the cash covering it from your customer. However, VAT can be reclaimed on bad debts, which in this case means amounts overdue by six months.

However, as a concession to small businesses with a taxable turnover (exclusive of VAT) of under £600,000, Customs will allow you to operate what is known as cash accounting. This enables small firms to account for tax when cash is paid and received rather than on presentation of an invoice.

It is also worth noting that if you are liable for VAT, inputs can be claimed on goods purchased for the business before it opens which are in place at the time of opening. VAT can also be claimed back on services such as professional advisers' fees supplied within six months of starting to trade.

Once you have registered for VAT, you will receive, at the end of each quarter, a form on which to make your return to Customs and Excise. It is very important to do this within the time stated, because there are financial penalties for making late returns, which can go as high as 15 per cent for repeated defaults.

There are also penalties for 'serious misdeclarations'. If you find, however, that you have accidentally underdeclared any of your taxable outputs, you can apply to the Customs and Excise to make a 'voluntary disclosure for accidental underpayment'. This would not make you liable to a penalty.

Before making a quarterly return, it is a good idea to check your own figures. Dividing the VAT total by the net total should show that the VAT is 17.5 per cent of the net, or at least very close to it. Customs and Excise will accept a tolerance like 0.25 per cent. But anything more than that suggests a mistake in your arithmetic somewhere. Better to pick it up yourself than to invite a visit from the VAT inspector.

As from 25 April 2002 certain small businesses have been able to account for VAT on a more straightforward basis: as a flat rate percentage of turnover. Ask Customs and Excise for details.

3.4 Other Taxation

How you are affected by taxation depends on the nature of the commercial activity in which you are engaged. Virtually everyone pays tax on income from some source, whether this be from full-time employment, from dividends or interest or from self-employment, or from a combination of several of these elements. The various kinds of income are assessed under several headings or schedules and the ones we will be particularly concerned with are:

1. Schedule D. Case I and Case II: Income from trades, professions or vocations. (In the interests of simplicity we will refer to this as Schedule D, though there are four other 'Cases' of Schedule D income.)
2. Schedule E: Wages and salaries from employment.

There are also other ways in which you may be involved in tax matters. You may be paying capital gains tax on the disposal of capital assets. If you are employing people full-time, you will be responsible for administering their PAYE payments; also, in certain circumstances, your own PAYE. If you are a shareholder in a limited company, it will be paying corporation tax on its profits. Lastly, you may – and if your turnover exceeds £55,000 a year, you must – for the supply of certain goods and services collect VAT from your customers and pay it over to Customs and Excise, less any VAT on goods and services supplied to you in the course of business (as discussed in the previous chapter). Essentially, if you are running your own business you will either run it directly yourself (as a 'sole trader'), or you will run it through the medium of a limited company.

One cannot, in a book of this nature, deal exhaustively with a subject as complex as taxation. But, with this proviso, let us look in broad outline at some of its principal implications. There are certain income tax advantages in working for yourself, or even in earning a supplementary income from part-time self-employment. For example you may be able to offset certain expenses (eg travelling expenses) against taxable income in a way that an ordinary employee cannot. If you carry on business via a limited company, the company will generally pay you a salary which will be liable to employee and employer National Insurance contributions in the normal way. However, if you carry on the business as a sole trader or a partnership, you will be subject to the specific National Insurance regime applicable to the self-employed. Essentially this consists of two parts: Class 4 National Insurance contributions, and flat rate Class 2 contributions. The amount of contribution is subject to a certain amount of annual tinkering. It is payable by men under 65 and women under 60 and it currently stands as a levy of 7 per cent of business profits between £4,615 and £30,420 in 2002/2003 – a maximum of £1,806 per year. It used to be the case that the self-employed could deduct 50 per cent of the Class 4 National Insurance contributions from their income for tax purposes, but this was abolished a few years back. Class 4 contributions are collected by the Inland Revenue. Contributions are payable if your profits exceed the threshold of £4,615 even if you work full-time or part-time in addition to being self-employed. However, there is a maximum amount of contributions that you have to pay in a year, so those who are employees and self-employed may be exempt from paying some or all of their Class 4 contributions. See below for details.

In addition, the self-employed must also pay a flat-rate weekly Class 2 National Insurance contribution if their profits are more than £4,025 a year. Those earning less than this can apply to be exempt. Ask for leaflet CA02 'National Insurance contributions for self-employed people with small earnings' from your local Contributions Agency (see your telephone directory) and fill in the exemption form CF10. The standard flat rate Class 2 contribution for 2002/2003 is £2.00 per week payable to the Department of Social Security. Most people pay this contribution by direct debit from their bank but alternatively you can be sent a quarterly bill.

As with Class 4 contributions, there is an overall maximum of

Class 2 contributions payable in any tax year if you are self-employed and an employee. If you have earnings as an employee taxed under PAYE you will pay Class 1 National Insurance contributions if you earn more than £89 a week in the 2002/2003 tax year.

If you earn £585 or more a week from employment (the so-called 'upper earnings limit' for 2002/2003, above which no further employee National Insurance contributions are payable) you will not normally have to pay any Class 2 or Class 4 contributions so you should ask for a deferral by asking for form CF259 from your local Contributions Agency office and send it to the Deferral Group of the Social Security office at Department for Work and Pensions, Newcastle upon Tyne, NE98 1YX. If your earnings are less than this amount you can either ask for a deferral or apply for a refund at the end of the tax year in respect of the appropriate part of the contributions.

In general terms, and in terms of maximising your entitlement to the state retirement pension, any Class 2 contributions for any one tax year count as a contribution year in terms of building up your entitlement to the state retirement pension in exactly the same way that employee National Insurance contributions build up the entitlement of an employee to the state retirement pension.

If you are self-employed, but you are not liable for Class 4 or Class 2 contributions as a result of having insufficient income, you can make a voluntary, contribution of £6.85 per week (2002/2003 level) in order to 'buy' the relevant year's contribution history to your state retirement pension entitlement.

As with income from employment, the profits of the self-employed are subject to an ascending rate of tax with income falling into different tax bands. If you have income from employment and self-employment, this is added together when calculating how much income falls into each tax band.

All income up to the basic Personal Allowance of £4,615 for the 2002/2003 tax year is tax free. If you are both an employee and self-employed, remember that you can have only one allowance which is offset against your total income. Income above this tax threshold then falls into tax bands starting with the first £1,920 of income (above your personal tax allowances) which is taxed at 10 per cent. The next £1,921 to £29,900 of income is taxed at 22 per cent and any income above £29,900 is taxed at 40 per cent. The total amount of income that will be taxed will also depend on any tax reliefs due – for example, personal pension contribution tax relief.

As discussed, the main difference between taxation of employees and taxation of the self-employed, is that the self-employed can deduct a vast array of costs and expenses when calculating their taxable profits. The self-employed can deduct any expenditure 'wholly and exclusively incurred' in carrying on a trade or profession. It is essential that you are aware of what you can – or cannot deduct – as it will enable you to reduce the amount of your taxable profits and therefore the amount of tax you will have to pay.

THE MAIN ALLOWABLE BUSINESS EXPENSES

You can deduct 100 per cent of the cost of buying the following items unless they are purchased for part business and part private use, in which case only the business proportion may be deducted.

1. *The cost of goods bought for resale and materials bought in manufacturing.* This does not include capital expenditure on items such as cars, machinery or computers, although you can deduct some of the cost of buying these via a 'capital allowance claim' (see page 150). However, small items of expenditure such as filing trays, software or small tools can be deducted.
2. *The running costs of the business or practice.* Under this heading come heating, lighting, rent, rates, telephone, postage, advertising, cleaning, repairs (but not improvements of a capital nature), insurance and the use of special clothing. If you are using your home as an office, you can claim up to two-thirds of the running costs of the premises as a business expense – provided you can convince the tax office that you are indeed using as high a proportion of your house as this exclusively for business purposes. Some people have been advised not to make this type of claim at all, because of the probability that,

on selling, they might have to pay capital gains tax on the 'business' part of the sale, thus outweighing any income tax advantage. One way round this is to use a room mainly for business rather than exclusively. You will generally need to agree with your tax office what proportion of costs you can deduct.

3. *Carriage, packing and delivery costs.*

4. *Wages and salaries.* Any sums paid to full-time or part-time employees. In circumstances where you carry on the business as a sole trader or partnership, however, you cannot count any salary you or your partners are taking from the business, but you can pay your spouse a salary (provided they are actually doing a reasonably convincing amount of work for you). This is an advantage if their income from other sources is less than £4,535 a year, because that first slice of earnings is free of tax.

5. *Travel.* Hotel and travelling expenses on business trips and in connection with soliciting business. You are not, however, allowed the cost of travel between home and office, if you have a regular place of work. In addition to these expenses you can claim for the running costs of your car (including petrol) in proportion to the extent to which you use it for business purposes. WARNING: you cannot deduct the cost of entertaining as this is a disallowable expense.

6. *Interest.* Interest on loans and overdraft incurred wholly in connection with your business. This does not include interest on any money you or your partners have lent to the business.

7. *Hire and hire purchase.* Hiring and leasing charges and interest element in hire-purchase agreement (not the actual cost, because this is a capital expense).

8. *Insurance.* Every kind of business insurance, including that taken out on behalf of employees, but excluding your own National Insurance contributions and premiums paid on your personal life insurance. You cannot deduct personal pension contributions as such when calculating your business profits, but when calculating your tax these contributions – which qualify for tax-relief at your highest rate of tax – can be used to reduce the amount of tax you will have to pay.

9. *The VAT element in allowable business expenses (unless you are a taxable trader for VAT purposes).* This would include, for instance, VAT on petrol for your car. The VAT on the purchase of a motor car is allowable (for the purposes of a capital allowances claim – see below) in all cases, since such VAT cannot be reclaimed in your VAT return.

10. *Certain legal and other professional fees.* You are allowed to claim for things like audit fees or court actions in connection with business, but not for penalties for breaking the law (eg parking fines!).

11. *Subscriptions to professional or trade bodies.*

12. *Bad debts.* These are bad debts actually incurred, though provision is generally allowed against tax in the case of specific customers whom you can show are unlikely to meet their obligations; for instance, if their account is overdue and they are failing to respond to reminders. A general provision for a percentage of unspecified bad debts is not allowable against tax, however sensible it may be to make such provision in your accounts.

   Trade debts owing to you count as income even if they have not been paid at the end of the accounting period. Likewise, debts owed by you count as costs, even if you are not going to pay them until the next accounting period.

13. *Gifts.* Business gifts costing up to £10 per recipient per year, provided they are marked with the firm's name (but excluding food, drink and tobacco). All gifts to employees are allowable, but generous employers should remember that the employee may have to declare them on her tax return and you will normally have to declare them on form P11D – see page 162).

Capital allowances

Generally you are allowed to write off against taxable profits 25 per cent of the cost of capital equipment on a reducing balance basis after the first year. For instance, in the year of purchase, if you buy a piece of equipment for £1,000, you will be granted £250 writing-down allowance. For the following year, it will be 25 per cent of £750 (£1,000–£250=£750) giving an allowance of £187.50

and so forth. However, a recent change means that small and medium-sized businesses may claim a first year allowance of 40 per cent on plant and machinery. In addition, small businesses that invest in various computers, software and Internet-enabled mobile phones during the 3 years from 1 April 2000 will be able to claim 100 per cent first-year allowances.

The writing-down allowance of 25 per cent per annum also extends to cars used for business, up to a maximum of £3,000 per annum.

Equipment bought on hire purchase is eligible for the writing-down allowance in respect of the capital element.

The interest charges inherent in the hire purchase agreement themselves can be claimed as business expenses, spread over the period of the agreement.

In calculating your writing-down allowances you will have to take into account whether or not you are a taxable trader for VAT purposes, which depends on whether your annual turnover exceeds £55,000. If you are, you will already have claimed the VAT on your purchase in your quarterly or monthly VAT return. Thus capital allowances will be calculated on the net amount excluding VAT (except in the case of motor cars in respect of which, as explained in Chapter 3.3, the input VAT is never reclaimable on your VAT return).

STOCK VALUATION

If you are in a business which involves holding stock (which may be either finished goods for resale, work in progress or materials for manufacture), it must be valued at each accounting date. The difference in value between opening stock and closing stock, when added to the value of purchases during the year, represents the cost of sales. Obviously, therefore, if you value your closing stock on a different basis from the opening stock, this will affect the profit you show. If you value the same kind of items more highly it will depress the cost of sales and increase the apparent profit. If you value them on a lower basis, the cost of sales will be increased and the profit decreased.

Table 3.4.1 *An example of stock valuation (assuming no purchases)*

Example A		Example B	
Sales	£150	Sales	£150
Opening Stock 100 Rose bushes @ £1.00: £100		*Opening Stock* 100 Rose bushes @ £1.00: £100	
Closing Stock 50 Rose bushes @ £1.50: £75		*Closing Stock* 50 Rose bushes @ 60p: £30	
Cost of Sales	£25	Cost of Sales	£70
Profit	£125	Profit	£80

Plainly, then, it does not make sense for you to up-value your closing stock in order to show a paper profit. Equally, you are not allowed to depress it artificially in order to achieve the reverse effect. However, if you can make a genuine case that some stock will have to be sold at a lower margin than the one you normally work to in order to be able to sell it within a reasonable time, a valuation in the light of this fact will generally be accepted by the tax office.

COMPUTING TAXABLE PROFIT

Normally your accountant will prepare a set of accounts for you for each year you are in business. Your accounting date need not coincide with the tax year (ending 5 April). The profits shown in these accounts will be the basis of your assessment.

As stated earlier, certain costs which are genuine enough from the point of view of your profit and loss account are nevertheless not allowable for tax purposes: for example, entertaining customers. You are also not allowed to charge depreciation against your profit (though remember that when claiming capital allowances you will receive a writing-down allowance which, in the end, has a similar effect). These and other non-allowable expenses must be added back to the profits.

Equally, certain profits which you have made are to be deducted for the purposes of Schedule D assessment because they are taxed on a different basis and are subject to a return under another heading. Examples are gains from the disposal of capital assets, income from sub-letting part of your premises or interest paid to you by the bank on money being held in a deposit account.

In recent years some new kinds of business spending have come in for tax relief, notably incidental costs of raising loan finance and start-up costs incurred before you begin trading.

LOSSES

If your business or professional occupation has made a loss in its accounting year (and remember that from the tax point of view non-allowable expenses are added back to profits and you will have to do the same in terms of computing any loss for tax purposes), you can have the loss set off against your other income for the tax year in which the loss was incurred and for the previous year. It is also possible for a trading loss to be offset against capital gains if you have no other income to offset it against.

If your income for the year in which you made the loss and that of the previous year still does not exceed that loss, you can set off the balance against future profits. There are special rules regarding losses incurred in the start-up years of the business, as set out below.

In the case of traders and partnerships, losses incurred in the first four years of business can be carried back against income from other sources, including salary, in the three years before commencing business as a self-employed person or partner. However, it should be noted that this does not apply to losses incurred by a limited company of which you are a shareholder – such losses can only be set off against profits chargeable in the form of corporation tax. However, if you carry on your business by a limited company, and you subscribe for new shares in it, and the company then goes bust, you would normally be able to offset the loss you make on the shares against your taxable income.

SELF-ASSESSMENT

In 1997 the taxation of the self-employed was radically changed. The main effect on the self-employed was that instead of being taxed on profits in their accounting year ending in the preceding tax year, they are now taxed on what is known as a 'current year basis'. This means that if, for example, your accounting year ends on 31 March 2003, you will be assessed for tax on those profits at the rates applying to the April 6 2002 to April 5 2003 tax year. Under the old regime you would not have been assessed until the following tax year. So, in effect the self-employed must pay tax on profits more quickly than they did under the old regime.

The self-employed pay tax on three different dates – two advance or 'interim' payments made by 31 January within the year of assessment and by 31 July following the end of the tax year of assessment. The third payment, the final balancing payment, is made by the following 31 January. To go back to the example above, a business with an accounting year to 31 March 2003, the first payment – usually half the tax on trading profits paid in respect of the previous tax year – will be payable on 31 January 2003, the second payment on 31 July 2003 and a final balancing payment (if any further tax is due) on 31 January 2004. If your profits are likely to be much lower than in the previous year you can apply to have your interim payments – also known as 'payments on account' – reduced.

The other change introduced by self-assessment is that you can calculate your own tax should you want to. However, this is not mandatory. If you want the Inland Revenue to calculate your tax liability you must complete and submit your Tax Return by 30 September following the end of the tax year on 5 April.

If you – or your accountant – wish to calculate the tax owed, the Tax Return does not have to be submitted until 31 January (see Table 3.4.2). If you miss this deadline, you will be fined (see Table 3.4.3).

Self-assessment also requires taxpayers to keep and retain records to support information on their Tax Return. The self-employed must keep records for five years after the 31 January following the end of the tax year of assessment concerned.

The amount of information you need to give on your Tax

Table 3.4.2   *Key dates to remember during the 2003/2004 tax year*

31 July 2003	Second interim payment on account for the 2002/2003 tax year now due
30 September 2003	Final deadline for 2002/2003 Tax Return to be submitted by those wanting the Inland Revenue to calculate their tax bill
5 October 2003	Deadline for those who need to inform the Inland Revenue of new sources of income in 2002/2003 tax year
31 January 2004	Final deadline to send back completed 2002/2003 Tax Return sent out following the end of the tax year on 5 April 2003
	First payment on account for the 2003/2004 tax year now due
	Final balancing payment for the 2002/2003 tax year now due

Return will depend on your turnover. Those with a turnover of less than £15,000 a year need only submit three line accounts – turnover, expenses and profit/loss. Other sole traders and partners have to produce more information including a detailed

Table 3.4.3   *Inland Revenue fines and penalties re 2002/2003 tax return*

Failure to submit Tax Return by 31 January 2003	£100
Failure to pay tax due on 31 January 2003	6% interest
Failure to pay tax by 28 February 2003	5% surcharge plus interest
Failure to submit 2002/2003 Tax Return by 31 July 2003	a further £100
Failure to pay tax by 31 July 2003	10% surcharge plus interest
Returns still not submitted after this date	up to £60 a day
Failure to keep accurate records	up to £3,000

breakdown of expenses claimed. As accountancy fees are tax deductible by the self-employed, you are strongly advised to use an accountant to help you – to ensure that you claim all that you can to reduce your taxable profits and to ensure you are not fined by the Inland Revenue.

SPARE-TIME WORK

Even though you have a full-time job which is being taxed under Schedule E and thus being taken care of under your employer's PAYE scheme, you may also have earnings from part-time employment in the evenings and weekends which you have to declare. Your employer need not know about this second income because you can establish with your tax inspector that the tax code which fixes the amount of PAYE you pay (see below) only relates to the income you receive from your employer.

Your spare-time income is also eligible for the allowances on expenses 'wholly and exclusively incurred' for business purposes. This means that it is most important that you should keep a proper record of incomings and outgoings. If your spare-time activities are on a small scale, you will not need to keep the kind of detailed books of account described in Chapter 3.1; but you should certainly maintain a simple cash book, from which at the end of the year you or your accountant can prepare a statement to append to your Income Tax Return.

Tax on spare-time work is payable in the same way described earlier in this chapter.

Probably the largest item you will be able to set off against spare-time income is any sums you can pay your spouse for assistance up to the level of their tax-free allowance of £4,535, provided they are not earning as much as this from another source.

PARTNERSHIPS

Partners pay tax on their share of the partnership profits in the same ratio as that in which they have agreed to split profits. Until the introduction of self-assessment in respect of tax year

1996/1997 *et seq.*, the partnership was taxed as a single entity with tax collected from the partnership as a whole, not the individual partners. However, the new rules stipulate that each partner is liable for his or her own tax. Most of the other tax rules relating to partners are the same as for the self-employed, so that means that salaries cannot be deducted when calculating profits and any interest on money put into the business by partners is considered as part of the partnership profits. Partners are deemed to start in business when they join the partnership and cease in business when they leave.

CORPORATION TAX

Corporation tax is payable by limited companies. Its provisions are somewhat complicated and it must be assumed, for the purposes of this brief chapter on taxation, that readers who are intending to set up businesses in this form will seek professional advice on tax aspects. However, the salient points are as follows:

1. For small companies corporation tax is currently charged at a rate of 0 per cent on taxable profits up to £10,000. Thereafter various effective overall rates apply up to 30 per cent for taxable profits over £1.5 million.
2. Unlike Schedule D income tax, corporation tax is normally payable nine months from the end of each accounting period, except for large companies where it is payable by instalments.
3. If you are a director of a limited company, any salary paid to you by the company will be subject to income tax under PAYE and to National Insurance contributions (see later in this chapter for a description of PAYE).

INHERITANCE TAX

This tax is in some ways similar to the older concept of death duties in that a charge is made on transfers of assets at death, up to a maximum of 40 per cent on amounts over £250,000 for the 2002/2003 tax year. If you make an outright gift more than seven years before death, no inheritance tax will be paid on this. Tax can become due on gifts made within seven years of death, although in certain cases such tax may be at a reduced rate. Such outright gifts are known as 'potentially exempt transfers'.

Business assets of those who have an interest in a small business or a farm qualify for substantial concessions which can reduce or eliminate the tax. You are advised to seek professional advice. However, generally, business relief means there is no inheritance tax to pay on business assets such as goodwill, land, buildings, plant, stock or patents (reduced by debts incurred in the business). What are regarded as private and business assets at death are, however, bound to be a subject of potential dispute with the Inland Revenue, so it is vital to seek professional advice on the implications of this tax when making a will.

CAPITAL GAINS TAX

If you sell or give away assets – usually cash, shares, property or other valuables – you are liable to capital gains tax on the gain made. This gain is generally calculated as the price you sell the asset for (or its market value) *less* the cost of purchasing the asset (or its value on 31 March 1982 if it was bought before then) and any costs incurred in buying, selling or improving the asset. However, you do not pay tax on gains to the extent that they do not exceed your annual exemption for capital gains purposes (£7,700 in the 2002/2003 tax year). If you are liable for capital gains tax it will be at your top rate of tax. So higher-rate taxpayers will pay it at 40 per cent.

The March 1998 Budget made significant changes to capital gains tax – with many of these new rules having a major impact on those running small businesses. Until the Budget, those selling assets could deduct the effects of inflation when calculating their gains. However, in future, inflation will only be deductible if the asset was bought before 1 April 1998 and then the effects of inflation can only be deducted until April 1998. For small businesses a major concession, retirement relief given to those selling their business after age 50 or retiring earlier due to ill-health, is being phased-out over five years until the tax year 2002/3. In the past this relief meant that the self-employed paid no capital gains tax if they owned the business for ten years before the sale and sold it for less than £250,000. Tax on gains between £250,000 and £1 million was halved. This relief is being replaced by a new tapering system of relief which will reduce the amount of tax paid the longer the asset is held. This taper relief is complex (a whole textbook has been written about it by accountants Tenon) and professional advice should always be taken.

Other tax concessions include relief if a business is sold and another one is bought within three years. As reliefs vary and provide valuable tax breaks, you are advised to consult an accountant.

One area where those running a business can be caught out is if they run a business from home. Profits made on the sale of your main residence are generally exempt from tax. However, if you use your home for business and have been claiming part of the costs of running the business including a share of heating, lighting, rates and your mortgage or rent, you could have to pay capital gains tax. The easiest way to get round this is to not use a room 'exclusively' for business but only 'mainly'. So if you have three rooms in your home (other than bathrooms and kitchens) and use one for business, instead of claiming a third of the running costs of your home, claim slightly less than this. Always agree the business proportion of these costs with your Tax Office.

APPEALS

All taxpayers, be they an individual or a corporation, have the right to appeal against their tax assessment, if they have grounds for believing they are being asked to pay too much. Such appeals have to be made in writing to the Inspector of Taxes within 30 days of receiving an assessment. They are usually settled by more or less amicable correspondence, but ultimately can be taken to a hearing by the General or, in more complex cases, Special Commissioners.

PAY AS YOU EARN (PAYE)

If you employ staff you will be responsible for deducting PAYE from their wages. The same applies to your own salary from a limited company. The sums have to be paid monthly to the Inland Revenue by the employer.

You will receive from the tax office a tax deduction card for each employee, with spaces for each week or month (depending on how they are paid) for the year ending 5 April. On these cards, weekly or monthly as the case may be, you will have to enter under a number of headings, details of tax, pay for each period and for the year to date. You will know how much tax to deduct by reading off the employee's tax code number, which has been allotted to him by the tax office, against a set of tables with which you will also be issued. Without going into technicalities, the way the tables work is to provide a mechanism, self-correcting for possible fluctuations of earnings, of assessing the amount of tax due on any particular wage or salary at any given point of the year.

At the end of the tax year you will have to make out two forms:

1. Form P14 for each employee for whom a deductions working sheet has been used in the year just ended. Two copies are sent to the tax office. The third copy is called Form P60, and is issued to each employee. This gives details of pay and tax deducted during the year.
2. Form P35 for the Inland Revenue. This is a summary of tax and graduated National Insurance contributions for all employees during the year. It is a covering certificate sent with the Forms P14.

Both of the above have to be submitted to the Inland Revenue by 19 May following the tax year ended on the previous 5 April.

When an employee leaves, you should complete another form, P45, for her. Part of this form, showing her code number, pay and tax deducted for the year to date, is sent to the tax office. The other parts are to be handed by the employee to her new employer so that she can pick up the PAYE system where you left off.

Employers are also responsible for deducting Class 1 National Insurance contributions from their employees and will have to pay these along with their own employer's contributions (which are also based on a percentage of each employee's pay) at the same time as making PAYE tax payments. The introduction of the Small Business Service should ease this process with advice and an automated payroll service available to small businesses.

THE BLACK ECONOMY

One cannot these days write about taxation without some reference to the 'black economy'. There is a good deal of evidence to suggest that the response to the way rising wages and salaries are pulling an increasing number of people into higher tax brackets has been tax evasion on a large scale by a variety of means, such as straightforward non-declaration of earnings, making or receiving payments in cash, arranging remuneration in kind or, simply, barter deals. Some of these methods are easier for the tax inspectors to spot than others, but this is not the place to give advice on a highly contentious topic, except to say that all forms of tax evasion are illegal. In fact, there are enough loopholes and 'perks' available to self-employed people with a good tax consultant at their elbow to render law-breaking an unacceptable and unnecessary risk.

THE CHALLENGE TO SELF-EMPLOYED STATUS

In recent years there has been an increasing tendency for the Inland Revenue to challenge taxpayers' claims to be assessed under Schedule D and to try to bring them within the PAYE scheme. The challenge hinges round the nature of the relationship between the provider of work and the performer of it. If the provider of work is in a position to tell the performer the exact place, time and manner in which the job is to be done, then the relationship between them is, to use an old-fashioned phrase, a master-and-servant one and clearly does not qualify for Schedule

D taxation. On the other hand, if the performer of the work is merely given a job to do and is absolutely free as to how she does it, except in so far as it has to be completed within certain specifications of time, quality and price, then the performer can be regarded as self-employed. There are, however, some potential grey areas here; for instance, a freelance working mostly for one client may be straying into a master-and-servant situation. The Inland Revenue is also now treating any income derived under a contract of service as liable to PAYE – even if it is only for one or two days a month. This means that formal contractual arrangements should be avoided when worthwhile payments are involved. A guidance note has been issued (IR56) under the title *Tax – Employed or Self-Employed*, but the inspector of taxes is still entitled to take his own view of your situation.

By 6 July following the end of the tax year to 5 April the employer has to prepare:

☐ a form P9D in respect of each employee earning less than £8,500, covering expenses and benefits provided to the employee in the tax year concerned;
☐ a form P11D in respect of employees earning more than £8,500 per annum, again setting out information regarding expenses and benefits provided to the employee in the tax year concerned.

The above have to be submitted to the Inland Revenue by 6 July, with a copy to the employee in each case. You will need to follow the complex guidance notes which will be given to you by the Inland Revenue, and again you will be well advised to take professional advice where appropriate.

There has been much discussion in the media over the last few years regarding the dreaded 'IR35', which came into effect on 6 April 2000. IR35 only affects people who carry on a business via a limited company. Essentially, IR35 allows the Inland Revenue to treat the income of your company as that of you personally, in circumstances where the relationships between the company and its customers are similar to the relationships which you would have had as an employee of the respective customers concerned.

This is a complex area, and if you believe you might fall within IR35 you would be well advised to take professional advice, as indeed you should also do in circumstances where the Inland Revenue threaten to invoke IR35 on you.

The Inland Revenue has a degree of autonomy which is not generally realised by the general public. It is not, for instance, answerable to Parliament except in the widest political sense, so it is no use writing to your MP, no matter how unjustified you may feel a tax decision is. Your only recourse is to take the matter to an Independent Appeals Tribunal, but unless a large sum of money is involved it is probably not worth the trouble – though self-employed people who are members of a professional association may find it willing to take up on their behalf something that looks like a test case.

Complaints

If you have a complaint about the way your affairs have been dealt with by Customs & Excise, there is a leaflet about complaints procedures relating to VAT: _Complaints Against Customs & Excise_, available from any local VAT office.

Beyond that, there is a complaints supremo, who deals with Inland Revenue and Benefit Office as well as VAT matters: The Adjudicator's Office (see Appendix 1).

Checklist: taxation

1. Inform the Department of Social Security if you have recently become full-time or self-employed.
2. Collect receipts for allowable business expenses. Check with your accountant if you are not sure what is permissible.
3. Become acquainted with the important dates related to self-assessment and make sure that you do not miss the deadlines.
4. Contact your tax inspector if you have a second, self-employed, job and establish that your tax code fixes the amount of PAYE you pay only for the income you receive from your employer.

---

5. Be aware that you might be liable to pay Capital Gains Tax on the sale of your home if you claim tax relief on using part of it as a business premise.

6. If you are likely to exceed £55,000 a year taxable outputs, register with the Customs and Excise for VAT and consult your accountant.

Section 4

Personnel and Business Administration

4.1 Pensions and Health Insurance

Until eighteen months ago, it was scarcely possible to open the financial pages of any newspaper without seeing at least one advertisement for self-employed pensions. It is also a fair bet that these are studied more closely by financial advisers than by the self-employed at whom they are aimed, unless of course the latter are nearing the age at which pensions begin to become of immediate interest – by which time it may be too late to do anything about it. The trouble is that the self-employed, by temperament, are more interested in risk than security and tend to place provisions for retirement rather low on their scale of priorities.

However, there are compelling reasons why you should take self-employed pensions seriously and find out what they involve, to outline which is the object of this chapter. In urging you to read it, we promise to avoid the mind-boggling pension jargon which generally sends readers of newspaper articles on the subject straight to the less demanding pastures of the sports or fashion pages.

For the moment, pension plan salesmen and investment fund managers are under the microscope of public scrutiny. With the collapse of stock exchange equity values, pension fund assets have shrunk in all developed countries. In a study published in January 2003, Watson Wyatt, the international investment consultancy, reported that the world's hoard of retirement money had plunged by $1,400 billion in 2002 alone.

In the UK pension fund assets fell to $934 billion in 2002 from $1,400 billion in 1999. Several well-known life assurance companies, which have been household names in the pensions industry for decades, have had to declare severely reduced pension benefits and payouts. A host of well-known companies, such as Marks & Spencer, British Airways, Abbey National, Dixons and W H Smith have closed their traditional defined benefit final salary schemes to new entrants.

At the same time, the government has finally owned up to the scale of the medium and long-term problems of funding adequate state pensions. In a policy paper at the end of 2002, a new approach to state-funded pensions is foreshadowed, involving incentives to continue working beyond the present retirement age of 65 and an increased emphasis on personal pension plans to supplement state pensions. The comments which follow on existing pension schemes must be read in the light of confirmed changes as they are introduced.

Meanwhile, the Financial Services Authority (FSA) and the Association of British Insurers have jointly launched an online pensions calculator to encourage individuals to start saving earlier for retirement. The calculator, which is intended for those in the stakeholder salary range of £10,000 to £20,000 who have no retirement savings, may be found on www.pensioncalculator. org.uk. Age, gender and planned retirement age are the key determinants together with either the weekly retirement income required or the amount to be saved monthly. For example, a 35 year-old woman requiring £209 per week on retirement at 65 would need to save £150 a month, while a 25 year-old man saving £100 a month could expect to receive £218 per week on retirement at the same age. The model also provides for users to specify an amount of tax-free cash on maturity.

STATE SCHEMES

Everyone in the UK is entitled to the basic state pension provided they have built up a record of National Insurance Contributions for a quarter of their working life (from age 16 through to state pension age). Contrary to popular belief, not everyone qualifies for the full state pension – only those with a record of contributions for nine-tenths of their working life. The self-employed should take particular care to ensure that they build up adequate contributions as they generally do not have a company pension to rely on when they retire. However, the primary state pension is very basic: just £77.45 a week for a single pensioner and £123.80 for a couple from April 2003, rising only at the higher rate of 2.5 per cent a year or the retail price index.

The second state pension was the top up scheme known as SERPS – the state earnings related pension scheme – but this has been replaced by an equally complicated scheme called the State Second Pension (SSP) since April 2002. The self-employed are not members of this scheme as the contributions to it are made from Class 1 National Insurance Contributions paid by employees (however, if you were an employee in the past you may have built up some SERPS entitlement). Only a quarter of working people are members of SERPS, the rest have opted out (known as contracting out) either through a personal pension plan or their company pension scheme. If you have past SERPS entitlement check how much pension this will provide. If you also have earnings from employment and are under age 45 and a man, or under 40 and a woman, and earn at least £10–12,000, a year you should consider contracting out of SERPS and investing rebates in a personal pension plan (provided you are not a member of a company pension scheme). This is because the SERPS pension (particularly that of the spouse after the pension-holder's death) has been reduced and you may be better off investing this cash to provide your own pension.

STAKEHOLDER PENSIONS

Stakeholder pension schemes offer a low cost option for people who do not currently have the right pensions provision, particularly those who cannot join an occupational pension scheme. They are a good option for people earning less than around £10,000 a year, but the maximum contribution is only £3,600 per annum. The schemes are offered by commercial companies and are registered with Inland Revenue and the Occupational Pensions Regulatory Authority (OPRA). The rules are designed to ensure that schemes offer value for money and flexibility. For example:

☐ A stakeholder pensions scheme cannot charge more than 1 per cent a year on the value of each member's funds.

☐ Members must be able to transfer into or out of a stakeholder pension, or stop paying for a time, without facing any extra charge.

☐ All stakeholder pensions schemes must accept contributions of £20 or more, though some may accept lower payments.

Advice is available from the Department for Work and Pensions (the successor to the DSS) Web site, www.pensionguide.gov.uk, or their Pensions Info-Line on: 0845 7 31 32 33. OPRA keeps a register of approved schemes, and can be contacted at http://www. opra.gov.uk.

As an employer, you may have to provide access to a stakeholder pension scheme for any employees over the age of 18 who earn more than the National Insurance lower earnings limit. This is the case if you have five or more employees (of any age or wage level) and do not already offer specific pension plans. Eligible employees can join the scheme if they so choose, though they do not have to do so. You do not necessarily have to make contributions as an employer. You do not yourself run the scheme, and are not responsible for its performance, although if you are dissatisfied you can change to a different scheme.

Similarly, if you take on a fifth employee, you must provide access to a scheme for all eligible employees within three months. To do this, you must:

☐ choose a registered stakeholder pension scheme or schemes from the OPRA list;

☐ discuss your choice of scheme with employees who qualify for access;

☐ designate (formally choose) the stakeholder pension scheme and give your employees its name and address;

☐ arrange to deduct contributions from employees' pay for those who wish to join (how much they pay is their decision), and inform them in writing of the arrangements;

☐ send your employee contributions (and any employer contributions) to the stakeholder pension scheme provider within the given time limits; schemes must accept payments of £20 or over, and some schemes accept lower amounts;

☐ record the payments you make to the stakeholder pension scheme provider.

New employees who already have a stakeholder scheme can continue to pay directly to that scheme, or elect to join your designated scheme and have deductions made through the payroll.

During this process, you should offer help and information but must not advise employees that they should or must join this (or any other) scheme; the FSA has strict rules on who is entitled to give advice.

Guidance on stakeholder pensions is available from the Inland Revenue Employer's Helpline, 08457 143143 (textphone 08456 021380), and the Occupational Pensions Regulatory Authority, 01273 627600.

TAX BENEFITS

Not being eligible for earnings-related benefit is in itself a reason why you should make additional arrangements as soon as you possibly can, but for the self-employed there is another compelling incentive. Investing in a pension scheme is probably the most tax-beneficial saving and investment vehicle available to you at this time. Here are some of its key features:

1. Tax relief is given on your contributions at your top rate of tax on earned income. This means that if you are paying tax at the top rate of 40 per cent you can get £1,000 worth of contributions to your pension for an outlay of only £600.
2. Pension funds are in themselves tax exempt – unlike any company in whose shares you might invest. Thus your capital builds up considerably more quickly than it would in stocks and shares.
3. When you finally come to take your benefits – and you can take part of them as a lump sum and part as a regular pension payment (of which more later) the lump sum will not be liable to capital gains tax and the pension will be

> treated as earned income from a tax point of view, as
> distinct from investment income, which is regarded as
> 'unearned' and taxed much more severely.
> 4. Lump sum benefits arising in the event of your death are
>   paid out to your dependants free of inheritance tax. This
>   may enable you to build up pension funds to the extent
>   where liability to inheritance tax is reduced quite drasti-
>   cally on other assets from which income has been
>   siphoned to provide a pension.

The advantage of all this over various DIY efforts to build up a
portfolio of stocks and shares – even if you are more knowledge-
able about the stock market than most – should be obvious;
you are contributing in that case out of taxed income, the resultant
investment income is taxed at unearned rates and capital gains
tax is payable on the profits you make from selling your holdings.

The convinced adherent of the DIY road may at this point say:
'Ah, but under my own provisions I can contribute as, when and
how much I can afford and I am not obliged to make regular
payments to a pension plan when it might be highly inconvenient
for me to do so.' Pensions, however, are not like life insurance,
though misguided or less scrupulous sales reps sometimes try to
make out that they are. You need not contribute a regular amount
at all. You can pay a lump sum or a regular amount. In fact, you
need not make a payment every year. There are even a number of
plans now available under which you are entitled to borrow from
your pension plan.

The only restriction that is put on you is imposed by the
government and relates to tax benefits. In order for self-employed
pensions not to become a vehicle for tax avoidance, the amount
you can contribute to them is limited to 17.5 per cent of your
income. You are, however, allowed to 'average out' your contributions over any six-year period to arrive at an overall percentage
per year of 17.5 per cent.

There is also a further concession for older people making their
own pension plans. Since an increasing number of self-employed
people – and their financial advisers – have come to recognise the
merits of these schemes, a great many companies have moved

Table 4.1.1 _Maximum payments qualifying for relief for personal pensions and retirement annuities expressed as percentage of net relevant earnings_

Age at 6 April 2000	Personal pensions limit	Retirement annuities limit
35 or less	17.5%	17.5%
36–45	20.0%	17.5%
46–50	25.0%	17.5%
51–55	30.0%	20.0%
56–60	35.0%	22.5%
61–74	40.0%	27.5%

Source: Inland Revenue, Tax Return guide for the year ended 5 April 2002.

Notes: For personal pensions the percentage limits apply to earnings up to a maximum of £95,400. Any personal payments made by your employer count towards your percentage limit, but you do not get tax relief on them.

There is no limit on the amount of earnings to which the percentage applies if you pay into a retirement annuity contract only.

into the market for self-employed pensions (see Table 4.1.1). Under a fair amount of jargon and often confused lineage of print, the plans they offer boil down to the following options.

1. _Pension policy with profits._ In essence this is a method of investing in a life assurance company, who then use your money to invest in stocks, shares, government securities or whatever. As we said earlier, the advantage from your point of view is that pension funds are tax exempt, so the profits from their investments build up more quickly. These profits are used to build up, in turn, the pension fund you stand to get at the end of the period over which you can contribute. There is no time limit on this period, though obviously the more you do contribute the greater your benefits will be and vice versa; also, you can elect to retire any time between 50 and 75. The downside, of course, is what has happened in the past two years as equity values have fallen, 'profits' have been wiped out and retirement expectations have been destroyed.

At retirement you can choose to have part of your pension paid as a lump sum and use it to buy an annuity. This could in some circumstances have a tax advantage over an ordinary pension, but the situation on it is quite complicated and you should seek professional advice in making your decision. What happens with an annuity, however, is that you can use it to buy an additional pension, the provider of which takes the risk that if you live to a ripe old age he might be out of pocket. Equally, you might die within six months, in which case the reverse would be true. The statistical probabilities of either of these extremes have been calculated by actuaries and the annuities on offer are based on their conclusions.

One important point about a conventional with-profits pension that often confuses people is that it is not really a form of life insurance. If you die before pensionable age, your dependants and your estate will not usually get back more than the value of the premiums you have paid, plus interest. The best way of insuring your life is through term assurance, of which more later.

2. *Unit linked pensions.* Unit linked policies are a variant of unit trust investment, where you make a regular monthly payment (or one outright purchase) to buy stocks and shares across a variety of investments through a fund, the managers of which are supposed to have a special skill in investing in the stock market.

Combining investment with a pension plan sounds extremely attractive and much more exciting than a conventional with-profits policy, and it is true that in some instances unit linked policies have shown a better return than their more staid rivals. However, as unit trust managers are at pains to warn you (usually in the small print), units can go down as well as up and if you get into one of the less successful unit trust funds – and there are quite wide variances in their performance – you may do less well than with a conventional policy.

Although the current period of stock market depreciation has affected the value of holdings adversely, over a period of time these fluctuations should even themselves out – you can get more units for your money when the market is down, and fewer when share prices are high. The only problem is that if your policy terminates at a time when share prices are low, you will do worse than if you cash in on a boom. However, there is nothing to compel you to sell your holdings when they mature. Unless you desperately need the money you can keep it invested until times are better. Remember, though, since this policy is for your pension, you may not be able to delay using the funds for too long.

Most unit trust companies run a number of funds, invested in different types of shares and in different markets: for instance, there are funds that are invested in the United States, Australia or Japan, or in specialist sectors such as mining or energy. If you find that the trust you are in is not performing as well as you had hoped (prices are quoted daily in the press), most trusts will allow you to switch from one fund to another at quite a modest administration charge.

3. _Unitised with profits._ This is a newer type of pension, which combines elements of with-profits and unit linked pensions. Your investment is given in terms of units (as with unit linked policies) but you also earn bonuses which, once added to your pension fund every year, cannot be taken away or fall in value should the stock market perform badly (these bonuses are added to with-profits policies each year and on retirement).

4. _Term assurance._ While this is not a form of pension at all, it may be attractive to add term assurance to your pension policy for tax purposes. Term assurance is a way of insuring your life for a given period by paying an annual premium. The more you pay, the more you (or rather your dependants) get. If you do not die before the end of the fixed term (eg 20 years) nothing is paid out. As with any other form of insurance, your premiums are simply, if you like, a bet against some untoward event occurring.

There is one indirect but useful connection between pensions and term assurance. The tax people allow you a scheme under which you pay term assurance premiums along with your pension premiums, both of them being relieved of tax at your top earned income rate.

The one thing that all types of pension scheme have in common is that their sales forces are all eagerly competing for the self-employed person's notional dollar. They will be anxious to extol the virtues of their own schemes, to withhold any unfavourable information about them and to make no comparisons, which could be odious, with other schemes. Although the Financial Services Authority (FSA) is clamping down on misleading information and selling practices, your best plan in making your selection is to work through a broker and to let her make the recommendation, but that does not mean that you can abdicate responsibility altogether. For one thing, in order for a broker to make the right selection of pension plans appropriate to your circumstances, you have to describe what your needs and constraints are:

1. Can you afford to make regular payments?
2. Does the irregular nature of your earnings mean that the occasional lump sum payment would be better?
3. Do you have any existing pension arrangements – eg from previous employment?
4. When do you want to retire?
5. What provision do you want to make for dependants?

Very likely the broker will come up with a mix of solutions – for instance, a small regular payment to a pension scheme, topped up by single premium payments. The suggestion may also be made that you should split your arrangements between a conventional with-profits policy and some sort of unit linked scheme; certainly you will be recommended to review your arrangements periodically to take care of inflation and possible changes in your circumstances.

Brokers have to be registered nowadays, so it is unlikely that you will be unlucky enough to land up with someone dishonest. Check that the person you are dealing with really is a *registered* broker – not a consultant, because anyone can call themselves that. Some very big household names among brokers are not, in fact, registered, but the majority are, although whoever you deal with, there are, as in other things in life, differences in the quality of what you get, which in this case is advice. It is as well to have a few checks at your elbow which will enable you to assess the value of the advice you are being given. For instance, national quality newspapers such as *The Daily Telegraph*, *The Guardian*, *The*

Independent and the *Financial Times*, as well as some specialist publications such as *The Economist* and *Investors Chronicle*, publish occasional surveys of the pension business which include performance charts of the various unit funds, showing those at the top and bottom of the league table over one-, five- and ten-year periods. There are also tables of benefits offered by the various life companies showing what happens in each case if, for instance, you invest £500 a year over ten years. There are quite considerable differences between what you get for your money from the most to the least generous firms. If your broker is advising you to put your money in a scheme that appears to give you less than the best deal going, you should not commit yourself to it without talking to your accountant; but with brokers, as with many other professional advisers, the best recommendation is word of mouth from someone you can trust who can vouch for the ability of the person in question.

HEALTH INSURANCE

Running your own business requires stamina and good health. If you are unlucky enough to become ill it will be a priority to get back on your feet as quickly as possible. Private health insurance has become increasingly popular amongst the self-employed for this reason. There are four types of health insurance currently available on the market, as defined by the most recent Office of Fair Trading report:

☐ **Private medical insurance.** This insures against the cost of short-term acute conditions in a private hospital or as a private patient in an NHS ward.
☐ **Permanent health insurance.** Replaces some or all of the income lost when a person becomes sick or disabled and unable to work and is normally paid to retirement age.
☐ **Critical illness insurance.** Provides a lump sum in the event of a serious illness.
☐ **Long-term care insurance.** Covers the cost of long-term care for those who become unable to look after themselves.

However, an Office of Fair Trading report has criticised the insurance industry for its lack of standardised products and complicated jargon. Indeed, it might well be worth getting independent advice before you commit yourself to purchasing a policy. It is also worth keeping an eye out for products specifically geared towards the self-employed, as there has recently been a launch of a combined health insurance policy which caters more closely to the needs of individuals working for themselves.

Checklist: pensions and health insurance

1. Review your current pension arrangements and assess whether or not they are adequate for retirement needs.
2. Discuss with your accountant the most tax-efficient way to invest in a pension scheme and with your broker about what kind of scheme is most appropriate.
3. Consider whether regular payment and/or one-off lump sum investments are best suited to your financial arrangements.
4. Take account of the government's revisions to state pension schemes when published.
5. Check that you are receiving independent advice from a registered broker.
6. Examine surveys of pensions within the national press to ensure that you are receiving adequate advice from your broker.
7. Identify if it is speed, location or choice that you require within a private medical insurance policy – this will help determine which policy you will choose.
8. Check the qualifying period within a critical illness policy – many do not start to pay out until after an excess period of six weeks or three months. Could your business survive an absence of this length? If not, you will have to consider paying higher premiums.

4.2 Employing People

A fairly common observation about employing people has been to say that this is when your troubles begin. Apart from the difficulty of finding Mr or Ms Right – a task which even experienced personnel people admit, in their more candid moments, is something of a lottery – employers also have to comply with various articles of employment legislation. Whole books could be and have been written about the legal technicalities involved, but all we can do in this section is to draw your attention to some of the major pitfalls you should look out for when you start employing people.

THE TERMS OF EMPLOYMENT

The terms of employment statement which has to be issued in writing to every employee who is going to work for you for eight hours or more per week within eight weeks of joining is in fact not a pitfall, but a rather sensible document which clarifies right from the outset what the terms of employment are. From the employer's point of view, the necessity of drafting a terms of employment statement should concentrate the mind wonderfully on issues about which it is all too easy to be sloppy at the expense of subsequent aggravation, such as hours of work, holidays and, above all, exactly what it is the employee is supposed to be doing. The following points have to be covered in the contract, and you must say if you have not covered one or other of them:

- ☐ The normal hours of work and the terms and conditions relating to them.
- ☐ Holidays and holiday pay.
- ☐ Provision for sick pay and maternity leave.
- ☐ Pension and pension schemes.
- ☐ Notice required by both parties.
- ☐ The job title.
- ☐ Any disciplinary rules relating to the job.
- ☐ Grievance procedures.
- ☐ Rights to arrears of pay in the event of insolvency.

A further requirement is that employers must issue on or before each payday and for each employee an itemised statement showing:

- ☐ Gross wages/salary.
- ☐ Net wages/salary.
- ☐ Deductions and the reasons for them (unless these are a standard amount, in which case the reasons need only be repeated every 12 months).
- ☐ Details of part-payments, eg special overtime rates.
- ☐ The rate of pay and how it is calculated.
- ☐ Whether it is paid weekly or monthly.
- ☐ The period of employment, if it is temporary.

UNFAIR DISMISSAL

Probably the area of legislation which it is easiest and most common to fall foul of is that relating to unfair dismissal. Every employee, including part-timers, must be given a written statement of your reason if you want to dismiss him or her.

You must also give them one week's notice (or payment in lieu) if they have been with you continuously for four weeks or more and, after two years, one week's notice for every year of continuous employment. Fair enough, you might say, particularly as, on the face of things, what the law regards as fair grounds for dismissal are perfectly reasonable: incompetence, misconduct or genuine redundancy. The problem is that the employee is at liberty to disagree with you on the fairness issue and to take the case to an industrial tribunal, which stipulates that the employer's grounds for dismissal must be _reasonable._

There are four areas of employment law of particular relevance to small businesses employing staff:

1. The qualifying period for alleged unfair dismissal is one year (or one month in some medical cases or some disputes over statutory rights).
2. Employment tribunals are directed to take account of the size and resources of the employer. For example, where an employee proves unsatisfactory in one job, a large employer might be able to offer him another position, but a small employer would find this more difficult in most cases.
3. Post-maternity reinstatement is waived for firms of less than five employees, if reinstatement is not practicable.
4. Frivolous claims are to be deterred by a liability to costs.

If the employee has been guilty of gross misconduct, such as persistent lateness, you will probably win your case, provided you warned him in writing to mend his ways well before you dismissed him. The point here is that not only must you have good reasons for dismissing him, but also you must have acted reasonably in the dismissal situation. This means that you have got to follow a proper sequence of written warnings – not less than three is the number generally recommended – stating his inadequacies, telling him what he has to do to put them right and spelling out the consequences if he fails to do so.

When it comes to matters of competence, though, things are rather less clear-cut, particularly if the task involved is not one where performance can be readily quantified or where there are many imponderables. It would be relatively easy to argue a case against a machine operator who was consistently turning out less work than her colleagues on similar machines, but far more difficult in the case of a sales rep who could plead that a poor call-rate was the result of difficulties in finding car parking or inefficient back-up from the office.

The fact is that in all matters affecting competence you really have to do your homework very carefully before dismissing someone. The inexperienced employer may unwittingly contribute to an adverse judgement by the tribunal by such steps as including the person concerned in a general salary rise not long before informing him he is not up to the job.

There may be cases where you, as the employer, are satisfied that dismissal is fair, but where the law does not agree with you. One where you have to be very careful is dismissal on medical grounds. No reasonable employer would dismiss anyone in such circumstances if you could help it, but if you get stuck with someone who is persistently off sick and is able to provide satisfactory medical evidence, you would have to show proof that the absences were of such a nature as to cause disruption to your business before you could discharge him. Even more tricky is the case of employees who are engaged in public duties, such as being on the local council. You have to give them reasonable time off to attend to those duties, though not necessarily with pay.

The Sex Discrimination Act and the Equal Pay Act mean that women have in all respects to be treated on an equal footing with men, though since 1982 firms with fewer than five employees have been exempt from the former provisions. There are also occupations where discrimination is legal because of the nature of the work.

There are some additional conditions when employing women of child-bearing age. It used to be the case that women had to have had two years' continuous service with the same employer to qualify for maternity leave. These rules have now changed. Every expectant mother can take up to 18 weeks maternity leave and is entitled to Statutory Maternity Pay (SMP). Those employed for one year or more can take additional maternity leave from the end of the ordinary period up to the end of a period 29 weeks after the birth. This is 90 per cent of average weekly earnings for the first six weeks of maternity leave and £60.20 a week for the remaining 12 weeks. Businesses can recover 92 per cent of the SMP paid to employees, with smaller firms allowed to claim 100 per cent. Employees must give 21 days notice of their intention to take maternity leave and are entitled to get their old job back when they return – although these rules are slightly relaxed for the smallest firms who do not need to keep the job open if they can show it is not practicable to do so.

There is also now the right to take parental leave for a child born after 15 December 1999. Before the child reaches the age of five, parents are allowed 13 weeks leave in periods of not less than one week and up to a maximum of four weeks per year. Even male employees after 26 weeks employment are entitled to statutory paternity pay (SPP) for two weeks leave.

Nor does it end there. You will have to maintain all benefits other than remuneration… and if you bring in a replacement for her, or any other employee who is off for any longer period of time, be very careful. Her replacement could sue you for unlawful dismissal unless you notify him or her in writing that the appointment is a temporary one and give notice when it is coming to an end.

The penalties for losing an unfair dismissal case can be ruinous for a small firm. Under the new White Paper, *Fairness at Work*, there is no longer any limit to the amount that can be claimed. One effect may be a rise in substantial five-figure claims by aggrieved claimants with an aggressive lawyer. Thus if you are in any doubt at all about a dismissal, you should consult a solicitor who is versed in this aspect of the law.

REDUNDANCY

Redundancy is a ripe area for misunderstanding. Redundancy occurs when a job disappears, for example because a firm ceases trading or has to cut down on staff. It does not have the same restrictions as dismissal, but nevertheless does involve some financial penalties for employers if the employee has been continuously employed by the firm concerned for one year or more. In that case he will be entitled to redundancy pay on a formula based on length of service and rate of pay. About half of this can be recovered from the Department for Work and Pensions, which you should notify if you intend to make anyone redundant. As usual, there is a good deal of form-filling involved. The law also requires you to give advance warning to the relevant unions if any of their members are to be made redundant.

What happens if you buy a business, lock, stock and barrel, together with the staff? You may find that you do not like some of the people the previous owner took on, or that you want to change or drop some of the things that were being done, with the result that staff will be made redundant. Irrespective of the fact that you did not hire the people concerned, you are still stuck with the responsibility towards them as their current employer, so that being the proverbial new broom can be a very costly exercise. Before buying a business, therefore, it is very important to look at the staff and at the extent of any redundancy payments or dismissals situations you could get involved in.

STATUTORY SICK PAY

Under the Social Security Contributions and Benefits Act (1992), employers are responsible for paying Statutory Sick Pay (SSP) to virtually all employees earning £67 or more a week, for up to 28 weeks' sickness in the year, and note that there is no longer a minimum number of weeks for which an employee has to have worked, before being able to claim sick pay. The obligation begins after the employee has been off work sick for more than three consecutive days. These need not be working days, though. They could include the weekend, or days when he would not normally be working. SSP is treated as earnings, so you should deduct PAYE and pay the employer's National Insurance contribution on it.

After these three days, and once the employee starts qualifying for SSP, it is only payable for the days when she would have been working. This means that when you employ part-timers – a growing part of the workforce – you would be well advised to specify their working days in the terms of employment, rather than having a loose 'as and when needed' arrangement.

Good paperwork in SSP situations is all the more important because you can claim back the payments you have made provided they exceed 13 per cent of your gross National Insurance contribution for the month (that is, NIC for employer *and* employee). The excess is deducted from the employer's National Insurance contribution.

The employee can offer self-certification for up to seven days. After that the employer should ask for a doctor's certificate. Careful records have to be kept of SSP payments and retained for three years. When you start employing people, you should get guidance from the DSS on how they require this to be done.

Guidance leaflets on employment

A great many leaflets giving guidance on employment matters are available free from the Department for Work and Pensions. For an up-to-date list, write the General Office, Information 4, Department of Employment, Caxton House, Tothill Street, London SW1H 9NF.

In the same context, another Act of Parliament you should keep an eye open for when buying a business is the Health and Safety at Work Act, which lays down standards to which working premises have to conform. Before putting down your money you should check with the inspectors of the Health and Safety Executive that any premises you are buying or leasing as part of the deal meet those standards.

In this connection it is important to be aware of the concept of 'constructive dismissal'. If an employer changes the terms of employment by action such as substantively lengthening hours, reducing pay or benefits or even adversely changing the status of an employee, that can be tantamount to unfair dismissal. Working Time Regulations are discussed later in this Chapter.

RECRUITMENT

The cost of discharging staff, whether because of redundancy or by dismissal, makes it imperative that you should make the right decisions in picking people to work for you in the first place. We have said that the sphere of personnel selection is something of a lottery. It could equally be described as a gamble and there are ways in which you could cut down on the odds against you.

The most obvious question to ask yourself is whether you really do need to take someone on permanently at all. The principle we have put forward for the purchase of equipment – never buy anything outright unless you are sure you have a continuing use for it and that it will pay for itself over a reasonable interval of time – also applies to personnel. The legal constraints that cover part-time or full-time employees do not extend to freelancers, personnel from agencies or outside work done on contract, and this could well be the best way of tackling a particular problem such as an upward bump in demand until you are sure that it is going to last.* It is worth remembering, too, that when you take on staff you take on a good many payroll and administrative overheads in addition to their salary. These can add quite significantly to your costs. The introduction of the minimum wage in April, 1999, should also have made you consider the costs of recruitment. The standard rate is £4.20 an hour for those aged 22 and above. For those aged 18–21 the rate is now £3.60 an hour. Exemptions include 16 and 17 year olds and apprentices between the ages of 18 and 26 who are in the first year of their apprenticeship.

Sooner or later, though, if you want your business to grow (and growth of some kind seems to be an inevitable concomitant of success) you are going to need people. But even then you should ask yourself what exactly you need them for and how much you can afford to pay. Clarifying these two issues is not only important in itself, but will also give you the basis of a job description which you can use in your press advertising or approach to a recruitment agency, at the interview and, finally, in the contract of employment. Around it you should also build a series of questions to ask the interviewee that should give you some indication of competence to do the job. Such questions should call for a detailed response rather than a 'yes' or 'no' type of answer. For example:

---

* However, in some cases freelancers have successfully argued retrospectively that since they were subject to the same conditions as the ordinary employees of a firm, they were covered by employment law. It is not enough to say that 'A' is a freelance and 'B' is not; there must be recognisable differences in the way they work. The freelance must not be under your direct supervision and control, or he will be likely to be classified (for the purposes of redundancy pay, etc) as an employee.

- How many previous employers has he had? Has his progress been up, down or steady? Is this move part of the overall employment pattern?
- If he is willing to take a large drop in salary find out why – there could be a perfectly good reason, but it is worth being cautious.
- If you are interviewing a sales representative, as well as asking her how long she has been in the business, try to find out which buyers she knows and how well she knows them.
- Always ask for and check references. Telephone references are reckoned to be more reliable than written ones as referees are more forthcoming without the potential threat of libel.
- Be careful that the job specification stays within the growing range of employment protection legislation. Many employment agencies will advise you on the dos and don'ts of these contentious areas before you start interviewing candidates.

Both in framing your recruitment advertisements and in interviewing take care not to offend against provisions of the Sex Discrimination Act 1975 and 1986, the Race Relations Act 1976 and the more recent Disability Discrimination Act 1995.

WORKING TIME

Since 1 October 1998, The Working Time Regulations have given a wide range of rights to employees and other workers, including, for the first time, a statutory right to paid leave. This right arises after 13 weeks of continuous working or employment. The minimum annual paid leave is four weeks. Working time must be recorded – including overtime – and must not exceed an average of 48 hours (averaged over a period which is usually 17 weeks) unless there is a written agreement between the employer and employees opting out of this restriction. Night workers also have restrictions on hours worked and have the right to free health assessments. The Regulations also give workers rights to rest-breaks and daily and weekly rest periods.

CONDITIONS OF WORK

Numerous regulations affect working conditions and you should be conversant with those relevant to your area, particularly if it is a potentially dangerous trade. Length of hours, minimum wages, employment of young persons, etc will tend to apply to all businesses and, though you may escape prosecution for a while, to fall foul of the law is likely to be embarrassing and expensive.

Checklist: employing people

1. Do you really need to take on staff? Will there be enough to keep them busy a year from now?
2. Have you worked out a job description which sets out the purpose of the job, the duties involved and who the person appointed will report to?
3. Have you decided how much you can afford to pay?
4. Does your advertisement or approach to a recruiting agency spell out the job description, the salary and an indication of the age of the person you are looking for?
5. Does it in any way contravene the Sex Discrimination Act or the Race Relations Act?
6. Have you prepared a series of questions that will throw some light on the interviewee's competence, personality and previous record of employment?
7. Have you taken up and checked references?
8. Are you satisfied, before making the appointment, that you have seen enough applicants to give you an idea of the quality of staff available for this particular job?
9. Do you have a procedure for reviewing the employee's progress before the expiry of the 52-week period after which he can claim unfair dismissal if you decide he is not suitable?
10. Do you make a practice of putting important matters in writing to the employees concerned?

4.3 Using IT to Run Your Office

E-COMMERCE

Technological advances have made self-employment accessible to many more businesses and individuals. The range of new technologies and equipment can be quite daunting and it seems that, no sooner than something appears on the market, it is replaced by an updated and more efficient version. Whereas five years ago a personal computer, fax and answerphone were probably all the equipment that start-up businesses needed, the phenomenal growth of e-commerce has made it important for individuals and small businesses to re-examine their needs and to investigate the use of information and communication technologies (ICTs). The easy accessibility and affordability of ICTs have had a two-fold effect on small businesses. First, it has made working from home far easier and second it has provided even the smallest enterprise access to a global market.

This accessibility and the growing interest of SMEs in e-commerce is demonstrated by the fact that Web site ownership and the use of Web sites to sell online by SMEs between 1997 and 2000 more than doubled, according to government figures. Indeed, the Christmas of 1999 was known as the first 'e-xmas' with many small traders reporting phenomenal sales through their Web sites.

However, as much as there is plenty to be optimistic about there are still concerns over the ability of the Internet to be secure and to maintain confidentiality. Furthermore, many businesses have been the victim of their own success and found that although having Web sites has boosted sales, they have not been able to back this up properly with adequate distribution and warehousing facilities. An interesting example of this is that the online sales of books in the run-up to the Christmas of 1999 far outstripped conventional purchasing in shops. However, this dropped off rapidly in the ten days before Christmas as customers lacked confidence in the ability of online retailers to get them their goods on time. Indeed, high-street traders found that they made up the sales lost to their electronic counterparts. Experience will undoubtedly iron out some of these problems and many are convinced that unless small businesses adopt e-commerce into their work practices they cannot possibly remain competitive. Commenting on the 1998 report *Net Benefit: The Electronic Commerce Agenda for the UK*, the former DTI minister, Barbara Roche, identified why it is so important for companies and individuals to embrace these changes:

> The phenomenal speed of change poses huge challenges to business – the need to change working practices, open up new markets, create new products and new forms of distribution. In markets where the traditional model can be turned on its head overnight, where a business can move from start-up to global player in a matter of months, it is vital that all companies, whatever their sector of business, whether large or small, understand how electronic commerce can bring them competitive advantage and use that knowledge.

Definition of e-commerce

There is still debate about the true definition of e-commerce. The Information Society Initiative, a government scheme to encourage SMEs to adopt e-commerce practices into their businesses, identifies two definitions:

1. Narrow definition: focus on buying and selling of goods or services over electronic networks such as the Internet between businesses, business and consumers or between the public and private sector.
2. Broad definition: includes the above but also activities between businesses for intermediate goods and the elec-

tronic processing of information, ie how businesses are using information gathered electronically to improve their business processes and relationships with suppliers and consumers.

A simpler definition is offered by the Association for Standards and Practices in Electronic Trade on its extremely useful Web site 'eCentreuk' http://www.eca.org.uk:

> Electronic commerce covers any form of business or administrative transaction or information exchange that is executed using any information and communications technology.

E-commerce is subject of course to the normal rules governing trade as well as to laws such as the Data Protection Act. The Information Protection Commissioner has voiced concerns that most companies selling through the Web do not have a returns policy, proper small print and data protection policies, and has made it clear that sites will be targeted for compliance with e-law and regulations. An Office of Fair Trading Internet sweep found that 52 per cent of e-sales companies failed to fulfil the rules on returning goods (a business selling from a Web site has to allow a cooling-off period for customers to change their minds, even after the goods have been delivered). A guide to compliance produced by UK online for business is available from www.ukonlineforbusiness.gov.uk

Building an ICT infrastructure

Building an ICT infrastructure could be as easy as buying a suitable PC with a modem. This might set you up with an e-mail capability, access to the Internet, ordering facilities, etc. Alternatively, you might need additional technology to build your infrastructure, such as a mobile phone with a modem if you are on the road a lot.

The 1999 ISI review of usage trends internationally found that ICT uptake was growing in all areas of UK industry:

ICT Ownership and Use

	1997 %	1999 %
PCs	94	93
PCs with modems	73	79
Internet access	35	62
Web site	27	51
External e-mail	52	72
Electronic Data Interchange (EDI)	31	32
Selling online	3	9

Source: Moving into the Information Age 1999, ISI

The Office for National Statistics published a survey report on e-commerce in May 2001. It showed that 16 per cent of businesses were using computer networks for sales, and another 12 per cent intended to do so over the next year, 2002. Internet sales totalled £57 billion, but the bulk of this came from business to business sales; the value of sales to households was around £10 billion, including £9 billion from the financial sector. Concerns about delivery of orders to households and about the lack of face-to-face meetings have shown some of the limits of e-commerce, but there has been significant growth since 1999 when less than 10 per cent of companies were selling goods over the Internet. Figures for PC use and Web access had changed little from the 1999 survey, but the report pointed out that while 94 per cent of larger firms had Web access the figure for companies with less than 50 employees was only 59 per cent (10 per cent of businesses were planning to get Web access over the next year).

Before considering what equipment your business may need, it is worth carrying out a needs assessment. Peter Chatterton in *Your Home Office* advises that the process of purchasing technological tools should be carried out in a sensible and planned way. He advises that you should:

☐ find out what's available;
☐ work out your own needs;
☐ put a realistic plan together;
☐ buy with confidence;

☐ learn gradually;
☐ get yourself organised.

Advice on your ICT needs can be sought from both the ISI and eCentreuk. However, the following is a base-line guide to equipment necessary to join the information superhighway.

A computer with modem

Either a PC or Mac with at least enough memory to make full use of graphical interfaces, like Windows. However, if you want to use your computer for the Internet or other functions such as e-mail you should think big. Generally, the bigger the processor and more megabytes (Mbs) of RAM you have, the faster and more advanced your computer will be. Likewise, the speed of your modem is also important as it can affect the speed of connections and downloading of documents. Current modems are running at 56K and are unlikely to change in the near future. However, check the current system entry levels for your PC or Mac as these change almost monthly.

There are a vast number of personal computers on the market, all offering much the same features. Your choice boils down to the following criteria:

☐ what you actually want to do;
☐ cost;
☐ desktop, laptop or palmtop;
☐ PC or Mac;
☐ processor type and speed;
☐ peripherals (such as scanner);
☐ speed of modem;
☐ software applications.

Desktops are considerably cheaper than laptops or portables but if you are on the move a lot it may make more sense to buy a laptop. The current generation of laptops has impressive specifications and match desktops in terms of MHz and RAM. Nearly all recent models of PCs – both desktop and laptop – include a modem and a fax facility.

What you actually want the computer to do is probably the most important factor in choosing one, but the issue here is one of choosing software, rather than hardware. There are software packages for virtually every conceivable standard business application, but if you think yours is in any way different, make sure that you do buy the right software package. 'Bending' software to a particular application can be done, but it is extremely expensive and it may be cheaper to change your procedures, rather than to get a special program written. Before you buy a piece of software, prepare a very detailed specification of what you do and what you need – and what you might need or be doing in the foreseeable future.

Cost largely depends on the range of features that are available, like the modem and fax capability mentioned earlier; it will also depend on how much software is 'bundled in' with the purchase price, such as word processing, financial and desktop-publishing packages. It is not advisable to buy second-hand computers, unless you really know what you are doing and what to look for.

Telephone lines

Although a simple choice in the past, the option now exists to have an Integrated Services Digital Network – an ISDN line. This will speed up your connection to the Internet and is a high-speed digital equivalent to a normal telephone line. It is also advisable if you want to link several users to the Internet. It is estimated to be as much as four times as fast as most modems and can connect you to your Internet Service Provider (ISP) almost immediately, although you will have to check with your ISP to see if it supports ISDN links.

Mobile phones have also become essential to businesses on the move. The newest versions can offer Internet access and fax and e-mail functions. We will not attempt to list the different networks and handset providers here as they are far too numerous to mention. However, if a mobile phone is necessary to your business you should include it in your overall strategy to integrate it fully into your ICT infrastructure.

Internet Service Provider

To take advantage of the Internet and to install e-mail you will need to sign up with an ISP. There has been the recent emergence of free services. However, take heed, many of the free services charge over the odds for technical support and whatever you might save on a subscription (typically £12-15 a month) you might lose in this additional cost. An ISP will provide your access to the Internet and e-mail. Setting up a Web site is discussed fully in Chapter 5.3 'Marketing Your Work'. However, it is worth mentioning here that it is also your ISP that rents you the file space for your Web site.

E-mail

The provision of e-mail by your ISP is also an important consideration and one of the great innovations of recent years. It allows messages, files or documents to be sent electronically to other Internet users for the price of a local telephone call. It is incredibly easy to use and the instantaneous sending of material makes it extremely attractive. Your PC should have the appropriate software. The advantages of using e-mail over fax are that you can send high resolution colour and long documents. Any computer file can be attached to an e-mail including spreadsheets, pictures and audio files.

Networks

Local networks are used by companies to link their employees. This can be within a company building, or to teleworkers based in various locations. Local Area Network (LAN) allows files and resources to be shared. It can also provide access to the Internet by being connected to an ISP via an ISDN or leased line.

Videoconferencing

Using the Internet as a telephone or videoconference service, two or more people can be linked visually. Your PC will need to have a microphone, sound card, speakers, camera and video card. A fast link to the Internet is also advisable as it reduces the time it takes to update the video pictures.

Electronic Data Interchange (EDI)

EDI facilitates the exchange of business documents between computers of trading partners. It allows purchasers and suppliers to handle transactions down the phone lines by sending set forms and invoices in an electronic form. However, for the small business or start-up, where there are not a large number of transactions, EDI might not be cost-effective and using e-mail might be more appropriate.

Areas of activity

The rapid increase in Web sites also signifies that many businesses acknowledge the marketing benefits of being on the Internet. However, there are other areas of business to which ICTs can bring a competitive advantage.

1. E-mail
   - Efficient communication with customers and staff.
   - Images – photographs, technical details, etc – can be sent to anywhere in the world enabling faster design approval times.
   - Standardised forms can be e-mailed, cutting times given for estimates and quotes. Cuts paperwork and postage.
   - Electronic products can be exported quickly and easily overseas.
   - After-sales service can be made by processing queries and keeping customers informed by e-mail. Newsletters can also be sent.
2. Networks
   - Provides access to information which can be updated as often as necessary and can create contact lists and diaries.
   - Manufacturing information placed on a network will allow suppliers to adjust production accordingly and reduce lead and delivery times.
   - Home-working made more effective by allowing access to shared information.
   - Help with customer service by providing information and individual details and transactions quickly.

3. CD ROM
   - Electronic data storage reduces the need for shelving and warehousing and provides quick access to information.
   - Easier to tailor presentations to a customer's needs with addition of sound and video.
4. Videoconferencing
   - Brings in outside expertise and allows for better communication for businesses based in isolated or rural setting.
5. Mobile telephone
   - Allows sales reps to work efficiently on the move and linked to a laptop computer enables access to records and data in different settings.
6. EDI
   - Speeds up payment of invoices by trading partners.
   - Can simplify paperwork of shipping, dispatch and money transfer.
7. Internet
   - Online recruitment finds a global pool of applicants.
   - Company Web site could have descriptions and prices of your products. Orders can also be placed.
   - Suppliers' stock levels and delivery times can be checked via Web sites.
   - Sourcing cheaper or better goods and new suppliers becomes easier.
   - Large companies are beginning to tender on the Web and expect responses in the same way.
   - Research new export markets and overseas contacts.
   - A company Web site will provide a global presence and attract overseas sales.

Growth of e-commerce

E-commerce has encouraged small businesses to enter the global market. Although in its infancy, there is no doubt that its current growth is set to continue. Given the growing importance of Internet sales, it should be given serious consideration by anyone starting out in business today – no matter how small that concern might be. If in doubt as to where to start, get help from either the government or from private consultants to formulate a needs assessment for your company and remember that marketing is only one area in which an ICT infrastructure can help.

Checklist: ICT questions

1. Consider your business needs and how electronic equipment can reduce costs and introduce efficiency.
2. Consider how your business might grow in the near future and the equipment you will need to accommodate expansion.
3. What areas of your business could benefit from ICT? Contact the ISI or eCentreuk for advice.
4. Consider the impact of marketing and selling on the Internet – do you have adequate administrative systems, distribution and warehousing to back it up?
5. Try to integrate your equipment into one infrastructure and don't duplicate functions with different equipment eg if your PC has a fax, do you need to buy a separate one (you will if you need to fax separate items that aren't generated from your PC unless you also have a scanner)?
6. Think about the speed and capacity of your equipment when purchasing and try to buy as high an entry specification as possible. This also applies to the modem.
7. Consider carefully the pros and cons of a free ISP or whether it is better to subscribe to a fuller service.

4.4 Choosing Premises

The choice of premises tends to be determined by individual requirements. Over 400,000 businesses are currently home-based, accounting for over one in ten small businesses in this country. This chapter will mainly concentrate on the requirements of this group. However, for many, such as those in retailing, this simply is not an option and help is available at the end of this chapter for those who need to choose separate premises.

WORKING FROM HOME

Research by Barclays Small Business Banking has identified the growing trend amongst the self-employed to work from home. Key findings include:

☐ Businesses operating from home are generally smaller than those with separate premises and have a quarter of the average turnover of these businesses.

☐ The average start-up cost for small businesses operating from home is £5,000 compared with £13,000 for those operating from separate premises.

☐ Only a fifth of those business owners working from home see it as a stepping stone to operating from separate premises.

☐ Business owners working from home work on average 11 hours less each week than those working from separate premises.

Commenting on this research, Mike Davis, Managing Director of Barclays Small Business Banking, identifies the reasons for the increasing number of home workers:

> The way we work is changing. Technological advances, especially in the communications field – coupled with growing frustration with time wasted travelling to and from work – has meant that more and more people are choosing to work from home.

Working from home needs to be given careful consideration. While start-up costs are smaller than for businesses operating from premises, you should be aware of the effects on family life and the prospect of working in isolation. Furthermore, should you need to have business visitors, a home-based office might create a bad impression of your operation unless you think carefully about presentation. You should also check whether by claiming part of the costs of running your business from home you will incur capital gains tax.

Barclays identifies two types of home worker. The first spends most of the working day at home and the second uses the home as a base but works at clients' premises. The second group is older, with over half aged over 45. Typical occupations in this group are building and gardening.

On the other hand, the group using their home as an office tend to be women, of which a sixth were formerly housewives. The researchers observe:

> These characteristics suggest many of the owners of these businesses are trying to juggle domestic responsibilities with those of work, or have more than one job and set up in business to supplement the family income. It is more likely that they plan to maintain the size of their home-based business rather than expand it to become the main breadwinner.

Indeed, the above comment points to one of the biggest problems experienced by working from home: the difficulty in separating work from home life. Domestic distractions are one thing (the attractions of finishing off the dusting can far outweigh having to do your accounts), but if you only have one telephone for both home and business, a child acting as receptionist to potential clients will not present a professional image and might critically damage your prospects.

Setting aside a dedicated room to act as a separate office can help, if your home allows it. This will help to separate domestic and work life both physically and psychologically. Going to work in a separate space – even if it is the room next door – can help create the division. However, while there are problems in juggling domestic responsibilities and work in the same environment, one should not ignore the benefits. For example, the Barclays research found that nearly half of the women working from home stated that it was an important benefit because it allowed them to look after children and/or other dependants. Flexible working hours and practices, a reduction in travelling time and improved quality of life were also cited as benefits of home working. The following table identifies the perceived benefits of working from home:

Table 4.4.1 _Perceived benefits of working from home_

Perceived benefit	All	Men	Women
Lower overheads	26	37	16
Allows me to look after children/dependants	24	4	48
Allows me flexible working hours/practices	22	20	23
Allows me to be my own boss	17	21	13
No need for separate premises	16	20	12
Less travelling time	12	13	11
Lower start-up costs	8	10	6
Better quality of life	6	8	5
Greater potential profits	5	8	3

Choosing a room

What, then, should be taken into consideration when setting up an office from home? The following checklist should help:

- ☐ Noise – choose as quiet a room as possible, away from the distractions of family and other external noises.
- ☐ Position – try to think about heating and ventilation. A south-facing office might be appealing but will become a heat trap in the summer, as can uninsulated attics. Save on heating bills by purchasing a heater for your office rather than heating the whole house in winter.
- ☐ Lighting – be aware of the glare on computers and of the need for good lighting for close work such as design.
- ☐ Storage – you will never have enough space to store paperwork. However, consideration for the best use of storage facilities should be given.
- ☐ Security – being burgled is an unpleasant experience that could be disastrous if your means of making a living are also taken. Invest in a burglar alarm, good window and door locks and mark any equipment with an identifiable label.

Visitors

One of the main reasons cited by people who do not choose to work from home is that separate premises provide a professional image. Indeed, a visitor who has to negotiate children's toys and overeager pets might not leave with the image of the professional business that you would want. Should you expect your home business to have visitors, bear in mind the impression you are likely to give and clear passageways and the route through to your working area where possible. Your office can be a comfortable environment in which to meet clients and as they know that you work from home they will not expect otherwise. However, you can also arrange to meet elsewhere such as in a hotel or club such as the Institute of Directors, should you be a member. Furthermore, if you do not want to use your home address for business purposes, using a Post Office Box number can help to guard privacy and, should you move, maintain continuity for your customers.

Networking

One of the biggest problems for people working from home is the sense of isolation. Whereas going to work in separate premises automatically introduces contact with other individuals, it is quite possible not to see another adult in your working day if you work from home. This can impact on your work, as informal feedback from colleagues about ideas and projects is an underrated but invaluable source of advice and motivation. Daily discussion that occurs naturally in shared offices and workspaces can be helpful on a range of issues and is often sorely missed. The lack of this informal feedback is often neglected when considering how to work from home and it is important to build into your work practice a way of networking with other people in the same occupation or in similar circumstances. Being a member of a trade association or union can help, as regular local meetings can be attended; local chambers of commerce can also help you keep in contact with other businesses in your region. The Internet is also another way to contact people through user-groups and e-mail. However, non-professional communication is also important and building in a break to the day where contact is made with other people can also help. Peter Chatterton describes how he has overcome this problem in *Your Home Office* (Kogan Page), by forming a lunch society with other home-based workers:

> We get together on an ad-hoc basis for lunch or early evening drinks. This may sound trivial, but it is important to one's sanity in home working. But there are other benefits – our growing band of home workers have suddenly found that we can work together and give each other business. It's the start of a new wave of home business networking.

Chatterton also recommends putting adverts in local papers to make contact with other home workers and taking advantage of the flexible hours by going to a local sports club during the day when there isn't the weekend rush, adding: 'Think originally and openly – after all, you don't have the constraints of a normal job.'

CHOOSING SEPARATE PREMISES

Working from home simply isn't an option when space needs to be found for employees, machinery, vehicles and other equipment. Indeed a sixth of small business owners cite this as the reason for working from separate premises. Research has also found that a further 15 per cent believe that it is easier to keep business and private lives separate, while 8 per cent thought it would mean fewer distractions. However, choosing a premise can be a complicated matter. It is important to consider your own specific requirements and ask some key questions before committing yourself to a lease or purchase. For example:

- ☐ Is passing trade a requirement for your business?
- ☐ Is a prestigious/prominent building important to your needs?
- ☐ What can you afford and are you going to lease or purchase?
- ☐ Do you have specific space requirements such as the need for warehousing?
- ☐ Is there sufficient utility capacity for your needs (ie gas, electricity, water, drainage, waste disposal)?
- ☐ Does the property present security risks?
- ☐ Do you need unrestricted parking for deliveries and customers?
- ☐ Will you need planning permission for your usage?
- ☐ Will it accommodate your growing business?

LEASES

Whether you plan to trade from your home or a separate premise, if the property is rented you will need to look carefully at the terms of your lease. There are likely to be restrictive covenants in the lease which will prevent you from carrying on a trade in premises let to you for domestic use. This may not be an insuperable obstacle, but you would certainly have to get the owner's permission if you wanted to use your home for any purpose other than just living there.

Even when you rent commercial premises there are likely to be restrictions on the trade you carry on in them. An empty flower shop, for instance, could probably be used as a dress shop without complications, but its use as a furniture repair business might be disallowed because of the noise involved in running wood-working machinery. You and your solicitor should examine the lease closely for possible snags of this sort.

Equally important is the existence of any restrictions which would prohibit you from transferring the lease to a third party. This would mean that the purchaser would have to negotiate the lease element in the event of the sale of the business with the property owner, not with you, and this could drastically affect the value of what you have to sell. For instance, if you took a gamble on renting premises in an improving area which fulfilled your expectations by coming up in the world, you would not be able to reap the benefit of your foresight and courage if you could not transfer the unexpired portion of the lease.

Commercial leases, unlike most domestic ones, run for relatively short periods: usually between three and seven years, with rent reviews at the end of each term or sometimes even sooner. This adds an unknown factor to the long-term future of any business in rented premises and is one you need to take into account in buying a business – again, particularly in an improving area. In Covent Garden, for instance, a number of small shops which moved in when it was a very run-down part of central London with correspondingly low rents were hit by huge increases when these rents were reviewed in the light of the improved status of the area subsequent to the redevelopment of the market building and its surroundings.

The other point to watch for in leases is whether you are responsible for dilapidation during the period of your lease. If you are, you could be in for a hefty bill at its end and for this reason it is advisable to have a survey done and its findings agreed with the owner, before you take on the lease.

MEET YOUR OWN REQUIREMENTS

Whether working from home, or from a separate premise, your environment is an important element in being able to motivate yourself and work efficiently. If you are able to discipline yourself to set hours within your home office, then this might be the answer for you. However, if being in contact with people on a daily basis is important it might be worth looking at a shared space with other like-minded self-employed individuals. Your local paper should have details of workspaces, or try your trade association or trade union for contacts. Deciding to work from separate premises will need careful consideration. Requirements for specific trades, such as retailing or catering, are discussed in Part 2. However, the Royal Institution of Chartered Surveyors also publishes a book, *The Business Property Handbook*, which covers all of the main areas such as the complicated issue of signing a lease, planning permission and tax allowances. The choice of premises in relation to marketing is also discussed in this book in Chapter 5.3

Checklist: choosing premises and equipment

1. Are you able to separate domestic and work duties within your own home?
2. Are you able to work in isolation?
3. Have you identified forums for networking and are there other self-employed home workers with whom you can maintain contact?
4. Talk to your local crime prevention officer for advice on securing your office and equipment and inform your insurance company that you will be using part of your home for work.
5. Have you a room which allows adequate storage, good light, comfortable heat and ventilation and that is reasonably quiet? Check the route to your office to assess the impression a visitor might get.
6. Consider a separate telephone line for your business use.

7. Talk to other home workers in similar businesses about their equipment before you commit yourself to buying anything. If you have low usage of a piece of equipment, such as a photocopier, assess local availability before purchasing.

8. Assess your needs when considering separate premises. If passing trade is a requirement, think about parking restrictions. Is there enough room for equipment and any future growth in staff and business?

9. Seek out legal and professional advice whether you are considering purchasing or leasing a property.

10. Check if planning permission is required before altering the premises.

4.5 Legal Basics

Going to law is a process where the cure, in money terms, is often worse than the disease – which is why so many settlements are made out of court. Even seeking legal advice is an expensive business: £80 to £150 an hour is now the going rate, depending on where you are, and few legal bills come to less than this minimum, even for a short consultation. In complex disputes or where larger sums of money are involved, legal action may ultimately be the only course open. But at the more basic levels of trading law there are some straightforward principles laid down, though they are sometimes blurred by traditional tales – for instance, that a shopkeeper is obliged by law to sell anything he displays for sale. Knowing what the law actually says about this and other everyday trading transactions will help you to sort out minor disputes and, very often, save costly legal fees.

THE SALE OF GOODS ACT 1979

This Act and the more recent Sale and Supply of Goods Act 1994 place some clear but not unfair obligations on you as the seller once a contract has taken place, an event which occurs when goods have been exchanged for money. Nothing needs to be written or even said to make the contract legally binding and you cannot normally override it by putting up a notice saying things like 'No Refunds' or limiting your responsibilities in some other way. This is prohibited under the Unfair Contract Terms Act of 1977.

The Sale of Goods Act has three main provisions concerning what you sell.

1. The goods must be 'of satisfactory quality'. This means that they must be capable of doing what the buyer could reasonably expect them to do – for instance, an electric kettle should boil the water in it within a reasonable length of time.
2. The goods must be 'fit for any particular purpose' which you make known to the buyer. For instance, if you are asked whether a rucksack can carry 100 lb without the strap breaking and it fails to match up to your promise of performance, you will have broken your contract.
3. The goods must be 'as described'. If you sell a bicycle as having five speeds and it only has three, then again you are in breach of contract – as well as of the Trade Descriptions Act, if you do so knowingly.

But what happens if you yourself have been misled by the manufacturer from whom you bought the item in question? You cannot refer the buyer back to her: the Sale of Goods Act specifically places responsibility for compensating the buyer on the retailer, no matter from whom the retailer bought the goods in the first place.

Thus, if the goods fail on any of the three grounds shown above, you will have to take them back and issue a full refund, unless you can negotiate a partial refund, with the buyer keeping the goods about which he has complained. However, he need not accept such an offer, nor even a credit note. Furthermore, you may be obliged to pay any costs the buyer incurred in returning the goods, and even to compensate him if he had a justifiable reason to hire a replacement for the defective item; for instance, if he had to hire a ladder to do an urgent DIY job because the one you supplied was faulty.

The only let-out you have under the Act – which also covers secondhand goods – is if you warned the buyer about a specific fault, or if this was so obvious that he should have noticed it. In the case of the bike, he probably would have found it difficult to spot that a couple of the gears were not working, but he could reasonably be expected to notice a missing pedal.

THE SUPPLY OF GOODS AND SERVICES ACT 1982

This is essentially an extension of the Sale of Goods Act into the sphere of services. The point you have to watch out for is this: if you are offering a service, say, for repairs or some form of consultancy, the implied terms, which the Court will read into the arrangement whether they are written down or not, are: (1) that the supplier will carry out the service with reasonable care and skill; and (2) that it will be carried out in reasonable time and at reasonable cost.

A recent example of the Supply of Goods and Services Act in operation was when an architectural student carried out a small flat conversion job for a client. He neglected to obtain planning permission for some of the work and, even though he was not fully qualified at the time, it was held that, in offering his services, he should have known that this was a basic part of the service he had been offering.

Disclaiming responsibility for your actions under either of these Acts is not the answer; that would make you liable under the Unfair Terms in Consumer Contracts Regulations 1994.

THE CONSUMER PROTECTION ACT 1987

This is essentially a health and safety measure which says that where a defective product causes damage or injury, the supplier will be held liable unless he can show that not enough was known about its dangers at the time he supplied it.

OBLIGATION TO SELL

By law, all goods have to be priced but, contrary to some widely held beliefs, there is no obligation on you to sell goods on display for sale if you don't want to. For instance, an assistant in an antique shop might wrongly price a picture at £2.50 rather than £250. The intending buyer cannot force you to sell at that price, even though it is publicly displayed. However, once the goods have been sold at £2.50, even in error, a contract has taken place and cannot be revoked without the agreement of both parties.

This also applies when the buyer has paid a deposit and this has been accepted. Supposing she had paid £1 and offered to return with the balance, a bargain would have been made which you would be obliged to complete. It is, however, binding on both parties. If the buyer, having paid a deposit, decided to change her mind you would be within your rights in refusing to refund the money.

ESTIMATES AND QUOTATIONS

Self-employed people supplying services such as repairs are often asked for a quote or an estimate. How binding is the figure you give?

This is a grey area in which even the Office of Fair Trading finds it difficult to give legal ruling. They recommend, however, that a 'quote' should be a firm commitment to produce whatever the subject of the inquiry is at the price stated, whereas an 'estimate', while it should be a close guess, allows more leeway to depart from that figure. Therefore, if you are not sure how much a job is going to cost, you should describe your price as an estimate and say it is subject to revision. This may not, of course, satisfy the customer, in which case he would press you for a quote. If you really find it difficult to state a fixed sum because of unknown factors, you can either give some parameters (eg between £x and £y) or say that you will do £x-worth of work – which on present evidence is what you think it would take – but that you will notify the customer if that sum is likely to be exceeded to do the job properly. In general, though, an itemised firm quotation is the document that is least likely to produce disputes.

COMPLETION AND DELIVERY DATES

If you give a time for completing a job you will have to do it within that time – certainly if it is stated in writing.

In the case of delivery of goods ordered by customers the same is true. If you give a date you have to stick to it or the contract is broken and the customer can refuse the goods and even, in some cases, ask for compensation. Even if no date is given, you have to supply the article within a reasonable period of time, bearing in mind that what is reasonable in one case, such as making a dress, may not be reasonable in another – obtaining some ready-made article from a wholesaler, for example. The relevant law here is the Supply of Goods and Services Act 1982.

TRADING ASSOCIATIONS

In addition to legal obligations you may also belong to a trading association which imposes its own code of conduct. Such codes sometimes go beyond strict legal requirements, on the principle that 'the customer is always right'. This is not a bad principle to observe, within reason, whatever the legalities of the case. A reputation for fair dealing can be worth many times its cost in terms of advertising.

THE TRADE DESCRIPTIONS ACT 1968

Another piece of legislation you need to watch out for, especially in advertisements and brochures, is the Trade Descriptions Act. This makes it a criminal offence knowingly to make false or misleading claims, verbally or in writing, about any goods or services you are offering. That includes what is known as 'passing off' – using a brand name to which you are not entitled or implying an association with some better known product.

The notion of a trade description covers a wide range of characteristics, such as size, quantity, strength, method and place of manufacture, ingredients, testimonials from satisfied customers and claims that the goods or service are cheaper than the same bought elsewhere.

It is possible by cunning wording to stick to the letter of the law, but not its spirit. For instance, the words 'made with' some desirable substance or other may indicate that it was made with only a minute quantity of it. But on the whole it is better to stick to the truth, since a successful claim against you could result in a compensation award of up to £1,000 – not to speak of loss of reputation.

THE DATA PROTECTION ACT

The 1984 Act, followed by the 1998 Act that came into force in 2000, had the object of protecting individuals from unauthorised use of personal data about them; for instance, by computer bureaux selling mailing lists to direct sales organisations. Registration under the Act had to be completed by May 1986. Though failure to register is a criminal offence, the indications are that very few small businesses have actually done so, other than those which are directly affected, such as computer bureaux. In theory, though, the obligation to register is quite widespread, because anyone with a word processor that can store personal data may be liable to register at a cost of £35.

Application forms and guidance notes are available from post offices. Essentially, data users have to disclose to the Registrar what lists they hold, how and where they obtained the details on them and for what purposes they intend to use them. They must also undertake not to disclose them to any unspecified third party, or to use them for any purposes other than the declared ones. However, data used for internal administrative purposes, such as payrolls, are exempt if they are used only for that function.

THE PRICE MARKING ORDER 1991

This is an EC Directive. It obliges you to state the price of goods offered for sale in writing.

Checklist: legal basics

1. Find out about legislation that applies to your area of activity, and more generally to running a business of any kind.

2. If you are selling goods, make sure that they comply to the Sale of Goods Act and that you have made appropriate checks with your supplier that the goods are of suitable standard and 'as described'.

3. Be clear about the services you are offering and that you comply with the Supply of Goods and Services Act 1982.

4. Do not commit yourself to making a quote if you are unsure. An 'estimate' should be offered first, with a quote to follow once you have assessed costs etc.

5. Contact your trade association for codes of conduct and guidelines.

6. If you have personal data on individuals, collect forms from the post office to disclose this to the Registrar.

Section 5

Growing Your Business

Looking for a business account that offers you more?

Look no further than Alliance & Leicester

- Choice of award-winning current accounts – recently voted Moneyfact's Best Business Current Account Provider
- Business Deposit Accounts – paying high rates of interest on your surplus funds
- Merchant Acquiring – competitive and easy to use credit and debit card processing services
- Property and Contents Insurance – range of insurance products designed for small businesses
- Commercial lending – overdrafts, secured and unsecured loans
- Asset finance – for all your capital purchases including vehicles
- Business Credit Cards – with no need to pay off balance in full each month

Winner

Best Business Current Account Provider

Find out more today

☎ **0800 587 0800**

Quote ref. AD0147

 Visit your local branch

 www.mybusinessbank.co.uk/self

Alliance Leicester
Business Banking

5.1 Researching Your Market

To restate one of the opening remarks of Chapter 1.5 on the business planning process, it is unwise to rely on your instinct or perception of a business opportunity, however well you think you know the business or the territory, without carrying out basic research to support the case.

DIFFERENT TYPES OF RESEARCH

Market research falls broadly into two categories: desk research and field research. Desk research, which normally precedes field research, can be carried out from home by accessing published information and interrogating information sources by telephone, fax and, increasingly, via the Internet in order to develop a profile of the market you are seeking to enter and the past history and product offerings of market leaders who serve it.

Field research, as its name implies, involves person-to-person research 'in the field', either by face-to-face or telephone interview or sometimes – usually less successfully – by fax or e-mail questionnaire. Field research is conducted with potential customers and suppliers, or with product users in the case of research into new product design or packaging.

Of course, professional market research can be purchased from a market research agency, but this is expensive and it is unlikely that your personal funds or seed capital will stretch to having the work done for you by experts. However, you can achieve much by carrying out the research yourself provided that you follow the basic rules for researching objectively and thoroughly.

One research avenue that you should not neglect is established competitors who are in the same line of business but operating in locations outside the territory you have chosen. You will find that most people are happy to talk about how they have developed their businesses, current problems and opportunities, provided that you are not a direct competitor.

RESEARCH OBJECTIVES

The starting point is to construct your research brief, specifying the information that you need to evaluate your target market and the opportunity for you to gain entry: the same brief that you would give to a market research agency to develop its proposal. The following are 10 key questions that you need to answer:

1. What is the value of the market you propose to enter?
2. Is the market growing or shrinking?
3. What and where is the main competition?
4. What are the market shares of your main competitors?
5. Are your competitors profitable?
6. What are consumers/customers looking for?
7. Where in the market should you position your product/ service?
8. What is the profile of your average target customer and what market share could you capture?
9. How can you fulfil consumer/customer demand profitably?
10. How can you promote yourself economically to your target audience?

Depending on the nature of the business and its scope, there will be more or less information that you can gather by desk research before you begin to consider how to survey the target market yourself through field research.

CARRYING OUT DESK RESEARCH

Let us consider two completely different kinds of business, both service industries: the one a specialised form of consumer retailing, the other a service to industrial and commercial clients.

Business A is the operation of a local garden centre, for which you have no prior experience except as an enthusiastic amateur gardener.

Business B is a consultancy to train telephone call centre customer-service staff. (Suppose that before deciding to work for yourself you were a supervisor in a call centre servicing national companies.)

For Business A, desk research will enable you to answer just a few of the 10 key questions on a national basis. You will be able to identify the overall value of consumer expenditure at garden centres and on horticultural products, and to confirm the rate of growth of the overall market. Local competition is readily identifiable, but not market share or profitability. There are a few listed companies engaged in garden centre operations that are obliged to file detailed accounts, and an inspection of these will provide some indications of how profitable these activities may be and whether their profitability is increasing or declining. However, in the context of planning a local business, desk research alone will not provide answers to the last seven questions.

For Business B, your prior work experience will help you to conduct desk research and to answer more of the 10 key questions. You should not rely on your experience alone to answer Question 6 (What are consumers/customers looking for?) or Question 7 (Where in the market should you position your product/service?), although it may provide strong pointers that you can test at the next stage.

Indeed, there are two possible markets for your proposed call centre training services: one is in staff training on a freelance basis in call centres that subcontract for clients, the other working directly with clients who prefer to set up their own telephone customer service operations in-house and need expert consultancy to train new or reallocated staff. Within the latter market, there are probably a number of niches in terms of the size of clients and the nature of their products or services. You will have to check out both markets by direct contact with each one in your field research.

The sources for desk research are widespread. They include

statistical reports, trade and specialist consumer journals, competitors' catalogues and, increasingly, competitors' and target customers'/clients' Web sites.

ENGAGING IN FIELD RESEARCH

The most important feature of useful field research is that it should be completely objective. There is a great temptation, particularly if you are enthusiastic about your business concept, to wander round putting a few questions to possible customers and suppliers, perhaps people who know you quite well, and to fool yourself that you have conducted a useful research exercise. Worse still, you may phrase your questions so that the response you are hoping for is clearly evident, and people who know you and want to encourage you are likely to give you the answers you are looking for.

The best way to avoid these traps is to discipline yourself to draw up a representative sample of the market you are researching and to prepare formal questionnaires, whether you will be interviewing face-to-face or by telephone. It also helps to condition yourself to conduct interviews as if you were a professional researcher carrying out the assignment for clients rather than on your own behalf.

Sampling

A truly representative sample that accurately reflects the total market in terms of income and social groups, age groups, occupations and purchasing profiles is the ideal that researchers strive for when surveying consumer markets. But this is probably impossible to achieve. Instead, professional market research agencies often design 'quota' samples and instruct their researchers to interview fixed numbers of respondents, whose circumstances and buying habits conform to various templates. (The preliminary questions of each interview are used to establish into which quota definition the respondent falls.)

Alternatively, the research agency may decide to adopt 'random' sampling. For example, if a survey of 100 households was commissioned in a neighbourhood of 1,000 houses, interviewers would be instructed to call on every tenth house. A random sampling approach might be more appropriate in our Business B example, where you decide to interview potential clients for call centre training among a range of selected industries located within your local region. A simple way to pick your sample would be to refer to the telephone book _Yellow Pages_ or local _Thomson's_ directory and pick your interview targets according to the number of companies listed in each business category.

What size of sample should you pick? Statistically, you might think the bigger the sample the better. In practice, a sample of 100 is normally sufficient for consumer products or services if the sample is chosen carefully. For industrial products, as few as 30 interviews may suffice.

In the case of Business A, it should be possible to survey your local garden centre market and produce unambiguous findings from 100 interviews of customers leaving local garden centres, selected on a random basis. If there are two or three centres in serious competition, you should split interviewing between them.

For Business B, a quota of five or six extended telephone interviews in each of, say, six targeted industry sectors should give a clear picture of the market for your training services. If the findings are ambiguous, you may need to extend interviewing selectively.

Questionnaire design

Most of us have been interviewed from time to time in the street, in shopping centres, or at railway or bus stations – often when we are short of time and do not want to be stopped; so we know what to expect when the lady with the clipboard approaches!

Try to organise your questionnaire in a similar way to conventional interviewing techniques. Here are a few tips that may help you:

1. Use short introductory phrases for each question to 'lead in' your respondents, for example: 'I can see that you're a keen gardener; how often do you visit a garden centre?'

2. Arrange the topics for your questions in a logical order: proceed from the general to the particular. In the case of research for Business A:
   - frequency of garden centre visits;
   - weekend/weekday shopping;
   - with/without family or partner;
   - range of products purchased;
   - seasonal variations in purchasing;
   - opinion of this garden centre (product quality and range, price, service);
   - other garden centres used;
   - other sources for garden products (DIY centres, department stores, mail order and so on);
   - customer spend per visit (range/average).
3. Always position questions about money towards the end of the interview (they may be 'turn-offs' and cause the respondent to terminate).
4. Try to ask questions in open-ended form first and so that they cannot be answered just 'Yes' or 'No', before offering structured alternatives, for example: 'How many other garden centres do you visit regularly?' before:

   Which of these other local outlets for garden products do you visit?

	Regularly	Sometimes	Never
a.			
b.			
c.			

5. Include a few personal questions at the end of the interview to establish the demographic identity of the respondent (eg age group, occupation, residential neighbourhood, size of garden).

Other field research

Of course, you will want to carry out other fieldwork in addition to interviewing customers or prospective clients. For Business A, you will need to visit each competitor location, examine the layout, product range, quality and pricing, display, point of sale material and promotional offers, and observe store traffic. You will also need to approach potential suppliers to check the availability, lead times, prices and delivery terms that you could negotiate and the possibilities of growing your own stock from seed.

For Business B, you may want to sample the quality of the telephone customer service that potential clients offer currently in order to assess their training needs.

USING YOUR MARKET RESEARCH FINDINGS

The market research you carry out yourself will deepen your understanding of the business opportunity and provide much of the background data needed to support your business case. It may also throw up attractive niche market opportunities that you had not identified previously, or cause you to modify or extend your product or service offering.

The Business B example differs from Business A in another important respect. Interviewing by telephone may establish your first list of actual business prospects among those who register a demand for the services that you intend to offer: in this case, call centre training. The same outcome is likely in the case of most business consultancy services that you may research. You will be able to follow up on the prospect list later when your plan is complete, funding is in place and you are ready to launch your business.

The final test of objectivity, if your market research findings are negative in any important respect, is to decide whether you should proceed with the business concept or abandon it. It is a good idea, in any case, to write up your research succinctly and to show the report to an adviser or friend who will give you an unbiased second opinion. If you are in any serious doubt, abandon the concept and go back to the drawing board. The research exercise has not been wasted. It will stand you in good stead next time.

Checklist: researching your market

1. Do not rely on your instinct or perception of an opportunity without carrying out the basic research to support the business case.
2. Define your research objectives first in terms of the key questions you need to answer.
3. Carry out desk research first from home by accessing published information and interrogating sources by telephone, fax and the Internet.
4. Do not neglect others in the same line of business but operating in a different location. Unless you are competing directly, they will probably be informative.
5. Visit your competitors' locations and investigate product range, quality, pricing and activity levels. Approach potential suppliers.
6. Field research should be completely objective. Discipline yourself to draw up a representative sample of the market and to prepare formal questionnaires.
7. Arrange the topics for your questions in a logical order. Always ask questions about money at the end of the interview.
8. Ask questions in open-ended form first so that they cannot be answered just by 'Yes' or 'No'. Then ask them in structured form.
9. Include a few personal questions at the end to establish demographic identity.
10. If your research findings are negative, restructure the business concept and research again – or abandon it.

5.2 Costing, Pricing and Estimating

How much should you charge your customers? Or, to put it more searchingly, on what factors should your charges be based? It is surprising that many self-employed people would be hard put to it to give a clear answer to that question. There are such things as 'going rates' and 'recommended' (or generally accepted) prices, but often these are in the nature of broad guidelines and unless you know what all your costs are, not just the cost of materials, or how long the job took you, you are sooner or later going to be in the position of either under charging or making an actual loss.

There are some self-employed occupations where the scope for how much you can charge is either narrow or non-existent. This applies particularly to many areas of the retail trade, where goods tend to have recommended prices printed on them by the suppliers; but even there you may want to consider *reducing* some prices in order to undercut a competitor and the question arises whether you can afford to do so. This depends on your overall costs – rent, rates, power supplies and many other factors. Equally, some freelance jobs are subject to generally accepted 'going rates' and the more commonplace such jobs are (ie the smaller the degree of service or expertise that is involved) the more strictly you have to keep within that rate. But the corollary of this statement is also true: the more unique your product or service, the more you can afford to charge for it.

This can apply even in the ordinary retail trade where, on the face of things, the prospect of getting away with charging more than the competition is not promising. Recently a small supermarket opened near my house. It is open late at night, on Sundays and on public holidays and, quite rightly, it charges for that extra time. Most things cost a penny or two above what they do in the larger shops down the High Street, but it is offering something more than they are, and meets competition not by charging less, but by providing more – a much-needed neighbourhood service for out-of-hours shopping.

The same principle can be applied to even rather routine freelance jobs. Provide a straightforward typing service and you will have to stick pretty much to the going rate; but offer something special, like accurately typing mathematical material or unusually high turn-round speeds, and you can move into a different price bracket.

DETERMINING YOUR COSTS

You could say to yourself: 'I'm going to charge as much as I can get away with' or, 'I'm going to charge the standard rate for the job.' These are quite sensible guidelines to be going on with, but at some point you are probably going to be in the situation of wondering whether you should be charging a little more, or perhaps whether you can afford to reduce your price in order to land some work that you badly want. It is then that you have to get to grips with what your costs really are.

The most obvious one is your own time, and curiously enough it is an element that self-employed people are often confused about, because they tend to regard it as being somehow different from the time taken by employees. If a job involves your working flat out for a 100-hour week, you are underpricing the product of that work if your remuneration is less than that of an employed person doing the same kind of work at full overtime rates. There may be a reason why you *should* be undercharging: you may want a 'loss-leader' introduction to a particular customer, or to undercut a competitor, or you may simply need the money that week. But if you undercharge, you should be clear in your mind why you are doing so.

Another factor that is sometimes overlooked is that in most cases there are overhead costs incurred in running your business, irrespective of whether you have work coming in or not. We will deal with these overheads in more detail in a moment, but the point to be made here is to correct any misconception that the margin between what you charge and your basic costs in time and/or materials represents your profit. True, it is a profit of a kind – gross profit. But the real profit element in a job, the net profit, only emerges when the overhead costs have been met. So the right way to work out your price to the customer, or to determine whether a job is worth taking on, is to establish whether it will pay for materials, overheads, wages (if you employ others) and still leave you with a margin of net profit that adequately reflects the time and skill you are putting into it.

Once you have been in business for a few months you should have accumulated enough facts and figures to establish what your overhead costs are. To what extent you can control the situation beyond that depends, again, on what sort of business you are in. If you are running an ordinary retail shop, operating on margins that are more or less fixed by the supplier, there is not much you can do about pricing your goods, but at least you will know whether you can afford to spend more on extra fittings or take on more staff, or whether you should be staying open longer to attract extra trade. But if you are manufacturing something, you can work out a rule-of-thumb method in the form of a percentage to add on to your materials costs in quoting prices or, in the case of a service, an average hourly rate. It is important, though, to keep on monitoring these rule-of-thumb procedures against what actually happened, so you should keep a record detailing the specification of each job, in which actual costs can be compared against your original estimate. Over a period of time, in this way you should be able to build up a reliable set of costs which can be referred to when an assignment which sounds similar comes up.

At the beginning, though, you will have very little to go on, so let us look in more detail at the factors you will have to take into account.

Costs connected with your premises

Rent, heat, light, telephone, rates, insurance, finance (if you own or have bought a lease of the premises), cleaning and maintenance contracts and the uniform business rate.

Costs of finance

Interest charged on overdrafts or loans. You should include in this calculation interest on any money you yourself have put into the business, because it should be earning a rate of return equivalent to what you could get on the open market.

Costs of equipment

If you are renting equipment or buying it on hire purchase, this item of expenditure presents no problems. The issue is more complicated if you have bought equipment outright, because you have to figure out some way of recovering the purchase price and this is done by bringing in the concept of 'depreciation'. What this means is that you gradually write off, over a period of time based on the item's useful life, most of the amount you paid initially; not all, because it will have some resale value at the end of the depreciation period.

Supposing you bought a second-hand van for £6,000 and you think it will last you for four years, at the end of which time you could expect to get £1,000 for it. This leaves you with £5,000 to depreciate over four years – £1,250 per annum. There are also a number of other ways to calculate depreciation and your accountant will advise you on the method most advantageous to your kind of business. The important point to bear in mind, though, is that depreciation is a real factor, not just an accountancy device. Assets like motor cars and equipment do wear out and have to be replaced. Financial reserves should be built up to enable you to do this.

Administrative costs

Running your business will involve general expenditure which cannot be directly related to particular assignments: stationery, publicity, travel, postage, entertainment of clients, fees to professional advisers, and so forth.

Salaries and welfare

Salaries are best calculated at an hourly rate, based on an average working week. In the case of employees, these rates are usually determined by the market for that particular kind of employment. The problem is deciding how much you should pay to yourself. Again, this obviously varies with the kind of business you are in, but as a rough guideline you should, after meeting all your expenses, be earning at least as much as an employed person with the same degree of skill and responsibility. It is most important to cost your time properly; let us, therefore, look at a worked example of what might be involved in the case of a person in full-time self-employment.

Supposing you were aiming to earn £20,000 a year. To start with you would want to take into account four weeks' annual paid holiday (three weeks, plus statutory holidays) and you would assume an eight-hour day and a five-day working week. However, not all your time would be directly productive: some of it would be spent travelling, on administration and on getting work. So let us say your productive time is 32 hours a week. That would give you an hourly rate based on 32 × 48 hours a year: 1,536 hours. Divided into £20,000, that means a rate of about £13.02 per hour. On top of that you have to allow for welfare items: your National Insurance stamp, possibly contributions to a retirement pension scheme and certainly insurance against sickness or death. Let us assume this comes to another £1,000 a year. Divided by 1,536 working hours, this adds another 98 pence to your hourly rate.

Similarly, when costing the time of any full-time staff working for you, it is not just a question of calculating basic rates of pay. You have to allow for holidays, the employer's contribution to National Insurance stamps and to the graduated pension scheme. These items can add up to 20 per cent to the cost of wages.

Variable costs

All the costs we have just described are fixed costs. You incur them whether you have work coming in or not. Variable costs are items like materials which can be attributed to specific jobs. There are circumstances in which what we have described as fixed costs can vary slightly. If you are running a lot of overtime, this will mean an increase in your fuel bills and extra payments to your staff or to yourself. But the benefit of achieving properly costed increases in productivity, for example in the case of a shop staying open late to attract more trade, is that, provided you are able to keep fixed overheads stable, this element will form a smaller proportion relative to your turnover, and that means a more profitable business.

ESTABLISHING YOUR PRICES

You now have a set of basic data on costs which can be applied to your prices when you are asked to quote for a job or in making up your invoice. If you are supplying a service, the best way to do this is to take all your fixed costs, establish an hourly rate based on your usual working week and then estimate how long the job will take you. The effect of this is that if jobs do not materialise in the way the 'usual working week' concept implies, you yourself are going to be carrying the can for the fixed overheads which are being incurred during all the hours in that week when you are not working. And if you only get 20 hours' work during a week in which you had budgeted for 40, loading your charges to the customer to make up for the shortfall could mean that you will come up with an unacceptable quotation or a price that will discourage your customer in the future.

The other lesson to be learnt is that fixed overheads should be kept as low as possible. For instance, if you are planning a freelance design service to earn extra money in the evenings, you should be chary of acquiring expensive equipment. In the limited hours of work which a part-time freelance operation implies, you may never be able to charge enough money to do more than pay the overheads. As far as possible, keep your costs in the variable category by hiring or renting equipment only when and for as long as you need it.

This is also true of businesses that produce manufactured articles (and activities which operate on lines similar to manufacturing such as a restaurant, where the product is created in the form of a meal), though in these cases some machinery and equipment are usually essential. The price here will be based on a unit per item rather than on an hourly rate, but the principle is the same. Instead of fixing an hourly rate based on an expected working week, calculations should be made on a projected volume of costs spread over the number of units sold. Thus, if you aimed to sell in a week 20 chairs which cost you £5 each in materials your variable costs would be £100. If your fixed over-heads, including your own remuneration, came to £300 a week, you would have to charge £20 per chair. And do not forget that even if your object is only to make a living wage out of your business, you should still be putting aside reserves to replace equipment as it wears out, and that the cost of doing so will, in periods of inflation, be a great deal higher than its original cost.

PREPARING QUOTATIONS

With many jobs, whether they are a service or a commission to manufacture something, you will be asked to supply a quotation before a firm order is placed. Once that quotation has been accepted it is legally binding on both parties, so it is important not only to get your sums right but to make it clear in the wording attached to them what exactly you are providing for the money. In the case of a decorating job, for example, you should specify who is providing the materials and, if you are, to what standards they are going to be. Consider also whether any out-of-pocket expenses will be involved (travel, subsistence) and whether these are to be met by your customer or whether they have been allowed for in your quotation.

Apart from variable factors such as these, every quotation should set out the conditions of sale under which it is being offered. Different businesses will involve different kinds of conditions, but here are some basic points to bear in mind:

1. In particular, you should make it clear that the prices quoted are current ones and may have to go up if costs rise during the course of the job.
2. Terms of payment should be set out, for example 30 days net.
3. You will have to cover the not uncommon situation of the customer changing her mind about the way she wants the

job done subsequent to her accepting your quotation. You should leave yourself free to charge extra in such circumstances.

4. If you have agreed to complete a job within a certain length of time, set out the factors beyond your control which would prevent you from meeting the agreed date.

5. You should make it clear what circumstances of error, loss or damage will be your responsibility and what would fall outside it.

6. You should stipulate that once the quotation is accepted, the order cannot be cancelled except by mutual consent and that the customer will be liable for all charges up to that point.

7. You should mention that the total is subject to VAT at the rate ruling at the date of invoice. This is particularly important when the customer is a private person who is unable to claim back VAT inputs. (See Chapter 3.3 for details of VAT.)

Having gone to all the trouble to set out the quotation and conditions of sale, you should not neglect to check, before you start work, that the customer has actually accepted it in writing! It is all too easy to forget this or to imagine that an amicable verbal OK is sufficient. If a dispute arises, however, you will be very thankful to have carried out all the formal steps of documentation.

Every few months sit back for half an hour and consider your pricing policy. If you have set up as a consulting engineer and have no wish to get involved with renting offices and employing others, your workload capacity is limited to the number of hours you put in. To start with, you will probably be glad of work at any price, but as your business builds up to the point where you are working all hours, the only way you will be able to increase your real income is to increase your prices. So if you have a reliable supply of work coming in which is giving you a reasonable income, do not be afraid to put in some highish quotes for new work. It is not always the case that the lowest tender wins the job, particularly in the field of consultancy.

Checklist: costing, pricing and estimating

1. How unique is your product or service? If it is not particularly uncommon, how can you make it more so?
2. How essential is it to the customer?
3. What is the competition charging for the same or similar product or service?
4. How badly do you need the job or order?
5. Is your customer likely to come back for more if the price is right, or is it a one-off?
6. Will doing business with this customer enable you to break into a wider market, and thus enable you to reduce your unit costs?
7. What is the element of risk involved (ie is the customer, to your knowledge, a quick and certain payer)?
8. Do you have any idea how long the job will take you?
9. Can you relate the time element to your fixed costs?
10. Have you made a full assessment of all your fixed costs?
11. Do you have any idea what your materials are going to cost you?
12. Have you costed your own time properly?
13. Will the job leave you a margin of net profit? Or should you forgo this in the interest of meeting fixed costs?
14. Have you prepared a quote, specifying exactly what you are going to provide or do, including terms of payment?
15. Has the customer accepted your quotation?
16. Are you keeping records of what the job cost you so that you can adjust your prices or quote more accurately next time?

5.3 Marketing Your Work

Good ideas, it is sometimes dismissively said, are ten a penny, the implication being that the really difficult part is putting them into effect. Apart from the obvious virtues of persistence, hard work and technical know-how, this also requires a modicum of marketing skill. In other words, you will have to know whether there is a big enough demand for your product or service at the price you need to charge to make a living and how to identify and reach your potential customers.

MANUFACTURERS

You may be the world's most skilful maker of hand-carved model sailing ships, but unless enough people want them you are going to have a hard time trying to make a living out of producing them commercially. It is worth doing some research before you start in business and the following methods should help you direct your products more effectively:

☐ Look around. Go to gift shops, luxury stores or wherever it is that the kind of item you are aiming to produce is being sold and find out about prices, quality standards and the extent of the demand. Shop managers might help advise you on any modifications required to your idea.

☐ Consider whether there is a long-term future for your product. Are you able to keep ahead by being in a position to meet the next craze before the big manufacturers become aware of it?

☐ Keep an eye on competitors of your own size to ensure your own commercial viability and to see if there is a gap in the market for your product.

But no matter how good or unique your product may be, the ultimate key to success lies in effective sales and distribution. At the smallest level you might be selling direct to the public through your own shop, as is the case with many craft goods, but you have to bear in mind that you need to achieve a considerable turnover for a shop in a good location to be viable. This is difficult if the range of specialisation is very narrow, and many small-scale manufacturers, therefore, combine having their own shop with direct mail and mail order (which we shall come to in a moment) and with marketing to other retail outlets. Shop and workshop premises can be combined in the same floor area, so that you can switch readily from the sales counter to the workbench when the shop is empty. This requires permission from the local planning authority if a 'change of use' of what were originally shop premises is involved.

Starting-up costs will eat deeply into your capital, so unless you have enough experience of the marketing (as opposed to the manufacturing) end of your speciality to be absolutely convinced that you can sell it, it is a good idea to begin by making a few prototypes of the product and its packaging and by trying to get orders from retailers. Though your friends and family may think your idea is wonderful, the acid test is whether it will survive in the marketplace. In the course of investigating this, the natural conservatism of most branches of the retail trade may at times depress or irritate you, but it is worth listening to what people who are involved in it have to say. If the same criticisms keep on cropping up, you should think seriously of modifying your prototype to take them into account.

Distribution can be another big headache and your premises should be big enough to enable you to hold roughly as many days' or weeks' supply of stocks as it takes to replace it at its rate of demand. If a business is selling ten chairs a week and it takes two weeks to get that number of replacements, there should, ideally, be space for something like 20 chairs. A customer might be prepared to wait a week before delivery, but she is unlikely to wait a month.

Accessibility of non-selling areas is important too. Adequate entry for goods and materials at the rear or side of the premises is often essential and will always save time and energy.

DEALING WITH LARGE COMPANIES

Winning an order from a large company can put a small business on its feet at a stroke, not only directly but in terms of gaining credibility with other customers. But pursuing orders of that kind is not without its perils. For one thing, large firms are not necessarily rapid payers; nor, as some bankruptcies have shown, is a household name inevitably a sign of financial soundness. Careful checks with your bank are essential.

The implications of a big order also need to be thought out very fully in cash-flow terms, and if progress payments are not offered other forms of finance will have to be found. A further point to consider is that it is highly likely that a major customer will seek to impose conditions not only of price, but of quality and delivery. Fair enough; but in combination these three can make what seems like a high-value order look much less tempting on the bottom line of profitability.

The whole thing becomes even more complicated if you find you have to subcontract part of the job, as is often the case when a small business lands in the big time. Unless you can control the subcontractor's work very tightly by writing and being in a position to enforce a very clear set of specifications, you can land yourself in the position one small book publisher got into once. It won an order from a major chain of multiples for many tens of thousands of copies of a number of titles. For cost reasons these had to be manufactured in the Far East and when they were delivered they did not match up to the very strict merchandising standards that had been stipulated. What had looked like a wonderful stroke of good fortune turned into a horrifying, litigation-laden loss.

Of course, large companies are anxious to avoid this sort of thing, so they seldom deal with small companies whose approach is less than 100 per cent professional. A lot of them, by all accounts, fall down at this first hurdle. However good your idea or product, it will never even come up for discussion unless your letter is clearly and neatly presented, reasonably well written and, above all, sent to the right person. Firms are full of stories of letters being sent to executives who had long left the company and whose names had been gleaned from some out-of-date directory. One phone call would have done the trick.

The lesson that small things make big impressions is also worth remembering when the big customer you have been courting finally sends his inspection team or his purchasing officer round. Nothing looks worse than a scruffy reception area or sounds worse than badly briefed staff. Indeed, you yourself should make sure that you can answer convincingly all the questions you are likely to be asked on such things as capacity, delivery, the quality of your workforce and whatever is connected with the business you are trying to win.

SHOPS AND SERVICE INDUSTRIES

The first large shopping centre built in Britain was a flop because, among other disadvantages, it had no parking facilities and was situated in a working-class area a few minutes' walk away from a large, long-established and very popular street market. The developers, for all their vast financial resources, had ignored hotel magnate Conrad Hilton's three factors in siting a business serving the public: location, location and location. If you are thinking of setting up a shop, restaurant or some other service outlet, find out as much as possible about the area and ask:

☐ Who lives there?
☐ Is the area declining economically or is it on the up and up?
☐ What is the range of competitors and how well are they doing?
☐ If you are thinking of opening a high-class restaurant and there are nothing but fish and chip establishments in the neighbourhood, does this mean that there is no demand for a good restaurant or a crying need for one?

Take the case of a bookshop. You would want to conduct some rule-of-thumb market research about the area before going any further. For example, you would want to know whether there were enough people in the area to support such a venture, whether they were the sort of people who regularly bought books, and how good the local library was. You would also want to know what impact the result of your market investigations might have on your trading policies. Thus, if there were a lot of families with young children around, you should be considering getting to know, and stocking, children's books; or, if there were a lot of students in the neighbourhood, it would be worth your while finding out what textbooks were being used in local educational institutions. Alternatively, if your bookshop is highly specialised – medicine, academic history, chess, or some other specific activity – an expensive High Street location is likely to be wholly inappropriate. You will want to be near the centre of that activity, or, more likely, will want to sell to your well-defined audience through direct mail.

The same broad principles apply to almost every kind of retail or service outlet and you will have to conduct this kind of research, which is really just plain common sense, whatever your venture. Do not be tempted to overlook it just because you are buying what is supposed to be a 'going concern'. One reason why it is up for sale may be that, despite the owner's or agent's protestations to the contrary, it was doing badly. If that was because the previous owner was a poor manager or stocked the wrong kind of goods for the neighbourhood you might be able to turn the business around, but if there was simply too much competition in the area from similar shops and there is no chance of trading viably in something else from the same address, you would be well advised to forget about those premises, however good a buy they may seem from a purely cost point of view. You will also be able to check on the vendor's assertions by looking, preferably with your accountant, at his profit and loss accounts, not just for the past year but the previous three to five years, to get a picture of the general trend of things. On the whole, buying a going concern has to be approached with great caution, particularly by the inexperienced, because of the difficulties of valuing stock and goodwill with any accuracy. See Chapters 1.3 and 6 for more detailed treatment of these points.

FREELANCE SERVICES

Most freelancers agree that the way you get work is by knowing people who are in a position to give it to you. That sounds rather like a chicken-and-egg situation and, to begin with, so it is. You would be ill-advised to launch into freelance work, certainly on a full-time basis, until you have built up a range of contacts who can provide you with enough work to produce some sort of living for at least the first few months. Often these are people whom you have got to know in the course of a full-time job, or while doing temporary work. Many advertising agencies, for instance, have been started by a breakaway group taking a batch of clients with them when they start up.* And it may even be that your employer, having been compelled to make you redundant, will still be willing to put work out to you on a freelance basis.

Once you have got going and established a reputation for doing good, reliable work, things get much easier. For one thing, word-of-mouth recommendations have a strong effect in the freelance world. Moreover, you will be able to produce examples of work sold, or be able to refer prospects to other clients who have engaged you successfully. Evidence, for instance, that your fashion photographs have actually been used by national magazines is generally more impressive than a folder of prints, no matter how good they are. In freelance work, as in other spheres, nothing succeeds like success.

One problem with freelance work, though, is that clients often want something done in a hurry – over a weekend or even overnight. This can be highly inconvenient at times, but it is generally a bad idea to turn work down simply for this reason. If you have to be selective, turn away the smaller, less remunerative jobs or commissions from people who are slow to pay their bills. One thing you should never do is to let a client down. If you cannot, or do not want to, take on an assignment, say so immediately.

---

*To combat this trend many firms now include clauses in their employment contract expressly stating that it is not permissible to work for a client of the employer for two years after leaving that employer.

PRESS ADVERTISING

Advertising is a marketing tool and like any other tool you have to use it in the right place, at the right time and for the right job if it is going to be of any use to you. If you are a local building contractor, there is no point in advertising in national newspapers, because most of the circulation, which is what you are paying for in the rates charged, will be outside the geographical area you are working in. On the other hand, if you are making a product to sell by mail order, the bigger the circulation the better. There are, however, still provisos; there is, for example, no point in advertising a product aimed at 'top people' in a mass-circulation tabloid.

When considering advertising think about:

☐ The right medium for the product or service you have to sell.

☐ The quality of the circulation rather than the figures. A small specialist or local paper might provide as good a return as a mass circulation publication.

☐ A regular 'classified' insertion will remind readers of your services and will be relatively inexpensive.

☐ Display advertising can be placed in eye-catching positions. These are more expensive than classified adverts and will need to be designed by a graphic designer (look in *Yellow Pages* or *Thomson* local directory) but you can control where they are placed.

☐ Experiment with different days for your advert to appear as some days can produce a better response than others.

☐ Experiment with wording, but do not use too many words. Be specific about how goods and services can be obtained. Your address and availability times should be prominent.

☐ Include an order coupon stating price *and* postage. This will also provide information on where your sales come from and will help future marketing efforts.

PUBLIC RELATIONS

It may be possible, particularly if you have a specialist line of business, to obtain free coverage in trade journals and local newspapers by sending them press releases to mark events such as the opening of an extension or the provision of some unique service. You simply type the information on a slip marked PRESS RELEASE; 'embargo' it – ie prohibit its use – until a date that suits you, and send it to newspapers and magazines you choose as the likeliest to use it. Newspapers and other news media – don't forget about local radio and even local TV – are, however, only interested in *news* and the mere fact that you have opened a business may not interest them much. Try to find a news angle; for instance, that you have obtained a large export order, or are reviving a local craft or are giving employment to school-leavers. If you have any friends who are journalists, ask their advice on the sort of information that is likely to get the attention of editors. Better still, ask them if they will draft your press release for you.

There are many other PR activities – sponsorship, stunts, celebrity appearances at your premises, public speaking, and so on. All are designed to publicise who you are and what you do, and suggest to the public that you provide a worthwhile and reliable service. PR for the small business is covered thoroughly in Michael Bland's *Be Your Own PR Man* (published by Kogan Page).

DIRECT MAIL AND DIRECT RESPONSE PROMOTION

Direct mail selling is a considerable subject in its own right. It differs from mail order in that the latter consists of mailing goods direct to the customer from orders engendered by general press advertising, whereas in the case of direct mail selling the advertising is a brochure or sales letter specifically directed at the customer. Direct response promotion consists of an ad plus coupon placed in a newspaper or journal, to be posted to the manufacturer as an order. If you use these methods, remember to allow for postage in your pricing, and since the response to direct mail averages around 2 per cent, the postage cost per sale is quite a considerable factor. It can, however, be a very effective way of selling specialised, high-priced items (£15 is around the viable minimum these days) or of identifying people who are likely to buy from you regularly if you are selling variations on the same product. Unless you are very skilful at writing brochures or sales letters you should get this done for you by an expert. Such people are employed by mailing list brokers (you will find those in the *Yellow Pages*), who will often provide a complete package: they will sell to you, or compile for you, specialised lists, address and stuff envelopes and produce sales literature.

Their services are not cheap and before you plunge into a direct mail campaign there are relatively inexpensive ways of testing the market for yourself. Pick 100 specialist addresses of the type you want to reach on a bigger scale – again, you may find them in the *Yellow Pages*. A small want ad in one of the advertising industry's trade papers will soon raise the services of freelance copywriters and designers if you need such help. From the percentage reply to the sample mailing, you will be able to gauge whether a bigger campaign is worth mounting and you will also get some idea of how to price the product to take into account the likely mailing costs per sale. It is generally essential, by the way, with direct mail advertising, to include a reply paid card or envelope with your sales literature. Details of how to apply for reply paid and Freepost facilities are available from the Post Office.

Mail Order Protection Schemes

Before you can start selling by direct response advertising in a newspaper or periodical, you will have to get permission to do so from its mail order protection scheme (MOPS). These schemes have been set up under the auspices of the Office of Fair Trading to protect consumers from fraudulent advertisers. Essentially, the various media act as insurers and undertake to refund readers' money if the advertiser absconds or fails to deliver for some reason or other. Before accepting the insurance risk, papers and periodicals will therefore try to satisfy themselves that the advertiser is above board. In the case of national media their requirements will be quite searching; they may want to see accounts, take up credit and other references and even look over your premises. Applications for MOPS clearing at this end of the advertising market have to be accompanied by a fee which can go well into four figures and which has to be renewed every year. Requirements in local and trade media are less exacting, but you still need clearance before they will take your advertisement.

MARKETING ON THE INTERNET

The number of people on the Internet is exploding. If you have a product or a service which is of more than local interest, then getting on the Internet is becoming an essential part of your marketing strategy. You do this by having your own Web site which describes your product or activity, how much it costs and how to get it. You can also take orders over the Internet and even get customers to pay by credit card. The mechanics of this are complicated by issues of security – customers are naturally anxious about disclosing credit card details on a system which gives open access to millions of people – but they are not insurmountable. Other business uses offered by the Internet include:

☐ carrying out research before you launch a new marketing campaign;
☐ checking patents, demographics or statistics on a new sales area;
☐ researching new manufacturers and distributors;
☐ creating a new way of marketing your products to a niche group of users;
☐ publicising your company and its products;
☐ keeping in touch with your customers and employees;
☐ cutting long-distance phone bills.

Research can be carried out on the Internet before you market your product. You can visit government Web sites for statistics, look for information on search engines and carry out research through news services, newspapers, magazines and user groups.

User groups are a particularly useful source of information on the Internet and there are over 250,000 of them. They cover a wide range of subject areas and you can access them through a Web Browser and post messages to them. Mailing lists can also be bought and you can send information by e-mail on your new product through this method.

Creating a Web site

If you want to sell over the Internet, your best plan would be to hire a consultant to help you design a Web site and register it with various search engines so that your name comes up when customers are looking for information on products in your field. Ask the consultant to show you how to update it, how to record users, how to follow-up enquiries and which item is attracting the most interest from visitors to your site.

You should also have a look at other Web sites to see what works and what doesn't before discussing your own needs with your consultant. Your own visits to other people's Web sites should also warn you about trying to use graphics that take too long to download, as Internet users have a notoriously short attention span and are unlikely to wait for your three-dimensional revolving logo to appear on their screens. The following points should also be considered when discussing the design with your consultant:

☐ content should be of good quality and be up-to-date;
☐ try to encourage feedback by making the Web site interactive;
☐ remember that your audience is international and make sure that you include relevant information such as the contact details of your worldwide distributors;
☐ register your Web site with search engines;
☐ create links with other Web sites; two-way traffic is mutually beneficial;
☐ swap banner advertising.

You can also stimulate interest in your product or service on the Internet in other ways. The design of your site can build in a link to other sites so that if, for instance, you are selling antique tools, there is a link to sites about books on antique tools. A customer for the one may well also be interested in the other. User groups are not only useful as sources of information about topics in the interest field in which your business is located (for example, antiques) but can be used for discrete marketing. For example, it is considered bad form to advertise directly in a user group, but you could drop in some comment about antique repairs and refer interested parties to a Web site, which might just happen to be yours.

Online for Business is a public–private partnership run by the Department of Trade and Industry and provides hands-on information and communications technology experience for businesses. For more information and advice, telephone 08457 152000 or visit its Web site www.ukonlineforbusiness.gov.uk. For a full account of Internet marketing, see *Doing Business on the Internet*, by Simon Collin (Kogan Page).

Checklist: marketing your work

Manufacturers
1. Have you tested your idea by discussing your proposed product with potential customers? Or, better still, by showing it to them?
2. Is the market for it big enough? How accessible is it?
3. Can the customers you have in mind afford a price that will produce a profit for you?
4. Have you studied the competition from the point of view of price, design quality, reliability, delivery dates, etc?
5. Should you modify your product so as to get the edge on the competition? What will this do to your costs?
6. Is there a long-term future for your product? If not, do you have any ideas for a follow-up?
7. Can you handle distribution? Do you have access to a van if the market is local? Do you have adequate parking facilities if it requires dispatching?

8. Have you taken dispatching costs into account in working out how much the product will cost the customer?
9. Do you have adequate space to hold stock, taking into account production time?
10. Do you have someone who can deal with customer queries and complaints? Or have you allowed for the fact that you will have to take time out yourself to deal with them?

Shops and service industries
1. How much do you know about the area?
2. Is the location good from the point of view of attracting the kind of trade you are looking for?
3. What competitors do you have?
4. How are they doing?
5. Based on your study of the area, and the people who live in it, how does this affect the type of goods or the nature of the service you are going to offer?
6. If you are buying a going concern, have you checked it out thoroughly with your professional advisers?

Freelance services
1. Do you have any contacts who can give you work?
2. Have you made a realistic appraisal of how much you can expect to earn over the first six months?
3. Have you allowed for the fact that you will need spare time to go around looking for more business?
4. What evidence can you produce of your competence to do freelance work in your proposed field?
5. Have you shown that evidence to the sort of person who might be a customer to get her reaction on whether it is likely to impress?
6. Who are your competitors, what do they charge and what can you offer that is superior to their services?

Advertising and promotion
1. Have you chosen the right medium to promote your product or service?

2. Do you have any idea of the circulation and how this is broken down, geographically or by type of reader?
3. Have you worked out any way of monitoring results, for instance by including a coupon?
4. Have you included the cost of advertising and promotion in your cash-flow budget and in costing your product?
5. How many orders do you need to get from your advertising/promotion campaign to show a profit?
6. In the case of a display advertisement, have you specified a position in which it is to appear?
7. Again, in the case of a display ad or a brochure, have you had it properly designed?
8. Does your advertising/promotion material state where your product or service can be obtained and the price?
9. Is the wording compelling? Does it clearly describe the product or service and does it motivate the customer? Would you buy it, if you were a customer?
10. In the case of a classified advertisement, have you specified under which classification it is to appear?
11. Are all the statements and claims you are making about your product or service true to the best of your knowledge and belief, bearing in mind that untruths can leave you open to prosecution under the Trade Descriptions Acts?
12. Have you looked at other companies' Web sites to see what works for users?
13. Is your Web site attractive to customers and easy to use? Do you update it regularly?
14. Have you registered with search engines?

5.4 The Fun of Exporting

'Exporting is fun,' said Harold Macmillan when he was Prime Minister, though it may perhaps be doubted whether he knew much about filling in bills of lading in sextuplicate or waiting for an onward flight in a corrugated iron shed in Burkina Faso. At any rate, it has taken a long time for the export message to sink in with British firms and even now many small companies put export fairly low on their list of priorities. But while it is true that it is usually essential to get one's place established in the domestic market, there are many attractions about exporting.

- [ ] It increases sales and therefore lowers unit costs.
- [ ] It decreases dependence on the UK market.
- [ ] It can produce increased profits in countries where you can charge higher prices or where sterling has a poor exchange rate.
- [ ] It broadens one's awareness of other markets and sometimes gives warning of competing products being developed or on sale elsewhere.
- [ ] It gives you a chance to see the world 'on the company'.

Even if you find none of these reasons compelling enough to make you want to leave your home patch, there are circumstances under which you can become an exporter without really wishing to. If you have a good product, it is very possible that someone abroad will get to hear of it and want to buy it. Indeed, that is how many small companies first become involved, having made the wise decision that business should never be turned away.

If, however, you decide to play a more active role as an exporter than just meeting the demand as it occurs, what special factors should a small business look at? Actually, in many respects they are not very different from those that apply domestically: that the product has to be competitive in price and quality or that it has a unique feature which places it in a class of its own, but for which there is also a viable demand at a price you are reasonably sure the market will pay. Where export does raise special problems is that you also have to make sure that the product meets local specification in terms of technical requirements and consumer laws; that it can thrive under what may be quite different environmental and climatic conditions; that manuals and user instructions are intelligible, either in English or in translations; and that it does not breach any cultural taboos. The last named is often more important and wide ranging than people realise. One Australian meat company nearly lost a huge Middle East order because their house symbol was stamped on their cheques. It was a pig, an unclean animal in Moslem countries.

Indeed, all markets have their peculiarities and the advice generally given to exporters is first to visit one country or region and get to know it rather than trying to sell to the world. Even Sir Terence Conran, one of Britain's outstanding marketing men, lost heavily at first with his New York venture because he had not appreciated the Americans' appetite for continuing 'sales', however bogus. Apart from that, exporters to the US market often fail to realise that the United States is such a huge country that the characteristics of the Midwest are different from those of California and that both are different from the South or New York City. Freight is a factor there too – freight costs can eat deeply into margins and you have to consider that the price of your goods to the customer has to include the cost of physically getting them to her.

Similar lessons can be drawn from Africa with its widely different climatic conditions and its heavy ingredient of political risk, from Asia and Australia where sheer distance from the UK means that it can take months to get the goods there and further months to get payment, and even from the EU.

WHERE TO GET HELP

Fortunately, there are quite a few sources of help and advice for those who want to become exporters. Addresses and Web sites can be found at the back of this book.

☐ Local Chambers of Commerce are often well informed about major markets.

☐ Many of Britain's major trading partners maintain trade associations in London (eg the German-British Chamber of Industry and Commerce, the Arab-British Chamber of Commerce) and though some of them are more concerned with exporting to this country than importing into their own, they do also know what the requirements are in the latter case.

☐ The customer service division of the overseas departments of the big four banks.

☐ The Department of Trade and Industry (DTI). They produce inexpensive booklets of basic information on all the major countries which do business with British firms and you can also get special reports on particular countries, which cost somewhat more. They can also tell you about buying missions from overseas buying organisations established in this country by major foreign department stores, for instance.

Equally usefully, they organise trade missions through local Chambers of Commerce or trade associations. These enable you to visit major markets as part of a group with a substantial government subsidy. Since contacts can be arranged in advance, this is a considerable saving in time as well as money. Usually, if you go on your own to another country, it takes days simply to find your bearings and set up meetings.

☐ The Overseas Trade Services Department of the DTI produces a *Guide to Export Services* which is well spoken of. Through its Trade Partners UK trade division, the DTI also organises local seminars for small exporters – call 020 7215 5444 for details. When contacting Trade Partners UK, ask to be put through to the country desk dealing with the country you are planning to export to. The information Web site address is www.tradepartners.gov.uk.

SETTING UP SALES ARRANGEMENTS

Few firms will want to move so far, so fast, though. Usually it is a question of setting up some kind of sales operation by appointing a local agent; you may already have been approached by one keen to handle your business. Flattering though such interest is, and though it certainly helps to start out with someone who feels optimistic about your prospects, agents do have to be checked out. Bad ones may not only hinder your progress, but may cost you a lot of money by alienating dealers or by taking commission on business which you would have got anyway and which they have made little effort to expand.

For a small fee the DTI provides status reports on agents, but the best plan is undoubtedly to go out to the territory and meet the prospective agent personally. Apart from any impressions you form of him and his office – you should certainly see the latter – you should find out who else he is working for and preferably get a statement of that in writing. You will be known in that territory by the company you keep. Quite apart from the fact that the agent's other clients should be appropriate to your business – there is no point in having someone handling medical supplies when all their other agencies are office equipment – they should also be reputable. Preferably, the principals in some cases should be known to you so that you can make further inquiries back in the UK.

Once you have satisfied yourself of his bona fides, there should be a written agreement defining:

- [ ] The territory.
- [ ] The period of time the agreement is to run for.
- [ ] Payment terms.
- [ ] Whether the agency is exclusive or not; and, if customers are still free to buy direct from you, whether the agent gets commission on such business.
- [ ] Whether or not he is to be a stockist and, if he is, on what terms he has the right to return unsold goods.
- [ ] What you undertake to provide, free or otherwise, in the way of promotional back-up.

Once you have appointed an agent it is equally important to keep taking an interest in his activities. If he never hears from you, he will assume that you have forgotten his existence. A word of praise, or even complaint, never comes amiss. Remember the US saying, 'The wheel that squeaks loudest gets the most oil'.

DOCUMENTATION

What chiefly deters small businesses – and some larger ones – from actively pursuing export sales is the documentation it involves. This is particularly true in countries with a strong bureaucracy or where the purchasing is done by the State. Invoices have to be correct in every detail and to conform exactly to quotes or other documents to which they relate; otherwise the goods may not be collected or, worse, not paid for. There are also problems in some countries with certificates of origin of the goods, usually because of political considerations. Quite a number of countries, for instance, do not buy – or at any rate profess not to buy – goods from countries of which they disapprove politically, and demand certified invoices attested by a Chamber of Commerce in multiple copies. In some cases, it must be said, the documentation is literally not worth the trouble it costs – it has to be a matter of judgement related to the value of the goods being supplied or the importance of the customer other-wise.

As an exporter you will also have to familiarise yourself with the arcane vocabulary of export documentation – phrases like CIF, CIP, FOB, FRC and so forth. An excellent account of this and other matters is given in *Getting Started in Export* by Roger Bennett, published by Kogan Page.

Fortunately, freight forwarders – a list of them can be obtained from the British International Freight Association – will handle the documentation for you, for a fee, which is quite modest considering the hassles involved: about 5 per cent of the total freight costs. Some freight forwarders are less than competent, though. Ask your colleagues in other firms for their recom-mendations and the name of the person they deal with. Good service quite often depends on one particular individual who is well worth rewarding with some good Scotch at Christmas time.

Sales to VAT registered customers in other EU countries are zero rated. You must show their VAT number (with their country code prefix) on the invoice and the goods must be sent to a destination outside the UK. You cannot, for instance, zero rate goods which are being sent to a customer's hotel in the UK and which he intends to take with him on his journey home. The prefix GB has to be shown on your own VAT number, so if you do a lot of exporting it may be worthwhile using it for all your invoices. In that case, however, you will also have to make a further quarterly return to Customs & Excise, the so-called EU Sales List (ESL). This is a record of all the sales you have made to customers within the EU.

You can also claim refunds of VAT incurred while doing business in other EU countries, but the documentation involved is very cumbersome. The matter may not be worth pursuing unless very substantial sums are involved.

GETTING PAID

One thing freight forwarders cannot do for you is to collect payments, and the mechanics of this are a great deal more complicated than in the UK. The reason for this is largely that invoices, which trigger the payment process, also have to serve as a Customs clearance document and must therefore have all kinds of data on them which are not required in the UK: weight, value, origin of the goods and so forth. The requirements vary from country to country and are set out in a book called *Croner's Reference Book for Exporters*. Your bank should be able to help you with them. They should also be able to advise you on the best method of getting paid once the invoice has been presented. Generally, it involves some method of transferring money from the customer's bank to yours, so you need feel no hesitation in calling on your bank for assistance.

If you just receive the occasional order from abroad and don't want to get involved in extended payment procedures, the best plan is to send a *pro forma* invoice. This still has to have details which are shown on the commercial invoice, but it means the customer has to pay in advance if he wants the goods. However, you should wait to clear his cheque before despatching them unless payment is made by some form of mail transfer; again through the bank.

The devaluation of sterling on 'black Wednesday' in 1992 brought handsome profits for those who had quoted prices in one of the currencies that appreciated against the pound. However, sterling rose by a good 10 per cent against some of these currencies during 1993, so those who went on quoting in them lost some of the money they had gained earlier. Again, businesses which had quoted in local currencies lost out badly when sterling soared in 1997/8. Most exporters agree that the safest bet is to quote in your own currency. You won't make any windfall profits that way, but at least you know you will be able to pay your UK suppliers in the currency at which you have bought from them, namely pounds sterling.

THE SINGLE EUROPEAN CURRENCY

The single European currency was introduced by 11 European states on 1 January 1999. Although Britain is unlikely to adopt the single currency before 2005 at the earliest (if at all), businesses are advised to prepare for its introduction now. The 'euro' was introduced as hard currency on 1 January 2002. Many larger international firms had already switched all accounting across Europe – including the UK – to euros. Any British business trading with large European companies or exporting to Europe has come under pressure to adopt the euro for electronic payments and invoicing. The advantage of the euro – if the UK joins – will be an end to currency fluctuations. However, until we join, sterling could be in for a bumpy ride, so make sure you prepare for this when trading with the Continent. HM Treasury, the DTI, Trade Partners UK and the British Chambers of Commerce have combined to offer a new information service. The Euro – Now In Business, tel 08456 010199, and at www.euro.gov.uk. Fact sheets and short case studies of firms in a variety of industries are available on request.

Checklist: exporting

1. Have you considered local conditions and regulations to ensure your product is suitable for the market?
2. Seek out help from the DTI, your local Chamber of Commerce or your bank.
3. Have you researched the territory you are planning to export to and checked up on the local agent through the DTI status report for the area?
4. Make sure a written agreement specifies issues such as territory and the period of time the agreement will run for.
5. Contact the British International Freight Association for a list of freight forwarders and ask colleagues for recommendations.
6. Consider setting up a euro account if you are trading with EU members and ask your bank about the best way to receive foreign payments.

5.5 Planning for Growth

The final chapter in this part of the book is intended for those who have suffered the birth pangs of starting a business, are working successfully for themselves and have achieved the objectives of their original business plans. Where do you stand and where do you go from here?

It is time for a strategic rethink. Having surmounted the initial hurdles to working for yourself, there are three main issues affecting the future of your new business that should be addressed sooner rather than later:

☐ sustainability;
☐ growth;
☐ personal goals.

These three issues are interrelated.

SUSTAINABILITY

Will your business continue to prosper as it is? If you are a self-employed consultant or freelance operator, will your original clients or customers continue to support you? As you will have discovered, one of the problems of working for yourself – by yourself – is that the flow of business activity is uneven. Either your time is fully occupied in servicing the business that you have gained – so that there is little or no opportunity to prospect and gain new business – or all your assignments come to a close and there is a lapse in revenue while you focus on gaining new clients and contracts.

The peaks and troughs in revenue and, therefore, cash flow are a 'feast or famine' syndrome from which it is difficult to escape. Hopefully you have provided for this imbalance in your cash-flow projections, but this kind of one person business is hard to sustain unless you are able to generate a proportion of long-term contracts or a high level of repeat business.

The same problem arises in the case of partnerships providing services, unless the partners are able to phase their activities so that there is an appropriate proportion of partners' collective time always available for sales development.

Small companies in retailing, distribution and manufacturing face a different set of problems. First, they are vulnerable to changes in market conditions; when recession strikes, new entrants to a market are usually the first to feel the pinch. Second, after an initial period of success in a slow-growing market, they may become the target of backlash from competitors anxious to recapture the business they have lost. Most likely, the pressure will take the form of price undercutting, which an established company can maintain on a small proportion of a wider customer base. For your company, retaliation in the form of matching price cuts or offering added benefits is likely to result in an erosion of profit margins across a high proportion of your sales turnover. As a small company, you may find it impossible to counteract the loss of margin by a reduction in fixed costs (other than a reduction in your own salary). The only way forward may be to expand sales turnover, and that is sure to demand additional funding.

It is an often repeated maxim that 'in business you cannot stand still'. If you try to maintain your current level of activity and no more, the business inevitably declines.

The corollary is that growth is an essential ingredient of sustainability.

GROWTH

Financial analysts will tell you that there are two forms of corporate growth: organic growth and M&A (merger and acquisition). They are not necessarily mutually exclusive, but for the young, thriving business it is wise to examine the organic growth opportunities first.

Organic growth

Put simply, organic growth means expansion of the original business based on its core resources, broadening the range and depth of business activities but not straying too far from its original character. Thus, organic growth encompasses additions to the range of products or services, broadening the customer base, adding distribution channels, expanding territorially with new offices or outlets, licensing or franchising your branded products or service, appointing export agents or distributors.

Moving into a new kind of business involving different skills and expertise with a different market does not qualify as organic growth, even if there is an overlap in the target customer base and shared overheads. Returning to the garden centre Business A example of Chapter 5.1, taking the decision to grow your own stock or open a second outlet would be an organic growth activity. Adding a restaurant or a Christmas decorations department in season might just qualify; opening a ladies' hairdressing salon on the same premises would not.

Most kinds of organic growth involve additional funding. Even the appointment of a franchisee or an export agent will add cost in the form of management time expended and, possibly, working capital for additional stock and debtors. The real impact is likely to be on the burden of fixed cost until such time as the add-on activity has taken off and is contributing gross profit (revenue less direct cost) to cover incremental overheads.

At its simplest, suppose you decide to expand your consultancy business by taking on a second consultant to support your work on assignments and to free up some of your time for business development. The additional monthly fixed cost is £5,000 per month (salary, pension, national insurance, other benefits, non-recoverable office and travel expenses). Let us say that all direct costs are chargeable to the client so that revenue and gross profit are the same. Therefore, until you have generated an additional revenue of £5,000 per month in cash received, there is an unfavourable impact on your bottom line and, of more immediate concern, on your cash flow.

In more complex businesses organic growth may involve more than additional working capital. For example, the expansion of the chauffeur-driven limousine service used as an example in Chapter 1.5 would require the addition of at least one more quality car, so that there is either a substantial capital investment to be made or a significant addition to monthly overheads in leasing or hire purchase charges in addition to the cost of another driver. At this stage you will need to reconsider carefully the different sources of capital surveyed in Chapter 2.1. Indeed, the whole process is reiterative as you will need to prepare an updated business plan and possibly carry out further research to prove that there is a market demand for the extension of services or new products which you are planning to introduce.

Extension of premises

At some stage during periods of organic growth the issue of extending existing premises or moving into larger ones will arise. If growth involves increasing your staff, other than engaging home workers, and, in particular, if you started up your business with an office at home, you will need to face up to this problem sooner rather than later.

Buying a freehold or longer leasehold property is a major financial commitment and you will require faith in the long-term future of your business before making such an investment. The following are some of the key considerations:

☐ Can you afford an investment in premises that will tie up so much cash?

☐ Property is an investment for your business that may give a good return, but do you understand the commercial property market?

☐ The long-term cost of buying premises is generally less than the rent you would pay. (The overall cost of buying is usually higher for the first five years, equal for the second five years and cheaper after that.)

☐ If you have enough staff on your payroll to set up a 'small self-administered pension scheme' (SASS), its funds might be used to buy a commercial property for your company to occupy, provided that it pays a commercial rent.

☐ You may gain operational flexibility by owning your own premises; there may for instance be opportunities to let part of the premises, or remortgage or arrange a sale and leaseback deal.

☐ In the case of an industrial building, you may be able to claim capital allowances on plant.

By comparison, renting premises through a lease or licence is flexible and ties up a minimal amount of capital. However, property law is a minefield and verbal agreements do not count. All arrangements must be in writing and you are strongly advised to engage a solicitor with expertise in 'conveyancing' property.

Particular issues to watch out for in a lease are:

☐ How long is the period of the lease and, if more than a few years, is there a break clause for you and/or the landlord to terminate the lease early?

☐ Do you have the right to sub-let or assign the lease and, if so, what are the conditions? For example, is there a requirement to guarantee the next tenant's payments?

☐ When are the rent review dates? Is the rent review based on open market rent or changes in the Retail Price Index, and what happens if you cannot agree?

☐ What are the tenant's liabilities for repairs and maintenance, and what happens when the lease expires?

☐ What service charges are there and how are they calculated?

For businesses in the start-up and early stages where the future is uncertain it may be prudent to enter into an 'easy in, easy out' licence instead of a lease, as this will provide you with maximum flexibility. The particular features of a licence are as follows:

☐ Licences normally cover a period up to two years. You and your landlord usually have the right to give one month's notice of termination.

☐ Many licensed business premises provide support services, such as staffed reception and building security.

☐ The licence agreement should be short and simple in plain English.

☐ Your payment liabilities should be limited to payments for the licence fee (rent), rates and any extra services.

Avoid licences with complex terms or a long fixed licence period without the right to terminate, which are more like leases.

Diversification

Business growth can also take the form of diversification into unrelated businesses where any commonality may be restricted to shared overheads, distribution channels or an overlap of the customer base. Instead of trying to justify the new business as an extension of the original, you are better advised to treat it as a separate business for funding purposes, with an additional business plan and a separate bank account. Unless the expertise which you have deployed in starting the first business is directly relevant to the second, you are engaging in a different kind of entrepreneurial venture in which you will be more dependent on the knowledge and experience of others. If your people judgement proves poor, you want to insulate the first, successful business from the harmful side effects of a less successful venture or even a failure.

Expansion and alliances

While you need to be achieving organic growth with your original business for sustainability, you may aspire to own and manage a larger business and you will get there faster through merger or acquisition than by organic growth alone over a number of years. So, start thinking about possible acquisitions at an early stage. Alternatively, you can build alliances with companies that you might subsequently acquire. You might be able to gain greater geographical reach by aligning yourself with a similar business in a different location; similarly, you could form an alliance with a company offering something slightly different with opportunities to cross-sell to each other's customer base. On the whole you should avoid an alliance with a business that has a very different offering to your own, or with companies up or downstream from you in the process or supply chain. M&A professional advisers will tell you that such mergers and acquisitions seldom work well.

Before embarking on a merger or acquisition adventure it is important to analyse your strengths and weaknesses as well as the opportunities and threats that the deal represents; in other words, make a complete SWOT analysis. The following are just a few of the questions that you should consider:

☐ What are your strengths, and would the deal complement them or risk diluting them?
☐ How good are your product, your market position and your market share?
☐ Are you financially strong?
☐ Do you have advantages in technology or intellectual property?
☐ Are your overheads taking too high a proportion of your income?
☐ Do you have significant management weaknesses?

Buying a company or merging with another company larger than your own will probably involve you in negotiating capital investment from a venture capitalist or business angel as outlined in Chapter 2.1 if you want to remain the controlling shareholder in the enlarged enterprise. This is the point where you move beyond dependence on your bank alone and a whole new set of considerations apply.

The capital funding you will need will almost certainly be a mixture of loan capital and equity as described in Chapter 2.1. Remember that venture capitalists are looking for a return on their investment within an exit strategy of three to five years maximum; but before you address venture capitalists' needs, take time out to identify and articulate your own goals.

PERSONAL GOALS

What are your longer-term objectives? Do you want to go on running and building up your business for the foreseeable future, simply maintaining a livelihood up to pensionable retirement age? Or is your aim to build the business to a size where it can be sold for a substantial capital sum so that you will then have the option of living on the unearned income or even reinvesting in another business and starting again?

There is another well-worn investment maxim that says that you should 'never fall in love with the business you own'.

Without a personal exit strategy there is a very real risk that you will soldier on in an increasingly blinkered and self-indulgent manner and fail to maximise the business potential. If you were enough of an entrepreneur to start working for yourself, you will almost certainly want to maximise the value of your endeavour.

These are the reasons why you may choose the M&A route to growth and will need to become skilled in negotiating and operating the more sophisticated funding arrangements and in working with the investment community. But that, as they say, is another story and the subject matter for another book.

Checklist: planning for growth

1. Having started your business successfully, address the three main issues for the future: sustainability, growth and personal goals.
2. Plan how to smooth out the peaks and troughs of your cash-flow cycle.
3. Learn how to reduce your vulnerability to changes in market conditions and to counter aggressive competition.
4. Examine organic growth opportunities first before considering mergers and acquisitions.
5. Most kinds of organic growth involve additional funding. Calculate the effects on cash flow before you embark on expansion.
6. Organic growth may cause you to consider extending or moving your business premises.
7. Take expert legal advice on all leases and licences. For businesses in the start-up and early stages it may be prudent to enter into an 'easy in, easy out' licence.
8. If you diversify into an unrelated business, run it as a separate business and insulate your first business from any harmful effects if the second venture fails.
8. M&A may be a faster route to growth than organic development, but before embarking on a deal carry out a thorough SWOT analysis of your own business.
10. What are your long-term objectives? Develop your personal exit strategy.

Part 3
Businesses Requiring Investment

6 **Retailing**

BUYING A SHOP

No book can answer all the questions or anticipate all the problems that buying a shop or starting a retail business entails, but it can warn you of the main reasons for failure:

☐ Paying an unrealistic price for the business.
☐ Lack of experience in the trade you enter.
☐ Cash flow problems caused by underestimating current costs.
☐ Failure to recognise the level of competition to the type of goods you sell or the service you offer (are you setting up a general food store next to a round-the-clock supermarket?).
☐ Choice of a bad location: away from the shopping centre, in a commercial area with little weekend trade, etc.

The character of areas and shopping precincts changes rapidly. The 'centre' of your town is perhaps moving, through lack of space, to an open-plan area with a multi-storey car park and a wide range of shopping units. Long-established shops in the 'older' part of town are often unable to survive, so be wary of being offered this type of business. There are wide variations in the desirability and potential profitability of even apparently similar retail businesses.

Ask where the business you have seen advertised is sited. Is it well positioned or far from the centre of trading activity? What is its reputation? Be sceptical of the seller's claims to a fund of 'goodwill' from long-standing customers. There is no guarantee that they exist or, if they do, that they will be as loyal to you. How much stock have you been offered as part of the purchase price? Does the shop need redecoration? What terms are you being offered: freehold or leasehold? What is the nature of the competition to your enterprise?

Such questions do not allow simple answers. These vary according to the type of business you intend to conduct. For example, a more specialised shop (selling, say, good-quality hi-fi or photographic equipment at competitive prices) does not need to be as central as a grocer's, butcher's or general goods store. Customers will hear about it and seek it out and, having been satisfied once, will return for accessories, improved equipment and advice.

Think, too, about general location and the composition of the local population: is it predominantly young or old, middle class or working class, close to sports facilities or not, and so on? Is there a seasonal trade that you might capture? Are there shops nearby that may attract certain types of people, whose custom you might aim to tap? Would you have to work special hours to fit in with the habits of your potential customers (by, for example, staying open until 7 or 7.30 pm in suburban residential areas)? Would those habits affect your trade adversely at certain times (low 'traffic' at weekends in business areas, for instance)?

In short, you must consider a whole range of locational factors before choosing to buy an established business or deciding *where* to start a new shop. Four rules:

☐ Talk to people who know the trade and the locality.
☐ Take the advice of an accountant and solicitor who will, respectively, assess the financial worth of the purchase and the legal commitments you will enter into.
☐ Do not buy the first shop offered to you unless *everyone* thinks it is an unmissable opportunity (and, even then, think again!).
☐ Always assume the seller is asking too much.

This is not sophisticated business thinking; it is plain common sense.

> 'Even if you have to borrow money, do not be under-capitalised. Keep your shelves full and well stocked since this will attract customers ... Apart from fruit and veg, you will need to have five to seven times your weekly takings tied up in stock.'
> _George Thorpe, food retailer_

YOU AND YOUR BUSINESS

On a more personal level, can you and your family bear the strain of managing a shop: the hours of work, the tedium of filling in tax forms and keeping books, the problems of receiving early morning deliveries, the physical work that might be involved in taking and storing deliveries, the pressure of having always to be polite to the customers? (You might not wish to follow the dictum that the customer is always right, but would you survive? Small businesses depend on customers returning and on word-of-mouth promotion.)

Working hours are long, but made tolerable by a commitment to _your_ business. You may grow to dislike VAT returns and difficult customers and you will encounter a host of petty day-to-day administrative difficulties, but if you are serious about the move in the first place, you should survive these. But ask yourself: is my immediate family as dedicated to the project as I am? What is a challenge to you may be a burden to them. So, be as sensitive to their needs as you are to your own.

BUYING AN ESTABLISHED BUSINESS

Shops for sale are sometimes advertised in the local and national press and in some trade journals,* or you can consult a firm of business valuers and transfer agents. It is a good idea to write down the specific requirements that you are looking for: this will

---

* A full list of these is contained in _British Rate & Data_ (_BRAD_), a monthly listing of all commercial periodical publications and newspapers, which should be available in any reasonable business reference library.

not only help you to brief your agents and any other advisers such as your accountant and bank manager, but will also help you to clarify your ideas.

Shops are generally rented on a leasehold basis, and you should aim for a property with as long a lease as possible. In paying for the shop you will be buying the premises, fixtures and fittings, existing stock and 'goodwill'. How this price is arrived at depends on a number of factors, which you must analyse carefully before you commit yourself. *Stock* is generally valued for business sale purposes at current market cost price, and an independent valuation of the stock is desirable. *Fixtures and fittings* should also be independently valued, and an inventory of these should be made and attached to the contract of sale. *Goodwill* is a nebulous concept to which an exact value cannot be attached. Obviously, the more the shop relies on regular, established customers, the higher the value of the goodwill; conversely, the more it relies on casual, passing trade, the lower the goodwill value. The price of a shop will also to a large extent depend on the potential of the local area. You will need to make a careful assessment of factors such as:

1. Competition. Do not make the mistake of thinking that the absence of a nearby competitor *necessarily* guarantees success. A shop that has done reasonably well in the face of nearby competition is a safer bet than a shop with a similar record which has had a virtual monopoly of local trade. There is always a danger that if there is no competition, someone else may move in after you. Another common mistake is to see only shops of the same trade as competition. Indirectly, all other traders in the area are competition, since all are competing for a share of the consumers' spending power.
2. Nearness to railway stations, bus stops, etc: this may substantially increase the flow of passing trade. A map may help to clarify the exact potential of the location.
3. Any further local development plans – check with the local authority.

It is important that you and your accountant study the books thoroughly. In particular, examine the trend of the profit and loss account over the past few years to determine whether the business is improving. Another important point to note is whether the previous trader has been paying himself a salary, or whether this has to be deducted from the net profit figure.

> 'Location, potential competition and overheads are the three key points to watch. If you're buying an existing store, scrutinise the accounts minutely. Is it possible to run it with one less member of staff, for example? Are home deliveries being made? These can be very, very expensive. Don't try to compete on prices with the big boys – you'll lose! Stock lots of lines and if need be sell, say, sugar at a loss knowing you've got a good margin on shampoo. There's no guarantee that goodwill will pass over to you on completion of the sale – your face might not fit and there's little allegiance nowadays from customers.'
>
> _Owner of general goods shop_

STARTING FROM SCRATCH

You may want to take over premises which have previously been used for other purposes, in which case you should look closely at the previous owner's reasons for closing down and determine to what extent the same factors will affect you, even though you are engaged in a different trade. If you are going to use them for another type of business, you must get planning permission first. Or you may want to rent newly built premises, in which case you will probably have to pay a premium. The premium is based on the potential of the area, but try to get an _exact_ idea of what that potential is: the number of new flats being built nearby, for example. In general, the premium should be lower than the goodwill price you would pay for a going concern, since it only indicates potential, not a record of success.

LEGAL OBLIGATIONS

These fall into four categories: first, employment legislation (see Chapter 4.2). Check the ages of your employees; ensure that they are taxed, and that you pay your share of their National Insurance contributions; cover them regarding pensions and superannuation; know where they stand in relation to the Employment Protection Act.

Second, safety, security and planning. You should insure your premises and stock, and cover yourself against liability, including liability for defective goods (potentially liability will vary widely depending on the goods you sell and the services you offer). In the case of a food shop, you must satisfy a health inspector, and other types of premises will have to be passed fit by a fire officer. Check these and local planning laws before you start trading. The quickest way to find out which of these laws apply to you is to contact your local Shops Act Inspector. She will also provide details of by-laws on opening hours, Sunday trading, pavement displays, etc.

Third, fair trading. Know and follow the provisions of the Consumer Credit Act and the Trade Descriptions Act. There are strict rules on how you display prices, on recommended prices and 'special' offers, on the giving of guarantees, on the rates of hire-purchase you can offer and the other types of credit you make available, and so on. Again, cover yourself against expensive litigation by going through existing legislation with a solicitor, looking at standard practice in businesses similar to your own, and taking advice from the local Weights and Measures Inspector.

Finally, be aware of your standing under the Sale of Goods Act. When you sell something, the merchandise you sell should be in good condition and fit for its stated purpose. If it is not, your customer is entitled to a suitable replacement or a refund. When you provide a service, under contract law it should be up to the required standard; if it is not, the customer can claim compensation. The Supply of Goods and Services Act 1982 brings the sale of goods and the provision of services into line and makes all retailers responsible for the product or service they provide. You must also be aware of recent legislation that makes it illegal to trade in imperial measurements.

_____

KEEPING ACCOUNTS

A great deal of bookwork will be inevitable: keeping count of stock levels and daily sales (for personal use and for VAT purposes); an elementary statistical breakdown of what is selling; keeping tabs on credit customers, orders, returned goods, etc. Your accountant and bank manager will wish to see comprehensive and up-to-date accounts to check your progress. See Chapter 3.1 for an introduction to simple accounting, but be warned: for anything more than day-to-day bookkeeping it is worth using a qualified accountant.

LEASING

Leases are written in legal jargon and for that reason the vendor is sometimes apt to sign without really understanding what the lease says. This is a great mistake, and if you cannot follow the wording or are unclear about anything, you should ask your solicitor to explain it to you. Look out particularly for restrictive covenants that prevent you from transferring the lease to a third party or from carrying on certain trades and professions at those premises.

SECURITY

Never leave cash lying about. If there is a lot of money in the till, take out a round sum in notes and leave a chit in the till to remind yourself where it is. Watch out for shoplifters, and ensure against them as far as possible by not leaving small, valuable items in easily accessible positions. Do not leave customers or visitors unattended. Remember that you must be insured right from the start, even before you have opened up for business. The Home Office produces a pamphlet on theft by staff, a danger which must not be overlooked. Consult your local crime prevention officer, who will advise you on ways to combat both dangers.

STOCK

It is sensible to buy stock from a wholesaler, or cash and carry, or from a manufacturers' agent, since you will generally need frequent deliveries of small quantities of goods. Have as few sources of supply as possible, to cut down your workload. There are a few exceptions to this. In the case of cigarettes, for example, it is better to deal direct with the manufacturer.

Make sure you know at all times what your stock levels are, and devise a system whereby you know when to reorder, before stocks run too low. The stock should be cleaned and dusted regularly and any stock that remains unsold over a long period should be discarded. Stock-taking should be carried out regularly, depending on the type of business in which you are engaged.

LAYOUT AND DISPLAY

Cleanliness and hygiene are, of course, absolute musts. Layout too, will be important. Make the interior of the shop as attractive as you can: displays, however small, should have a focal point, and should be changed frequently. Allow space for your customers to move and, if necessary, push prams, and make sure that they have access to all the goods on your shelves. Think, also, about your window displays: manufacturers will often supply signs and special display items which may improve the look of your shop.

Useful information

National Association of Shopkeepers, Lynch House, 91 Mansfield Street, Nottingham NG1 3FN. Tel. 0115 947 5046.

---

7 Farming and Market Gardening

The 'back to the land' movement has been quite fashionable in recent years, with all kinds of people giving up their jobs and homes in cities to live on smallholdings (communal or otherwise) where they try to be completely self-sufficient. Others, more commercially minded, may take up market gardening, which gives them a pleasant life in the country while they sell the fruits of their labours to others. Some more conventional and hardy souls may simply decide to buy a farm and rear cattle, grow corn or keep pigs or poultry if they are undeterred by established farmers' experiences of the 2001 BSE crisis and the move towards diversification from farming.

In all cases, the romantic glow soon disappears. There are two essentials for any of these occupations, neither of them romantic: capital and the capacity for hard work. Take advice from professional bodies such as the Advisory Services of the Department for the Environment, Food and Rural Affairs (www.defra.gov.uk) or the local county office of the National Farmers' Union. The local authority is responsible for agricultural education and you should make inquiries about courses that might be available in your area. The soaring costs of fuel and animal foodstuffs have already put many market gardeners and farmers out of business, so it is obviously essential to go into the finances of the operation very thoroughly before making a decision.

It is also essential to have the complete support of your family. This can be a very hard life, getting up early in all weathers to feed animals, breaking your back hoeing and weeding, and you have to be extremely keen and enthusiastic to take it on. If your nearest and dearest are not equally enthusiastic, forget it, for you are going to need their active help, since labour is both expensive and hard to come by.

FARMING

Farming has become a technological occupation, requiring all kinds of special skills and knowledge. Unless you can convince a bank that you have this know-how (and some business experience) you are unlikely to get your money. Long-term loans for the purchase of land are available from the Agricultural Mortgage Corporation Ltd but, here again, properly prepared budgets and a realistic and comprehensive proposal will be required if the application is to be successful.

Now a highly risky occupation, farming gives only a 3 to 4 per cent return on tenanted land at best. The failure rate is very high, and to take it up with little or no experience almost guarantees failure. Unless you know about fertilisers, pesticides, animal husbandry and farm machinery, you are likely to make some expensive mistakes, and remember that two bad years could wipe you out financially. The farmers who are most successful are those who start young, probably in a family-owned business. By the time they take over, they have acquired the necessary experience, usually backed up these days with a course at one of the agricultural colleges. You should not contemplate farming without some practical experience, or a degree or diploma from an agricultural college, or preferably both.

Another idea which is very popular with the 'get-away-from-it-all' brigade is to buy a smallholding and try to be entirely self-sufficient, perhaps even setting up a commune. It is an attractive idea, and the initial cost need not be great, but be warned: this is subsistence farming and you will find yourself working as hard as the American pioneers did. Also, even on a commune you may need a tractor and, for that, you are going to need money. You really need to be dedicated or rich (preferably both).

If the foregoing has not deterred you, get some professional advice, either from ADAS (the Agricultural Development Advisory Service of the DEFRA) or from your local agricultural college or institute. There are also various farm management consultants and land agency firms who will (for a fee) give advice on what to do.

Even running a smallholding will demand considerable capital and expertise, as well as determination and immense hard work.

> 'You must start with sufficient capital to carry you through the first year, since you will almost certainly make nothing at all until your second year. All the self-employed work long hours but running a smallholding involves particularly long hours – weekends don't exist.'
>
> *Pat Burke, smallholding owner*

MARKET GARDENING

Unless you take over an established business, the main problems for the would-be market gardener are acquiring the necessary land and a greenhouse. You may be lucky enough to own a suitable piece of land already, or a garden big enough (two or three acres) to be worked commercially. However, if you have to purchase land the price of this will depend on the area, quality of soil and drainage, previous history and needs of use. This can cost anything between £1,500 and £5,000 per acre. A greenhouse is the other big expense. It is a vital piece of equipment, enabling you to grow tomatoes, bedding plants, pot plants for the winter months and seedlings for early vegetables. You can do without one, but you must then make enough money in the spring and summer to make up for the lean winter months when you have virtually nothing to offer except a few winter vegetables. You also have to make provision for the cost of heating a greenhouse: price increases in fuel have sent the cost sky-high, so you must make sure that every inch of space is working for you, if your profits are not going literally to disappear in smoke. You can expect to pay for a new, modern, glasshouse shell the minimum of £100,000 pro rata. The smaller the house the higher rate the cost per square metre.

If you are not a trained horticulturalist, it is a good idea to employ someone who is, or who has at least had practical experience of running a big garden and greenhouse. One full-time helper is probably all you will be able to afford in the early years. Seasonal help picking tomatoes, strawberries, beans, etc is often difficult to find and the minimum legal wage is £3.60 for younger workers and £4.20 for adults (plus extra costs such as National Insurance). You (and your family) must be prepared to work long hours and turn your hand to anything. On the other hand, there is a growing trend towards advertising 'pick your own' facilities during peak seasons. The amount people are willing to pay for the privilege of picking their own fruit compares favourably with the wholesale prices you would be able to obtain.

For general information, particularly on the economics of growing produce, contact the National Farmers' Union, which has a very good horticultural section. Another excellent source of information on what crops to grow, soil tests, etc is the Agricultural Development Advisory Service of the Ministry of Agriculture (ADAS).

One basic decision to be made, once you have decided on your crops, is how you are going to market your produce. If you are on a busy main road you may decide to rely heavily on local advertising and passing trade from tourists, etc, sending the surplus to the local market, or even taking a stall in the local market yourself. You can also send your produce to one of the big central markets, but you then have to pay a fee to the auctioneer, as well as transport costs.

ALTERNATIVE RURAL BUSINESSES

The recent problems in farming have seen many people previously employed in the sector looking for new opportunities within a rural context. Indeed, if one wanted to find evidence of how flexible and imaginative the self-employed can be, there are many examples in the industries that have sprung up in rural areas supporting, or in some cases replacing, the income lost from traditional farming. Some have turned to organic farming to find new markets, while others have found more unusual avenues. However, it is worth remembering if you are new to this sector, and to a rural environment, that conditions are often extremely hard.

Lesley Stimson started her angora farm with no previous experience of handling livestock apart from keeping a horse and pets. She now has a herd of 28 goats from which she makes angora products.

> 'It's not a 9-5 job. With animals, if it's cold at night you still have to go out at 10 o'clock and top up the water buckets. You're always here and you can't go away very easily if you have animals.'
>
> *Lesley Stimson, Silvermore Mohair*

An ex-teacher, she has found advice from the National Farmer's Union useful with help on matters such as insurance, and interestingly, she says that the Inland Revenue was particularly helpful.

> 'The tax inspector was extremely good. I put all my cards on the table and it was him who advised me not to be self-employed and to be in a partnership. It is important to make an appointment with the Inland Revenue and to go to them with your plans and books and they will help you.'
>
> *Lesley Stimson, Silvermore Mohair*

Business in a rural environment can be found if you look for obvious gaps in the market. That's what Gay Russell, Farm Administrator, did when she set up her business nine years ago.

> 'My business sense said, what can you do in East Anglia? What goes on here and what skills have you got that can be utilised here? We live in a very isolated position and this has always been a predominantly agricultural area. I'm used to working on my own and I wanted to be self-employed. I need to be able to choose my own times of working, when I work and how much I do to fit in with the other things in my life.'
>
> *Gay Russell, Farm Administrator*

Working as a sole trader the first thing she did was to join the local branch of her professional association the Institute of Agricultural Secretaries and Administrators. Conferences, seminars and continuous professional development are offered by the Institute; with half-day workshops on accountancy, VAT and other business issues. Marketing her services was also something she considered but she found that in an occupation where confidentiality was important it was word-of-mouth that helped her pick up work.

> 'At first I did put a few postcards around which were useless. Word-of-mouth worked best because it is quite a personalised job and people are very worried about confidentiality so to be recommended is much the best plan so that they can feel safe that their records and things will be secure. Being a member of a professional association also helps.'
>
> *Gay Russell, Farm Administrator*

Her professional institute helped, as did a local government sponsored organisation, MENTA. This involved local professionals giving help to start-ups with business plans, marketing and sales lectures, promotions and packaging.

These are just two examples of innovative enterprise in areas where traditional forms of industry are diminishing. The National Farmers Union's Countryside Division is particularly helpful for alternative rural businesses and can offer good advice and help.

Equally, the Country Land and Business Association is an

_____

invaluable source of advice for owners of agricultural land and rural buildings seeking to release added value from their assets.

Useful information

Agricultural Development Advisory Service, Woodthorne, Wergs Road, Wolverhampton WV6 8QT. Tel. 01902 754190. Web: www.adas.co.uk.

Agricultural Mortgage Corporation Ltd, AMC House, Chantry Street, Andover, Hants SP10 1DD. Tel. 01264 334747. Web: www.amconline.co.uk.

Country Land and Business Association, 16 Belgrave Square, London SW1X 8PQ. Tel. 020 234 0511. Web: http//www.cla.org.uk.

Royal Horticultural Society, 14–15 Belgrave Square, London SW1X 8PS. Tel. 020 7245 6943. Web: http://www.horticulture.demon.co.uk.

National Farmers' Union, 164 Shaftesbury Avenue, London WC2H 8HL. Tel. 020 7331 7200. Web: http://www.nfu.org.uk.

8 Hotels, Catering and Entertainment

Hotels, pubs, clubs and the range of independently owned eating places, from simple corner-shop cafés to long-established, expensive restaurants, constitute a vast business. There are over 30,000 hotels and large guest houses and a vast number of pubs and clubs in the UK, and in employment terms, catering is one of the biggest industries. The range of opportunities and business options is so wide that we can barely scratch the surface, but an outline of each area will be given and some general conclusions drawn.

THE BUSINESS

What is true of running a shop, that you need unstinting energy and commitment, is even truer in this field. Your hours will be long and irregular. You are likely to have to work 365 days a year. You may have to deal with dissatisfied and difficult customers. There is a mountain of paperwork to monitor and national and local regulations to understand and abide by. Your family, which is in any case likely to be directly involved in the running of your hotel, restaurant or café, should be as committed to succeeding as you are.

Offsetting these disadvantages, these areas, particularly owning a restaurant or hotel on which you can stamp your personality and deal very closely with your customers, have many attractions. Indeed, perhaps too many: new restaurants open with great frequency but often quickly collapse because of poor planning, bad management, lack of finance, or a simple lack of realism about the scope for _that_ type of restaurant in _that_ locality.

LOCATION

As in retailing, location is crucial. Decide what sort of operation you wish to conduct and then look for the premises. If you want to start a hotel or guest house, look for an expanding inland tourist spot or popular seaside resort. In the latter, think about the problems of surviving the winter, with only limited and erratic custom. Ask yourself what type of visitor the place attracts and who might be attracted by price reductions out of season (pensioners or disabled people perhaps). Understand the character of the area in which your business will be sited, and have some idea _whose_ needs you will cater for. This applies as much to services as to manufacturing firms, and is crucial when you decide how to market that service.

GETTING PLANNING PERMISSION

This is more difficult than you might think. Local authorities will want details not only of what you intend to do with the premises but of structural changes you intend to make, of the effect the development will have on other properties, of the safety factors involved, of the parking facilities available for your customers, and so on. You will have to submit detailed plans, and will probably need to consult a lawyer and a surveyor. Even then your application may not succeed, and you will have bought a good deal of expensive legal advice with no return. Remember that restaurants and clubs may be noisy, keep long hours and attract a large number of patrons – local authorities are naturally anxious to regulate these developments, and your application may therefore be lengthy and will need to be well planned and properly researched.

RESTAURANTS

New restaurants open every week, particularly in the London area. But almost as many close, and only the gifted and the adaptable survive. Establishing a restaurant is extremely expensive, particularly when you have to convert premises (as is usually the case). A good idea is not sufficient; you also need diligence and, above all, *money*. In a period of tight money and high interest rates, financial backing for enterprises as doubtful as restaurants is in short supply.

There are basically two kinds of people who open a restaurant – the gifted amateur or professional cook, and the 'ideas person' who knows how to fulfil a taste and buys premises and finds the staff to meet that need (many of the 'in places' in London are now more rated for décor, music and clientele than for their cuisine). The main problem for the amateur or professional is likely to be how to maintain standards without wasting an enormous amount of food and losing money. One answer is to have a *small* choice of dishes which are changed regularly. You will have to spend quite a lot of time finding the best sources locally for fresh meat, fish and vegetables, since your reputation depends on it. The restaurateur who has a speciality (such as steaks) and sticks to it will find life a lot simpler.

Where your restaurant is located is obviously essential. If it is in the centre of town, well and good. If not, you must set out advertising, make sure your friends spread the word around, find an eye-catching décor and try to get yourself written up in the local paper. If you are sufficiently confident, you could try writing to the restaurant critics on some of the big magazines (such as *Harpers & Queen*) or newspapers.

If your restaurant is quite small, you will probably find it more economical in the long run to be as mechanised as possible with chip machines, dishwashers, freezers, etc, rather than hiring a lot of expensive, possibly unreliable, staff. Costing can be quite difficult, with the rising price of food, but beware of undercharging. There is a temptation to court trade with low prices, but you will soon find it impossible to keep up standards. Moreover, do not undercharge when you first open simply to attract customers; when your prices rise they will see through your scheme and look elsewhere. Charge the going rate: decent food, pleasant surroundings, efficient and friendly service and a reasonable location should guarantee some degree of success.

It is a good idea, too, to realise your limitations and not try to be grander than you are – if you are basically steak and chips there is no point in trying to produce cordon bleu menus: you will soon be found out!

We spoke to a restaurateur, who points to seven problem areas:

1. Wastage.
2. Overheads – heating and lighting cost £80 per week for a 30-seat restaurant!
3. Payment of VAT.
4. Establishing good and appropriate décor.
5. The need to change the menu – don't let yourself or your customers get bored with it.
6. Maintaining your profit margins.
7. Coping with fluctuations in demand – no customers one night, 50 the next!

CAFÉS, SNACK BARS, ETC

The large restaurant has very different problems from the small, unpretentious café. The former provides particular foods with (one hopes) a distinctive touch, and will seek to build up a clientele. It may encounter problems in employing staff, dealing with alcohol licensing, regulations on opening hours, fire precautions, and so on. Moreover, it may be vulnerable to economic downturns and changing consumer tastes. By contrast, the café offers a simple service to the local workforce and others at a reasonable price. Fads of taste and the vagaries of economics count for little.

Owning a café is more closely allied to general retailing than to being a restaurateur. True, you must be able to prepare a reasonably wide range of good food cheaply, quickly, efficiently and hygienically. But this should not be beyond the capabilities of the average person.

Reread the retailing section: location will be important and your business must be located in heavy 'traffic' areas. Recognise that each day will have peaks and troughs – a rush at noon to 2 pm perhaps? Can you cope and, if you can, will you then be overstaffed for the rest of the day?

Think carefully about why you have chosen the location and what will make your café different from any other in the area. For example, the owner of an Internet café in a small town in the Peak District saw the chance to marry two needs in her new venture:

> 'There was a gap in the market in the sense that New Mills was crying out for another café. Also, the Internet was just emerging as a new technology. The idea at the time was to combine a beautiful location with the technology, training and accessibility necessary to enable teleworking, or working from home.'
>
> *Eleanor Chronnell, Peak Art Cyber Café, New Mills*

However, her vision was not always shared by the people she went to for advice and help:

> 'Business Link High Peak has been the most helpful in terms of information both at the setting-up stage and with ongoing advice. I also have a very good accountant, and, of necessity, a bank manager! The banks were probably the least helpful, and asked useless questions like 'What is the Internet?' and 'Why will people use it?' Little foresight and no leeway whatsoever!'
>
> *Eleanor Chronnell, Peak Art Cyber Café, New Mills*

Whatever makes your café stand out from the crowd, uniform legislation applies to the whole sector without exceptions. For example, your business must be covered by health and safety regulations and must be passed by a food inspector and a fire officer. Regulations on bookkeeping and VAT returns apply to you with equal force as to any other retail business.

THE HOTEL BUSINESS

You must choose your hotel or guest house with great care. It is a big investment to make, so be sure to examine the following points:

The area

What is the competition like? Are there any plans for redevelopment locally which might involve one of the big hotel groups? Is it on a main road or tourist route, or is it hidden in the back streets or down a country lane? Does the area as a whole seem to be coming up in the world, or going down?

The customers

Ideally, you want to attract a variety of clientele, so that you are fairly busy all year round. Seaside hotels are full up for most of the summer, but virtually deserted in the winter: are you going to make enough profit to cover those lean winter months? Other hotels in industrial or commercial areas will find that they are full of business travellers during the week, but that the weekends are very quiet. The most successful hotels are those which have a good mix of commercial, holiday, conference and banqueting business. Study the accounts if you can and see what the pattern of business is.

The fabric

What state is your hotel in? You must find out how much renovating or decorating needs to be done and how much this is going to cost. What are the maintenance costs likely to be?

The law

There are a number of laws that the hotelier is subject to, particularly health and safety legislation. Insure your property and protect yourself against liability; make sure you meet the necessary safety levels for fireproofing and hygiene, or your insurance

_____

may be worthless. Another important set of regulations, if you are opening a new hotel, covers licensing. There are various guides to the licensing laws, but if you have to apply for a new licence it is wise to do it through a solicitor.

Also very important is the Fire Precautions Act of 1971. Every hotel, if it sleeps more than six people, must have a fire certificate from the local fire authority. When buying a going concern, find out if it has a fire certificate, or if an application for one has been made (if not, the hotel is being run illegally). If the fire authority has already inspected the building, check on the cost of any alterations required to bring the premises into line with the Act.

Staff

Good staff are obviously essential for the smooth and efficient running of a hotel, but they are very difficult to come by. This is an industry with a very high staff turnover, especially among unskilled staff, and you must expect to spend a lot of time interviewing, supervising and training. Everyone in the business agrees that it pays to take your time (however inconvenient) and select staff very carefully, rather than always employing the first person you see because you are busy.

Goodwill

Does the hotel you are considering buying have a good reputation? Will regular visitors return even though the hotel has changed ownership?

Past performance and potential

How has it operated in the past: could you improve on it? What is the sleeping capacity? Could it be increased without reducing standards? Can seasonal fluctuations be reduced by good marketing? How great are staff expenses and other overheads as a proportion of turnover? What is the hotel's net profit as a percentage of turnover?

PUBS

The following section refers to brewery tenants, not to pub managers (who are not self-employed) or to the owners of free houses, which are now so few and far between as to make the possibility of finding a vacant one very unlikely.

Tenants rent their pubs from the brewery company, paying an agreed sum to the outgoing tenant for fittings, equipment and stock. They agree to buy their beer from the brewery, and generally cannot buy stock (even of items other than liquor) from any other source without the brewery's permission. They keep their own profits and are responsible for their own losses, the brewery receiving only the rent on the premises and the guaranteed outlet for its product.

There are more applications from prospective tenants than there are tenancies available, so the breweries are able to 'pick and choose' to some extent. The qualities they look for in a prospective tenant are:

1. Sufficient capital resources to purchase fittings, equipment and stock in hand, to cover immediate running expenses, and to provide a sufficient reserve to cover the tenant in the event of a temporary reduction in trade.
2. A preference for married tenants. Running a pub is very much a family affair, and your spouse's experience and attitude can be a decisive factor.
3. Good health, since running a pub involves hard physical work and long hours.
4. Some managerial experience, in any trade – this would count in the applicant's favour, though it is not strictly necessary. Similarly, experience or training in the liquor trade would be useful, and though not a mandatory requirement it would be useful from your point of view to have experienced the trade in various capacities first.

> 'Watch the optics, the fiddles and the free drinks to friends. Watch that the brewers don't send you lines you don't want. Don't commit yourself to loans and brewers' discounts – there'll be conditions in the fine print you won't like. The Weights and Measures boys will be calling often to check your measures and make sure you have price notices and age warnings up.'
>
> *Publican*

Tenancy agreements

Most breweries have a standard form of agreement to be signed by the tenant. The procedure for taking over the fittings, furniture and equipment is the only area in which there may be a substantial difference between breweries: some require the new tenant to buy these items from the outgoing tenant, while in other cases they remain the property of the brewery and the tenant lodges a deposit, returnable when the tenancy is given up. Other items covered in the tenancy agreement include rent (usually paid quarterly), the term of the tenancy, responsibility for repairs, a requirement that the tenant must take out employees' and public liability insurance, the terms on which the stock is purchased, the brewery company's right of access to the premises, requirements connected with transfer of the licence, and terms on which the tenancy can be terminated.

Licences

The tenant usually takes over premises that are already licensed, so you have to negotiate the transfer of the licence from the outgoing tenant to yourself. It is advisable to be represented by a solicitor in your application for transfer of the licence.

Training

If you are accepted by a brewery for a tenancy, and neither you nor your spouse has any experience of the trade, it is likely that both of you will be asked to attend a short residential course, run by the brewery company and lasting from one to two weeks. While you are waiting for a suitable tenancy, or applying to different breweries, it is advisable, if you have no experience, to work part-time in a pub. This will give you some experience, and will help you to decide whether you are really suited to what is in fact a very arduous job.

OTHER OPPORTUNITIES

It is possible to run clubs, cinemas, theatres and so on independently. Indeed, the attractions for the music lover or cinema buff are considerable, as it seems to be possible to mix business with pleasure. But base any decision on *business* sense, not on a romantic notion of making your leisure interest pay. Can the town support another cinema, particularly if you intend to show nothing but *avant garde* and experimental films? (Whether you want to show more obscure films or not, if the major companies have tied up the distribution of the money-spinning movies you may have no option!)

You will face the same problems as the hotelier and restaurateur in choosing the right location, employing staff, perhaps getting restrictions on opening hours lifted, obtaining a licence to serve alcohol and meeting fire regulations.* (Some of these problems can be circumvented if you make your institution a private club, admitting members only at some sort of fee, though future legislation may close this loophole.) And do not forget the less well-known legislation on health, hygiene, noise abatement, etc, which may involve you in short-term inconvenience or, worse, long-term and expensive rounds of litigation.

WHICH BUSINESS?

Whatever type of service you provide, you will need sound financial backing, commercial acumen, the ability to offer something distinctive and market it accordingly, and patience in choosing the right opening. Fix on a 'target' population: advertise in newspapers and periodicals which they are likely to read, and be prepared for an initial struggle while you attempt to build up the business. The business field you choose to enter should be one in which you have some expertise, something distinctive to offer and a practical marketing strategy. But, even then, you will need resilience and the ability to work hard for long periods.

Useful information

British Institute of Innkeeping, Wessex House, 80 Park Street, Camberley, Surrey GU15 3PT. Tel. 01276 684449. Web site: www.bii.org.

Careers Information Service, Hotel and Catering Training Company, International House, High Street, London W5 5DB. Tel. 020 8579 2400. Web site: www.htf.org.uk.

Hotel and Catering International Management Association, 191 Trinity Road, London SW17 7HN. Tel. 020 8772 7400. Web site: www.hcima.org.uk/.

British Beer and Pub Association (formerly Brewers and Licensed Retailers Association), Market Towers, 1 Nine Elms Lane, London SW8 5NQ. Tel. 020 7627 9191. Web site: www.beerandpub.com.

Careers in Catering and Management, Kogan Page
Guide to Careers in the Catering, Travel and Leisure Industries, Kogan Page
The Publican's Handbook, Kogan Page

---

* This could be extremely expensive if alterations to a club or cinema have to be made to comply with regulations. Consider this when you buy a property which you hope to convert, and check that an established business has a fire certificate.

9 Construction, Building, Maintenance and Distribution Services

Builders, carpenters, plumbers and electricians are in constant demand. Established firms charge high labour rates, and people qualified in these trades can obtain a steady income by taking on extra work at reasonable rates. Alternatively, if you are more ambitious, you may start a building or redecoration company. You will need some capital, the necessary equipment, some means of transport, and a rudimentary administrative system – to take commissions for work, send invoices, check payments, keep tabs on costs, etc.

Following the new tax arrangements for the construction industry that came into effect on 1 August 1999, you will most likely fit within the 'registration card' regime. You will need to obtain a registration card from the Inland Revenue in order to receive payments from main contractors. The payments they then make to you will have tax withheld at the rate of 18 per cent on the element of each invoice that does not relate to materials.

Substantial sub contractors may apply for a sub contractors tax certificate, which enables main contractors to pay them gross.

The Inland Revenue publish guidance on how to apply for and use registration cards and sub contractors tax certificates.

TRAINING

The orthodox training for these trades is by entering into apprenticeship after leaving school, but it is now sometimes possible for older people to learn these skills at government training centres (details from your local employment office).

Much of the work available in private households consists either of very small jobs, such as putting up shelves or wallpapering, or conversion work, for which you must take into account building regulations and you or the house owner should get planning permission if applicable. You will find that the wider the range of skills you can offer, the more you will be in demand, since one job might involve both carpentry and decorating, for example.

It is advisable to work with a partner, since you will often need help with lifting, measurement, etc. You will also find that it is invaluable to have contacts who specialise in other, related trades, since you will often find that you cannot complete a job without the help of, say, an electrician. Contacts will also help you to find work since they will get in touch with you to finish jobs that they themselves cannot complete.

THE BUILDING REGULATIONS

Major structural changes must conform with national and local building regulations. If in doubt, consult your local authority (ask for the District Surveyor or Building Inspector).

Planning permission needs to be granted for external extensions exceeding 1,300 cubic feet. If the building you are working on is listed as being of historic interest there may be regulations against changing its external appearance – again, check with the local authority. These problems concern the person who commissioned the work more than they affect you, but it is as well to guard yourself against liability.

HOW TO GET WORK

As explained above, contacts in related trades are invaluable. You might also obtain subcontracted work from small building firms. Landlords and property agents are useful people to cultivate, as they often provide a great deal of maintenance and conversion work. You may also wish to advertise in the local press. But beware of making claims which you cannot support: do not, for example, say that you are a master builder if you hold no such certificate.

Sources of information

1. The Department of the Environment publishes a leaflet called *How To Find Out: Getting the Best from Building Information Services*, listing 80 important information sources for the construction industry. They also publish free leaflets on a wide range of subjects such as paint, water supply, mortar and rendering which may be of interest. Contact the Department of the Environment, Food and Rural Affairs' free publication line on 0870 122 6236 and ask for leaflets to be sent to you covering the subject areas you require.

2. The Building Centre is at 26 Store Street, London WC1E 7BT(tel: 020 7692 4000). There is a bookshop and displays.

3. The Building Research Establishment is the largest and most comprehensive source of technical advice available to the construction industry. It operates from Watford.

PAINTING, DECORATING, PLUMBING AND ELECTRICAL WORK

These are areas which attract numerous 'cowboys' offering little or no expertise and a generally poor service. Fortunately, because continued custom depends so much on word of mouth, the

---

rogues tend to fall by the wayside and only those offering a professional service survive. If you are experienced in one of these areas, try it for a while on a part-time basis and, if you have a steady stream of jobs and apparently satisfied customers, enter the profession full-time.

You will probably have been employed with a firm in this capacity and may at first worry about days (or weeks) without work and a long-term shortage of orders. But you must learn to live with the downturns, and price your work for jobs accordingly. These services are always in demand, and if you do a competent job at a competitive price you will survive. Word of mouth will win you most orders but, if you can cope with additional work, go out and look for it: put ads in the windows of local shops, in local newspapers and in the *Yellow Pages*.

'It's silly to start with no work in hand so make sure you have sufficient work before you take the plunge. By "sufficient" I don't mean bits and pieces but solid full-time jobs. Recommendation is better than advertising, and do a good job for a fair price.'

Painter and decorator

Useful information

Federation of Master Builders, 14–15 Great James Street, London WC1N 3DP. Tel. 020 7242 7583. Web: www.fmb.org.uk. Construction Industry Training Board, Bircham Newton, King's Lynn, Norfolk PE31 6RH. Tel. 01485 577577, Web: www.citb.org.uk.

Appendices

SECTOR INFORMATION FOR LOW INVESTMENT, PART-TIME AND FREELANCE OPPORTUNITIES

This is not an exhaustive list. However, it is an indicator of the range of opportunities available to people who want to work for themselves. Where possible details of trade associations and other sources of useful information are included. Information on training, qualifications and industry codes of conduct can generally be obtained from these sources. Further information can be obtained from *The A-Z of Careers and Jobs*, Kogan Page.

ACUPUNCTURIST

The British Acupuncture Council, 63 Jeddo Road, London W12 9HQ; tel: 020 8735 0400; Web site: www.acupuncture.org.uk
British Medical Acupuncture Society, Admin, 12 Marbury House, Higher Whitley, Warrington, Chesire WA4 4QW; tel: 01925 730727; Web site www.medical-acupuncture.co.uk
Working in Complementary and Alternative Medicine, Kogan Page.

AERIAL ERECTOR

Confederation of Aerial Industries Ltd (CAI), Fulton House Business Centre, Fulton Road, Wembley Park, Middlesex HA9 0TF; tel: 020 8902 8998; Web site: www.cai.org.uk

ANTIQUE DEALER

British Antique Dealer's Association, 20 Rutland Gate, London SW7 1BD; tel: 020 7589 4128; Web site: www.bada.org

ART THERAPY

The British Association of Art Therapists, Mary Ward House, 5 Tavistock Place, London WC1H 9SN; tel: 020 7383 3774; Web site: www.baat.org
Careers in Art and Design, Kogan Page.

BEAUTICIAN

British Association of Beauty Therapy and Cosmetology, BABTAC House, 70 Eastgate Street, Gloucester GL1 1QN; tel: 01452 421114; Web site: www.babtac.com
International Health and Beauty Council, 46 Aldwick Road, Bognor Regis, West Sussex PO21 2PN; tel: 01243 842064
International Federation of Health and Beauty Therapists, 3rd Floor, Eastleigh House, Upper Market Street, Eastleigh Hampshire SO50 9FD; tel: 023 8048 8900; Web site: www.fht.org.uk
Careers in the Hairdressing, Beauty and Fitness Industries, Kogan Page.

BLACKSMITH

The Farriers Registration Council, Sefton House, Adam Court, Newark Road, Peterborough PE1 5PP; tel: 01733 319911; Web site: www.farrier-reg.gov.uk

BOAT BUILDER

British Marine Federation, Marine House, Thorpe Lea Road, Egham, Surrey TW20 8BF; tel: 01784 473377; Web site: www.britishmarine.co.uk

BOOKSELLER

Booksellers Association of Great Britain and Ireland, Minster House, 272-274 Vauxhall Bridge Road, London SW1V 1BA; tel: 020 7802 0802; Web site: www.booksellers.org.uk

CARPENTER AND BENCH JOINER

Construction Industry Training Board, Bircham Newton, King's Lynn, Norfolk PE31 6RH; tel: 01485 577577; Web site: www.citb.org.uk

Institute of Carpenters, Central Office, 35 Hayworth Road, Sandiacre, Nottingham NG10 5LL; tel: 0115 949 0641; Web site: www.central-office.co.uk

Practical Guide to Woodworking Careers and Educational Facilities, Guild of Master Craftsmen.

CARPET FITTER

National Institute of Carpet Fitters and Floorlayers, 4d St Mary's Place, The Lace Market, Nottingham NG1 1PH; tel: 0115 958 3077; Web site: www.nicfltd.org.uk

COMPUTERS/IT CONSULTANT

Association of Computer Professionals, 204 Barnett Wood Lane, Ashtead Surrey KT21 2DB; tel: 01372 273442; Web site: www.acpexamboard.com

British Computer Society, 1 Sanford Street, Swindon, Wiltshire
SN1 1HJ; tel: 01793 417 424; Web site: www.bcs.org.uk
Freelance Informer, Reed Publications, 01753 567567

CONFERENCE ORGANISING

The Association of Conferences and Events, ACE International,
Riverside House, High Street, Huntingdon, Cambridgeshire PE18
6SG; tel: 01480 457595; Web site: www.martex.co.uk/ace

CONSERVATION (HISTORICAL)

The British Association of Painting Conservator-Restorers, PO
Box 32, Hayling Island, PO11 9WE; tel: 0239 246 5115; Web site:
www.abpr.co.uk
Historic Scotland, Longmore House, Salsibury Place, Edinburgh
EH9 1SH; tel: 0131 668 8600; Web site: www. historic-
scotland.gov.uk
Institute of Paper Conservation, Bridge House, Waterside, Upton-
upon-Severn WR8 0HG; tel: 01684 591150; Web site: http://
palimpsest.stanford.edu/ipc
Museums Association, 24 Calvin Street, London E1 6NW; tel: 020
7426 6970; Web site: www.museumsassociation.org
Scottish Society for Conservation and Restoration, Chantstoun,
Tartraven, Bathgate Hills, West Lothian EH48 4NP; tel: 01506 811
777; Web site: www.sscr.demon.co.uk
Society of Archivists, 40 Northampton Road, London EC1R 0HB;
tel: 020 7278 8630; Web site: www.archives.org.uk
United Kingdom Institute for Conservation, 109 The Chandlery,
50 Westminster Bridge Road, London SE1 7QY; tel: 020 7721 8721;
Web site: www.ukic.org.uk

COOKING

British Hospitality Association, Queens House, 55-56 Lincoln's
Inn Fields, London WC2A 3BH; tel: 020 7404 7744; Web site:
www.bha-online.org.uk

Careers Information Service, Hospitality Training Foundation, Third Floor, International House, High Street, London W5 5DB; tel: 020 8579 2400; Web site: www.htf.org.uk
The Catering Management Handbook, Kogan Page.

DESIGNER

Chartered Society of Designers, 5 Bermondsey Exchange, 197-81 Bermondsey Street, London SE1 3UW; tel: 020 7357 8088; Web site: www.csd.org.uk
Design Council, 34 Bow Street, London, WC2E 7DL; tel: 020 7420 5200; Web site: www.design-council.org.uk
Careers in Art and Design, Kogan Page.

DETECTIVE/PRIVATE INVESTIGATOR

Association of British Investigators, 48 Queens Road, Basing-stoke, Hampshire RG21 7RE; tel: 01256 816390; Web site: www.theabi.org.uk
The Institute of Professional Investigators, 21 Bloomsbury Way, London WC1A 2TH; tel: 020 7242 6696; Web site: ww.ipi.org.uk

DISC JOCKEY

Phonographic Performance Ltd, 1 Upper James Street, London W1F 9DE; tel: 020 7534 1000; Web site: www.ppluk.com

DOG GROOMER

Petcare Trust, Bedford Business Centre, 170 Mile Road, Bedford MK42 9TW; tel: 01234 273933; Web site: www.petcare.org.uk

DRAMA THERAPIST

British Association for Dramatherapists, 41 Broomhouse Lane, London SW6 3DP; tel: 020 7731 0160; Web site: www. badth.ision.co.uk

DRIVING INSTRUCTOR

Driving Instructor's Association, Safety House, Beddington Farm Road, Croydon CR0 4XZ; tel: 0845 345 5151; Web site: www. driving.org
Register of Approved Driving Instructors, Driving Standards Agency, Stanley House, 56 Talbot Street, Nottingham NG1 5GU; tel: 0115 901 2500; Web site: www.dsa.gov.uk
The Driving Instructor's Handbook, Kogan Page.

EDITING

The Society of Freelance Editors and Proofreaders, Riverbank House, 1 Putney Bridge Approach, Fulham, London SW6 3JD; tel: 020 7736 3278; Web site: www.sfep.org.uk

ESTATE AGENT

The College of Estate Management, Whiteknights, Reading, Berkshire RG6 6AW; tel: 0118 986 1101; Web site: www.cem.ac.uk
The National Association of Estate Agents, Arbon House, 21 Jury Street, Warwick CV34 4EH; tel: 01926 496800; Web site: www. propertylive.co.uk and www.naea.co.uk

FILM PRODUCTION

Broadcasting, Entertainment, Cinematograph and Theatre Union (BECTU), 373–377 Clapham Road, London SW9 9BT; tel: 020 7346 0900; Web site: www.bectu.org.uk

FT2 (Film and Television Freelance Training), Fourth Floor, Warwick House, 9 Warwick Street, London W1B 5LY; tel: 020 7734 5141; Web site: www.ft2.org.uk

Skillset – The Sector Skills Council for the Audio Visual Industries, Prospect House, 80–110 New Oxford Street, London WC1A 1HB; tel: 020 7520 5757; Web site: www.skillset.org

FLORIST

Floristry Training Council, Roebuck House, Hampstead Norreys Road, Hermitage, Thatcham, Berkshire RG18 9RX; tel: 01635 200465

GARDENER

Askham Bryan College of Agriculture and Horticulture, Askham Bryan, York YO23 3FR; tel: 01904 772211; Web site: www.askham-bryan.ac.uk

Institute of Horticulture, 14–15 Belgrave Square, London SW1X 8PS; tel: 020 7245 6943; Web site: www.horticulture.org.uk

Careers Working Outdoors, Kogan Page.

GENEALOGIST

The Institute of Heraldic and Genealogical Studies, 79–82 Northgate, Canterbury, Kent CT1 1BA; tel: 01227 768664; Web site: www.ihgs.ac.uk

The Society of Genealogists, 14 Charterhouse Buildings, Goswell Road, London EC1M 7BA; tel: 020 7251 8799; Web site: www.sog.org.uk

GLAZIER

Construction Industry Training Board, Bircham Newton, King's Lynn, Norfolk PE31 6RH; tel: 01553 577577; Web site: www.citb.org.uk

HAIRDRESSER

Hairdressing and Beauty Industry Authority, Fraser House, Nether Hall Road, Doncaster DN1 2PH; tel: 01302 380000; Web site: www.habia.org

National Hairdressers' Federation, 11 Goldington Road, Bedford MK40 3JY; tel: 0845 3456 500; Web site: www.the-nhf.org

Careers in the Hairdressing, Beauty and Fitness Industries, Kogan Page.

Running Your Own Hairdressing Salon, Kogan Page.

HOMEOPATH

British School of Homeopathy, Lily Cottage, Townsend, Chittle-hampton, Umberleigh EX37 9PU; tel: 01769 540155; Web site: www.homoeopathy.co.uk

Society of Homeopaths, 4a Artizan Road, Northampton NN1 4HU; tel: 01604 621400; Web site: www.homeopathy-soh.org

HORTICULTURIST

See 'Gardener'.

ILLUSTRATOR

The Association of Illustrators, 81 Leonard Street, London EC2A 4QS; tel: 020 7613 4328; Web site: www.theaoi.com

Careers in Art and Design, Kogan Page.

INDEXER

Society of Indexers, Blades Enterprise Centre, John Street, Sheffield S2 4SU; tel: 0114 292 2350; Web site: www.indexers. org.uk

INTERIOR DECORATOR/DESIGNER

British Interior Design Association, 1–4 Chelsea Harbour Design Centre, Chelsea Harbour, London SW10 0XE; tel: 020 7349 0800; Web site: www.bida.org
Chartered Society of Designers, 5 Bermondsey Exchange, 179–181 Bermondsey Street, London SE1 3UW; tel: 020 7357 8088; Web site: www.csd.org.uk

INTERPRETER

Institute of Linguists, Saxon House, 48 Southwark Street, London SE1 1UN; tel: 020 7940 3100; Web site: www.iol.org.uk
Institute of Translation and Interpreting, Exchange House, Fortuna House, South Fifth Street, Milton Keynes MK9 2EU; 01908 325250; Web site: www.iti.org.uk
Careers Using Languages, Kogan Page.

JEWELLERY

British Jewellers' Association, 10 Vyse Street, Birmingham B18 6LT; tel: 0121 233 2121; Web site: www.bja.org.uk
National Association of Goldsmiths, 78a Luke Street, London EC2A 4XG; tel: 020 7613 4445; Web site: www.progold.net

JOURNALIST

Chartered Institute of Journalists, 2 Dock Offices, Surrey Quays Road, London SE16 2XU; tel: 020 7252 1187; Web site: www.ioj.co.uk
National Council for the Training of Journalists, Latton Bush Centre, Southern Way, Harlow, Essex CM18 7BL; tel: 01279 430009; Web site: www.nctj.com

LANDSCAPE ARCHITECT

The Landscape Institute, 6–8 Barnard Mews, London SW11 1QU; tel: 020 7350 5200; Web site: www.l-i.org.uk
Careers Working Outdoors, Kogan Page.

MANAGEMENT CONSULTANT

Institute of Management Consultancy, 3rd Floor, 17–18 Haywards Place, London EC1R 0EQ; tel: 020 7566 5220; Web site: www.imc.co.uk
Management Consultancies Association, 49 Whitehall, London SW1A 2BX; tel: 020 7231 3990; Web site: www.mca.org.uk

MARKET RESEARCH

Market Research Society, 15 Northburgh Street, London EC1V 0JR; tel: 020 7490 4911; Web Site: www.mrs.org.uk

MASSEUR

British School of Complementary Therapy, 140 Harley Street, London W1N 1AH; tel: 020 7224 2393; Web site: www.bsct.co.uk
The Northern Institute of Massage, 14–16 St Marys Place, Bury, Lancashire BL9 0DZ; tel: 0161 797 1800; Web site: www.nim56.co.uk

MUSICIAN

Incorporated Society of Musicians, 10 Stratford Place, London W1C 1AA; tel: 020 7629 4413; Web site: www.ism.org
Musicians' Union, 60–62 Clapham Road, London SW9 0JJ; tel: 020 7582 5566; Web site: www.musiciansunion.org.uk

MUSIC THERAPIST

Association of Professional Music Therapists, Administrator, 26 Hamlyn Road, Glastonbury, Somerset BA6 8HT; tel: 01458 832839; Web site: www.apmt.org

British Society for Music Therapy, 25 Rosslyn Avenue, East Barnet, Hertfordshire EN4 8DH; tel: 020 8368 8879; Web site: www.bsmt.org

NATUROPATH

The British College of Osteopathic Medicine, Lief House, 120–122 Finchley Road, London NW3 5HR; tel: 020 7435 6464; Web site: www.bcom.ac.uk

OFFICE SKILLS

Institute of Qualified Private Secretaries, First Floor, 6 Bridge Avenue, Maidenhead FL6 1RR; tel: 01628 625007; Web site: www.iqps.org

OSTEOPATH

See 'Naturopath'
Working in Complementary and Alternative Medicine, Kogan Page.

PHOTOGRAPHER

Association of Photographers Ltd, 81 Leonard Street, London EC2A 4QS; tel: 020 7739 6669; Web site: www.the-aop.org

British Institute of Professional Photography, Fox Talbot House, Amwell End, Ware, Hertfordshire SG12 9HN; tel: 01920 464011; Web site: www.bipp.com

The National Council for the Training of Journalists – see 'Journalist'

PIANO TUNER

Pianoforte Tuners' Association, c/o 10 Reculver Road, Herne Bay, Kent CT6 6LD; tel: 01227 368808; Web site: www.pianotuner. org.uk

PLAYGROUP LEADER

Council for Awards in Children's Care and Education, 8 Chequer Street, St Albans, Hertfordshire AL1 3XZ; tel: 01727 738308; Web site: www.cache.org.uk
Pre-School Learning Alliance, 2nd Floor, Tabard House, 116 Southwark Street, London SE1 0TA; tel: 020 7620 0550;Web site: www.pre-school.org.uk

PLUMBER

Institute of Plumbing, 64 Station Lane, Hornchurch, Essex RM12 6NB; tel: 01708 472791; Web site: www.plumbers.org.uk

POTTER

Crafts Council, 44a Pentonville Road, London N1 9BY; tel: 020 7278 7700; Web site: www.craftscouncil.org.uk
Contemporary Ceramics, 7 Marshall Street, W1F 7EH; tel: 020 7437 7605

RIDING INSTRUCTOR

The British Horse Society, British Equestrian Centre, Stoneleigh Deer Park, Kenilworth, Warwickshire CV8 2XZ; tel: 08701 202 244; Web site: www.bhs.org.uk

SELLING

The Direct Selling Association, 29 Floral Street, London WC2E
9DP; tel: 020 7497 1234; Web site: www.dsa.org.uk

SPORTS COACH/PERSONAL TRAINER

Sports England, 16 Upper Woburn Place, London WC1H 0QP; tel:
020 7273 1500; Web site: www.sportengland.org
SportScotland, Caledonia House, South Gyle, Edinburgh EH12
9DQ; tel: 0131 317 7200; Web site: www.sportscotland.org.uk
Careers in Sport, Kogan Page.

STEEPLEJACK

National Federation of Master Steeplejacks and Lightning
Conductor Engineers, 4d St Mary's Place, The Lace Market,
Nottingham NG1 1PH; tel: 0115 955 8818; Web site: www.
nfmslce.co.uk

STONEMASON

Building Crafts College, Kennard Road, Stratford, London E15
1AH; tel: 020 8522 1705; Web site: www.thecarpenterscompany.
co.uk

TAXI DRIVER

Licensed Taxi Drivers Association, LTDA Taxi House, Wood-
field Road, London W9 2BA; tel: 020 7286 1046; Web site:
www.ltda.co.uk

THATCHER

National Council of Master Thatchers Association, Foxhill, Hillside, South Brent, Devon TQ10 9AU; tel: 07000 781909; Web site: www.buildingconservation.com/ad390.htm

TOUR OPERATOR

Institute of Travel and Tourism, Mill Studio, Crane Mead, Ware, Hertfordshire SG12 9PY; tel: 0870 770 7960; Web site: www.itt.co.uk
The Tourism Society, 1–2 Queen Victoria Terrace, Sovereign Court, London E1 3HA; tel: 020 7488 2789; Web site: www.tourismsociety.org

TRANSLATOR

See 'Interpreter'.
Careers Using Languages, Kogan Page.

UPHOLSTERER

London Guildhall University, Old Castle Street, London E1 7NT; tel: 020 7320 1000; Web site: www.lgu.uk
Association of Master Upholders and Soft Furnishers, 102a Commercial Street, Newport, South Wales NP20 1LU; tel: 01633 215454; Web site: www.upholsterers.co.uk

WINE TRADE

Wine and Spirit Education Trust, Five Kings House, 1 Queen Street Place, London EC4R 1QS; tel: 020 7236 3551; Web site: www.wset.co.uk

WRITER

Institute of Scientific and Technical Communicators, PO Box 522, Peterborough PE2 5WX; tel: 01733 390141; Web site: www.istc. org.uk

Society of Authors, 84 Drayton Gardens, London SW10 9SB; tel: 020 7373 6642; Web site: www.writer.org.uk/society

The Writers' Guild of Great Britain, 15 Britannia Street, London WC1X 9JN; tel: 020 7833 0777; Web site: www.writersguild.org.uk

See 'Journalist'

USEFUL CONTACTS

Government

The Adjudicator's Office
(For complaints against rulings by
Customs and Excise)
Haymarket House
28 Haymarket
London SW1Y 4SP
Tel: 020 7930 2292
Web site:www.adjudicatorsoffice.
gov.uk

**ADAS (formerly the Agricultural
Development Advisory Service
(DEFRA))**
ADAS HQ, Woodthorne
Wergs Road
Wolverhampton WV6 8TQ
Tel: 0845 766 0085
Web site: www.adas.co.uk

**Central Office of Information
Communications**
Hercules House
Hercules Road
London SE1 7DU
Tel: 020 7928 2345
Web site: www.coi.gov.uk

The Countryside Agency
John Dower House
Crescent Place
Cheltenham GL50 3RA
Tel: 01242 521381
Web site: www.countryside.gov.uk

Customs and Excise
New King's Beam House
22 Upper Ground
London SE1 9PJ
Tel: 020 7865 3000
Web site: www.hmce.gov.uk

**Customs and Excise – National
Advice Service**
Tel: 0845 010 9000

The Data Protection Registrar
Wycliffe House
Water Lane
Wilmslow
Cheshire SK9 5AF
Tel: 01625 545740
Web site: www.dpr.gov.uk

Department for Education and Skills
Sanctuary Buildings
Great Smith Street
London SW1P 3BT
Tel: 0870 000 2288
Web site: www.dfes.gov.uk

**Department for Environment, Food
and Rural Affairs (DEFRA)**
Nobel House
17 Smith Square
London SW1P 3JR
Tel: 020 7238 6000
Web site: www.defra.gov.uk

Department of Trade and Industry
DTI Enquiry Unit
1 Victoria Street
London SW1H 0ET
Tel: 020 7215 5000

Small Business Service Enquiry Line
(for details of local and other services)
1 Victoria Street
London SW1H OET
Tel: 08456 045 678

Department of Transport
Eland House
Bressenden Place
London SW1E 5DU
Tel: 020 7944 3000
Web site: www.dft.gov.uk

**Exports Credits Guarantee
Department (ECGD)**
PO Box 2200
2 Exchange Tower
Harbour Exchange Square
London E14 9GS
Tel: 020 7512 7000
Web site: www.ecgd.gov.uk

Her Majesty's Treasury
The Public Enquiries Unit
Room 110/2
Treasury Chambers
Parliament Street
London SW1P 3AG
Tel: 020 7270 4558
Web site: www.hm-treasury.gov.uk

Inland Revenue
The Inland Revenue has a number of
helplines for enquiries, a listing of
which can be found on its Web site at
www.inlandrevenue.gov.uk

Learning and Skills Council
Cheylesmore House
Quinton Road
Coventry CV1 2WT
Tel: 0845 019 4170
Web site: www.lsc.gov.uk

Office of Fair Trading
Fleetbank House
2-6 Salisbury Square
London EC4Y 8JX
Tel: 08457 224 499
Web site: www.oft.gov.uk

Office for National Statistics
The Library
1 Drummond Gate
London SW1V 2QQ
Tel: 08456 013 034 Web site:
www.statistics.gov.uk

Small Business Service
Kingsgate House
66–74 Victoria Street
London SW1E 6SW
Tel: 0845 600 9006
Web site: www.sbs.gov.uk

**Training and Enterprise Councils
(TECs) and Local Enterprise
Companies**
List obtained from: Small Business
Service Enquiry Line
1 Victoria Street
London SW1H 0ET
Tel: 08456 045 678
Web site: www.tec.co.uk

UK Online
A gateway to all Government
Department Web sites:
www.open.gov.uk

Government Offices for the Regions

Four departments (Employment,
Trade and Industry, Environment and
Transport) have been organised into
integrated offices known as
Government Offices (GOs for the
Regions).

Government Office for the East
Westbrook Centre
Milton Road
Cambridge CB4 1YG
Tel: 01223 346700
Web site: www.go-east.gov.uk

**Government Office for the East
Midlands**
The Belgrave Centre
Stanley Place
Talbot Street
Nottingham NG1 5GG
Tel: 0115 971 9971
Web site: www.go-em.gov.uk

Government Office for London
Riverwalk House
157–161 Millbank
London SW1P 4RR
Tel: 020 7217 3328
Web site: www.go-london.gov.uk

**Government Office for the
North East**
Wellbar House
Gallowgate
Newcastle Upon Tyne NE1 4TD
Tel: 0191 201 3300
Web site: www.go-ne.gov.uk

**Government Office for the
North West**
Sunley Tower
Piccadilly Plaza
Manchester M1 4BE
Tel: 0161 952 4000
Web site: www.go-nw.gov.uk

Cunard Building
Pier Head
Water Street
Liverpool L3 1QB
Tel: 0151 224 6300

**Government Office for the
South East**
Bridge House
1 Walnut Tree Close
Guildford GU1 4GA
Tel: 01483 882 255
Web site: www.go-se.gov.uk

**Government Office for the
South West**
2 Rivergate
Temple Quay
Bristol BS1 6ED
Tel: 0117 900 700
Web site: www.gosw.gov.uk

Mast House
Shepherds Wharf
24 Sutton Road
Plymouth PL4 0HJ
Tel: 01752 635000

**Government Office for the
West Midlands**
77 Paradise Circus
Queensway
Birmingham B1 2DT
Tel: 0121 212 5050
Web site: www.go-wm.gov.uk

**Government Office for Yorkshire and
The Humber**
PO Box 213
City House
New Station Street
Leeds LS1 4US
Tel: 0113 280 0600
Web site: www.goyh.gov.uk

Government Office for Northern Ireland

**Department of Enterprise Trade and
Investment**
Netherleigh
Massey Avenue
Belfast BT4 2TP
Tel: 028 9052 9900
Web site: www.detini.gov.uk

Government Office for Scotland

Scotland Office – Edinburgh
Finance and Administration Division
1 Melville Crescent
Edinburgh EH3 7HW
Tel: 0131 244 9010
Web site:
www.scottishsecretary.gov.uk

Scotland Office – Glasgow
Economic and Industry Division
1st Floor Meridian Court
5 Cadogan Street
Glasgow G2 6AT
Tel: 0141 242 5958

London Office
Ministerial Offices
Parlimentary and Constitutional
Divison
Dover House
Whitehall
London SW1A 2AU
Tel: 020 7270 6754

Government Office for Wales

The Wales Office
Office of the Secretary of State for
Wales
Gwydyr House
Whitehall
London SW1A 2ER
Web site: www.ossw.wales.gov.uk

Start-up advice
England and Wales

Business in the Community
137 Shepherdess Walk
London N1 7RQ
Tel: 0870 600 2482
Web site: www.bitc.org.uk

The National Assembly for Wales
Cardiff Bay
Cardiff CF99 1NA
Tel: 029 2082 5111
Web site: www.wales.gov.uk

Welsh Development Agency
Plas Glyndwr
Kingsway
Cardiff
South Glamorgan CF10 3AH
Tel: 01443 845500
Web site: www.wda.co.uk

Scotland

Highlands and Islands Enterprise
Cowan House
Inverness Retail and Business Park
Inverness IV2 7GF
Tel: 01463 234171
Web site: www.hie.co.uk

The Office of the Scottish Executive
Enterprise and Lifelong Learning
Department
Meridian Court
5 Cadogan Street
Glasgow G2 6AT
Tel: 0141 248 2855
Web site: www.scotland.gov.uk

Education Department
Victoria Quay
Edinburgh EH6 6QQ
Tel: 0131 566 8400

Scottish Business in the Community
PO Box 408
Bankhead Avenue
Edinburgh EH11 4HE
Tel: 0131 442 2020
Web site: www.sbcscot.com

Scottish Enterprise
5 Atlantic Quay
150 Broomielaw
Glasgow G2 8LU
Tel: 08456 078 787 Web site:
www.scottish-enterprise.com

Small Business Gateway (Scottish
Enterprise's small business
information service)
Tel: 0845 609 6611
Web site: sbgateway.com

Northern Ireland

Invest Northern Ireland
64 Chichester Street
Belfast BT1 4JX
Tel: 028 9023 9090
Web site: www.investni.com

For a list of Local Enterprise Agencies in Northern Ireland and information, advice and resources for businesses contact:

Oak Tree Press
19 Rutland Street
Cork
Ireland
Tel: +351 21 431 3855
Web site:
www.startingabusinessinireland.
com/dirlea.htm

National associations representing small firms

British Chambers of Commerce
50 Broadway
St James' Park
London SW1H 0RG
Web site: www.chamberonline.co.uk

British Franchise Association
Thames View
Newton Road
Henley on Thames
Oxfordshire RG9 1HG
Tel: 01491 578050
Web site: www.british-franchise.org.uk

Confederation of British Industry (CBI)
Centre Point
103 New Oxford Street
London WC1A 1DU
Tel: 020 7395 8247
Web site: www.cbi.org.uk

Federation of Small Businesses Ltd
Sir Frank Whittle Way
Blackpool Business Park
Blackpool
Lancashire FY4 2FE
Tel: 01253 336000
Web site: www.fsb.org.uk

The Forum of Private Business Ltd
Ruskin Chambers
Drury Lane
Knutsford
Cheshire WA16 6HA
Tel: 01565 634467
Web site: www.fpb.co.uk

Smaller Firms Council (CBI)
Centre Point
103 New Oxford Street
London WC1A 1DU
Tel: 020 7379 7400
Web site: www.cbi.org.uk

The Work Foundation and Industrial Society Learning and Development
Peter Runge House
3 Carlton House Terrace
London SW1Y 5DG
Tel: 0870 165 6700
Web site:
www.theworkfoundation.com

Forming a company

Companies Limited/Rapid Refunds
376 Euston Road
London NW1 3BL
Tel: 020 7383 2323
Web site: www.companies-ltd.co.uk
To buy an off-the-shelf company.

Industrial Common Ownership Movement (ICOM)
Holyoake House
Hanover Street
Manchester M60 0AS
Tel: 0161 246 2959
Web site: www.icof.co.uk/icom/index
Advice on setting up worker co-operatives.

The Institute of Business Advisers
Response House
Queen Street North
Chesterfield S41 9AB
Tel: 01246 453322
Web site: www.iba.org.uk

The Institute of Directors
116 Pall Mall
London SW1Y 5ED
Tel: 020 7766 8866
Web site: www.iod.co.uk

Lawyers for Your Business
Law Society
113 Chancery Lane
London WC2A 1P
Tel: 020 7405 9075
Web site: www.lfyb.lawsociety.org.uk

The Patent Office
Concept House
Cardiff Road
Newport
Gwent NP10 8QQ
Tel: 01633 814000
Web site: www.patent.gov.uk

Registrar of Companies
Companies Registration Office
Crown Way
Maindy
Cardiff CF14 3UZ
Tel: 0870 333 3636
Web site:
www.companies-house.gov.uk

Registrar of Companies – London:
Companies Registration Office
PO Box 29019
21 Bloomsbury Street
London WC1B 3XD
Tel: 0870 333 3636

Registrar of Companies – Manchester
75 Mosley Street
Manchester M2 3HR
Tel: 0870 333 3636

Registrar of Companies – Scotland
37 Castle Terrace
Edinburgh EH1 2EB
Tel: 0870 333 3636

Banks

Alliance and Leicester Business Banking
Bridle Road
Bootle
Merseyside L20 1PH
Tel: 0800 587 0800
Web site: www.mybusinessbank.co.uk

Bank of Scotland and Halifax Business
Business Banking eCommerce
1st Floor
New Uberior House
11 Earl Grey Street
Edinburgh EH3 9BN
Tel: 01244 624 100
Web site: www.bankofscotland.co.uk/
business

Barclays Bank plc Small Business Banking
PO Box 120
Longwood Close
Westwood Business Park
Coventry CV4 8JN
Tel: 024 76 694242
Web site: www.barclays.co.uk

HSBC Bank plc Business Unit
Tel: 08457 43 44 45
For advice and business start-up pack
Web site: www.banking.hsbc.co.uk

Lloyds TSB Bank plc, Small Business Advice
PO Box 112
Canons House
Canons Way
Bristol BS99 7LB
Tel: 08000 560 056
Web site: www.smallbusiness.co.uk

National Westminster Bank plc, Business Banking
Level 20 Drapers Gardens
12 Throgmorton Avenue
London EC2N 2DL
Tel: 020 7920 5555
Web site: www.natwest.com

329

Royal Bank of Scotland Small Business
Tel: Helpdesk 0131 523 4069
Web site: www.royalbankscot.co.uk/Small_Business

Raising capital

Association of British Credit Unions Ltd
Holyoake House
Hanover Street
Manchester M60 0AS
Tel: 0161 832 3694
Web site: www.abcul.org

British Insurance Brokers Association
BIBA House
14 Bevis Marks
London EC3A 7NT
Tel: 020 7623 9043
Web site: www.biba.org.uk

British Venture Capital Association
3 Clements Inn
London WC2A 2AZ
Tel: 020 7025 2950
Web site: www.bvca.co.uk

European Grants Ltd
Gallands Close
2 Swanland
East Yorkshire HU14 3GE
Tel: 01482 651695
Web site: www.europeangrants.com

Factors and Discounters Association
Boston House
The Little Green
Richmond
Surrey TW9 1QE
Tel: 020 8332 9955
Web site: www.factors.org.uk

Finance and Leasing Association
Imperial House
2nd Floor
15–19 Kings Way
London WC2B 6UN
Tel: 020 7836 6511
Web site: www.fla.org.uk

Institute of Patentees and Investors
Suite 505a
Triumph House
189 Regent Street
London W1B 4JY
Tel: 020 7434 1818
Web site: www.invent.org.uk

Local Investment Networking Co (LINC)
London Enterprise Agency
4 Snow Hill
London EC1A 2BS
Tel: 020 7403 0300

The Prince's Youth Business Trust
18 Park Square East
London NW1 4LH
Tel: 0800 842 842
Web site: www.princes-trust.org.uk

3I plc
91 Waterloo Road
London SE1 8XP
Tel: 020 7928 3131
Web site: www.3i.com

Venture Capital Report Ltd
7 Old Park Lane
London W1K 1QR
Tel: 020 7629 9949
Web site: www.vcr1978.com

Managing finance

Association of Chartered Certified Accountants
29 Lincoln's Inn Fields
London WC2A 3EE
Tel: 020 7396 7000
Web site: www.acca.co.uk

Chartered Accountants Directory
Datacomp
4 Houldsworth Square
Reddish
Stockport
Cheshire SK5 7AF
Tel: 0161 442 5233
Web site:
www.chartered-accountants.co.uk

Chartered Institute of Taxation
12 Upper Belgrave Street
London SW1X 8BB
Tel: 020 7235 9381
Web site: www.tax.org.uk

Institute of Chartered Accountants in England and Wales
PO Box 433
Chartered Accountants Hall
Moorgate Place
London EC2P 2BJ
Tel: 020 7920 8100
Web site: www.icaew.co.uk

Institute of Chartered Accountants of Scotland
CA House
21 Haymarket Yards
Edinburgh EH12 5BH
Tel: 0131 347 0100
Web site: www.icas.org.uk

Institute of Company Accountants
40 Tyndales Road
Clifton
Bristol BS8 1PL
Tel: 0117 973 8261

The International Association of Book-keepers
44 Burford House
London Road
Sevenoaks
Kent TN13 1AS
Tel: 01732 458080
Web site:
www.accountingweb.co.uk/iab

Marketing and sales

The Advertising Association
Abford House
15 Wilton Road
London SW1V 1NJ
Tel: 020 7828 2771
Web site: www.adassoc.org.uk

British Safety Council
70 Chancellor's Road
London W6 9RS
Tel: 020 8741 1231
Web site:
www.britishsafetycouncil.org

British Standards Institution
389 Chiswick High Road
London W4 4AL
Tel: 020 8996 9000
Web site: www.bsi-global.com

Chartered Institute of Marketing
Moor Hall
Cookham
Maidenhead
Berkshire SL6 9QH
Tel: 01628 427500
Web site: www.cim.co.uk

Direct Marketing Association UK Ltd
DMA House
70 Margaret Street
London W1W 8SS
Tel: 020 7291 3300
Web site: www.dma.org.uk

Institute of Direct Marketing
1 Park Road
Teddington
Middlesex TW11 0AR
Tel: 020 8614 0277
Web site: www.theidm.com

Institute of Public Relations
The Old Trading House
15 Northburgh Street
London EC1V 0PR
Tel: 020 7253 5151
Web site: www.ipr.org.uk

Market Research Society
15 Northburgh Street
London EC1V 0JR
Tel: 020 7490 0608
Web site: www.mrs.org.uk

Marketing Society
St George's House
3–5 Pepys Road
London SW20 8NJ
Tel: 020 8879 3464
Web site:
www.marketing-society.org.uk

Export

Association of British Chambers of Commerce
International Division
4 Westwood House
Westwood Business Park
Coventry CV4 8HS
Tel: 024 7669 4484
Web site: www.britishchambers.org.uk/exportzone

British Exporters Association
Broadway House
Tothill Street
London SW1H 9NQ
Tel: 020 7222 5419
Web site: www.bexa.co.uk

British International Freight Association
Redfem House
Browells Lane
Feltham
Middlesex TW13 7EP
Tel: 020 8844 2266
Web site: www.bifa.org

Department of Trade and Industry
Export Control Organisation
4th Floor
Abbey Orchard Street
London SW1P 2HT
Tel: 020 7215 8070
Web site:
www.dti.gov.uk/export.control

Euler Trade Indemnity plc
1 Canada Square
Canary Wharf
London E14 5DX
Tel: 020 7512 9333
Web site: www.eulerhermes.com/eti

Euro Info Centre
33 Queen Street
London EC4R 1AP
Tel 020 7489 1992
Web site: www.euro-info.org.uk

European Commission Representation in the United Kingdom
Jean Monet House
8 Storey's Gate
London SW1P 3AT
Tel: 020 7973 1992
Web site: www.cec.org.uk and http://europa.eu.int

Export Credits Guarantee Department
PO Box 2200
2 Exchange Tower
Harbour Exchange Square
London E14 9GS
Tel: 020 7512 7000
Web site: www.ecgd.gov.uk

Lamborne House
Lamborne Crescent
Llanishen
Cardiff CF14 5GG
Tel: 029 2032 8500

Institute of Export
Export House
Minerva Business Park
Lynch Wood
Peterborough PE2 6FT
Tel: 01733 404400
Web site: www.export.org.uk

London Chamber of Commerce and Industry
33 Queen Street
London EC4R 1AP
Tel: 020 7248 4444
Web site: www.londonchamber.co.uk

Simplifying International Trade Ltd
Oxford House
8th Floor
76 Oxford Street
London W1D 1BS
Tel: 020 7467 7280
Web site: www.sitpro.org

Technical Information Group
British Standards Institution – Import and Export
389 Chiswick High Road
London W4 4AL
Tel: 020 8996 7111
Web site: www.bsi-global.com/Import +Export+Advice

Trade Partners UK
Kingsgate House
66–74 Victoria Street
London SW1E 6SW
Tel: 020 7215 5444/5
Web site: www.tradepartners.gov.uk

TradeUK
Web site: www.tradeuk.com
Online advice on export issues and e-commerce.

Labour relations and personnel management

Advisory, Conciliation and Arbitration Service (ACAS)
Brandon House
180 Borough High Street
London SE1 1LW
Tel: 020 7210 3613
Web site: www.acas.org.uk

The Chartered Institute of Management
Small Firms Information Service
Management House
Cottingham Road
Corby
Northants NN17 7IT
Tel: 01536 204222
Web site: www.inst-mgt.org.uk

Chartered Institute of Personnel and Development
CIPD House
35 Camp Road
Wimbledon
London SW19 4UX
Tel: 020 8971 9000
Web site: www.ipd.co.uk

Health and Safety Executive
Public Enquiry Centre
Caerphilly Business Park
Caerphilly
Tel: 08701 545500
Web site: www.hse.gov.uk

The Institute of Management Consultancy
3rd Floor
17–18 Haywards Place
London EC1R 0EQ
Tel: 020 7566 5220
Web site: www.imc.co.uk

Recruitment and Employment Confederation
33–36 Mortimer Street
London W1W 7RG
Tel: 020 8212 8260
Web site: www.rec.uk.com

Premises

Country Land and Business Association
16 Belgrave Square
London SW1X 8PQ
Tel: 020 7235 0511
Web site: www.cla.org.uk

English Partnership
St George's House
Kingsway
Team Valley
Gateshead
Tyne and Wear NE11 0NA
Tel: 0191 487 6565
Web site: www.englishpartnerships.
co.uk

Estates Today
84–86 Regent Street
London W1R 6AJ
Tel: 01483 855568
Web site: www.estatestoday.co.uk
Online commercial estate agent.

Royal Institution of Chartered Surveyors
Contact Centre
Surveyor Court
Westwood Way
Coventry CV4 8JE
Tel: 0870 333 1600
Web site: www.rics.org

Information and communication technologies

Central Small Business Solutions
Web site: www.bcentral.com
Exchange advertising banner with other sites.

British Telecom
Web: www.britishtelecom.co.uk
Advice on communications and information technologies for business.

Digits.comWebCounter
Web Site: www.digits.com
Adds visitor counter to your Web site.

e.centre
10 Maltravers Street
London WC2R 3BX
Tel: 020 7655 9000
Web site: www.eca.org.uk

Exploit
Web site: www.exploit.com

List universe
Web site: www.list-universe.com
Provides details of mailing lists and joining details.

Nominet
To register Internet domain names.
Web site: www.nic.uk

SubmitIt
Web site: www.submitit.com
This company will submit your Web site address to online search engines.

Technologies for Training
71–73 Woodbridge Road
Guildford GU1 4YZ
Web site: www.tft.co.uk
Gateway to IT help with links to numerous organisations working in IT.

UK Online for Business
Web site: www.ukonlineforbusiness.
gov.uk
Offers IT advice and support for businesses.

FURTHER SOURCES OF INFORMATION

Specialist libraries

Business Information Service
British Library
96 Euston Road
London NW1 2DB
Tel: 020 7412 7454
Web site: www.bl.uk

Chartered Institute of Marketing Library
Moor Hall
Cookham
Maidenhead
Berkshire SL6 9QH
Tel: 01628 427333
Web site: www.cim.co.uk

Chartered Institute of Management Library
Management House
Cottingham Road
Corby
Northants NN17 1TT
Tel: 01536 204222
Web site: www.inst-mgt.org.uk

Competition Commission Information Centre
New Court
48 Carey Street
London WC2A 2JT
Tel: 020 7271 0243
Web site:
www.competition-commission.org.uk

Cyril Kleinwort Library
The Cass Learning Resource Centre
106 Bunhill Row
London EC1Y 8TZ
Tel: 020 7477 8787
Web site: www.city.ac.uk/library/ckl

Department of Trade and Industry Library
Information and Library Services
1 Victoria Street
London SW1H 0ET
Tel: 020 7215 5006

Information Centre of Trade Partners UK
Kingsgate House
66–74 Victoria Street
London SW1E 6SW
Tel: 020 7215 5444
Web site: www.tradepartners.gov.uk

Institute of Management Library
Management House
Cottingham Road
Corby
Northants NN17 1TT
Tel: 01536 204222
Web site: www.inst-mgt.org.uk

London Business School Library
25 Tauton Place
London NW1 4SA
Tel: 020 7262 5050
Web site: www.lbs.lon.ac.uk/library

London Guildhall University
School of Business Studies
84 Moorgate
London EC2M 6SQ
Tel: 020 7320 1000
Web site: www.lgu.ac.uk

Office of Fair Trading Library
Fleetbank House
2–6 Salisbury Square
London EC4Y 8JX
Tel: 020 7211 8941
Web site: www.oft.gov.uk

Office for National Statistics
The Library
1 Drummond Gate
London SW1V 2QQ
Tel: 08456 013 034
Web site: www.statistics.gov.uk

Web sites of interest

Better Business
Web site: www.better-business.co.uk
Offers independent and impartial advice to small businesses.

Business Clubs UK
Web site: www.onlinebusinessclub.net
A federation of clubs, groups and associations that provides advice, contacts and government links.

DTI
Web site: www.dti.gov.uk
Good links to government-sponsored
schemes.

Electronic Telegraph
Web site: www.telegraph.co.uk
Access to full text of *Daily Telegraph*
and directory listing of British business.

Financial Times
Web site: www.ft.com
Business directory and up-to-date
financial information.

**Keele University Management Web
Resources Database**
Web site: www.keele.ac.uk
Well resourced database of business
and management Web sites with good
links.

Kogan Page
Web site: www.kogan-page.co.uk
Extensive list of publications for start-
ups and SMEs.

Law Links
Provides links to relevant government
legislation, TUC reports and DTI
guides
Web site: www.lawlinks.co.uk

**Strathclyde University Business
Information Sources on the Internet**
Web site: www.dis.strath.ac.uk
Thoroughly recommended Web site
with extensive listings of sites and
general sources of business
information.

WhoWhere
Web site: www.whowhere.lycos.com
E-mail address, telephone number and
street address directory.

Yahoo
Web site: www.yahoo.com
Search engine with extensive business
directory.

Yell
Web: www.yell.co.uk
Online version of the *Yellow Pages*.

Appendix 2 — Select Bibliography

Accounting for Non-Accountants, 5th edition, Graham Mott (Kogan Page)
All About Selling, A Williams (McGraw-Hill)
The Allied Dunbar Tax Guide, W I Sinclair (Longman, published annually)
Be Your Own Boss!, David McMullan (Kogan Page)
Be Your Own P R Man, Michael Bland (Kogan Page)
British Rate & Data (monthly)
The Business Property Handbook (Royal Institution of Chartered Surveyors)
Careers in Catering and Management (Kogan Page)
The Catering Management Handbook 1994, Judy Ridgway and Brian Ridgway (Kogan Page)
Croner's Reference Book for Exporters (Croner Publications Ltd)
Croner's Reference Book for the Self-employed and Smaller Business (Croner Publications Ltd)
Directory of Enterprise Agencies (Business in the Community)
Doing Business on the Internet, 3rd edition, Simon Collin (Kogan Page)
Effective PR Management, 2nd edition, Paul Winner (Kogan Page)
Fair Deal: A Shopper's Guide (Office of Fair Trading)
Forming a Limited Company, 7th edition, Patricia Clayton (Kogan Page)
Getting Started in Export, Roger Bennett (Kogan Page)
Getting Started in Importing, John R Wilson (Kogan Page)
Going Freelance, 5th edition, Godfrey Golzen (Kogan Page)
Guide to Careers in the Catering, Travel and Leisure Industries (Kogan Page)
A Guide to Franchising, Martin Mendelsohn (Cassell)
A Guide to Sources of Finance for SMEs, Michael Brand (Kogan Page)
The Handbook of World Trade, Jonathan Reuvid (Kogan Page)
How to Run Your Own Restaurant, B Sim and William Gleeson (Kogan Page)
Looking Ahead: A Guide to Retirement, Fred Kemp and Bernard Buttle (Springfield)
Management of Trade Credit, T G Hutson and J Butterworth (Gower Press)
Managing for Results, Peter F Drucker (Pan Books)
Money, Health and Your Retirement, E V Eves (Paperback Choice)
The Publican's Handbook (Kogan Page)

Self-Employment in the United Kingdom, Nigel Meager (Institute of Employment Studies)
Setting up a Workshop (Crafts Council)
The Small Business Casebook, Sue Birley (Macmillan Press)
The Small Business Guide, 4th edition, C Barrow (BBC Publications)
Small Business Guide, S Williams (Penguin)
Writers' & Artists' Yearbook (A & C Black)
Writing for the BBC, Norman Longmate (BBC Publications)
Your Home Office, Peter Chatterton (Kogan Page)

Many of the pamphlets produced by the Department of Trade and Industry, the Department of Social Security, the Inland Revenue, the Department for Education and Skills and the Department of the Environment will also be of value.

Also, a useful magazine is *Better Business*, Cribau Mill, Llanvair Discoed, Chepstow, Gwent NP6 6RD. Tel: 01291 641222; Fax: 01291 61777; Web site: www.better-business.co.uk

OTHER USEFUL BOOKS FROM KOGAN PAGE

Business Plans, 2nd edition, Brian Finch
Law for the Small Business, 10th edition, Patricia Clayton
Running Your Own Boarding Kennels, 3rd edition, Sheila Zabawa
The Small Business Action Kit, 4th edition, John Rosthorn *et al*
Taking up a Franchise, 14th edition, Colin Barrow and Godfrey Golzen
Understand Your Accounts, 4th edition, A St John Price

PUBLICATIONS FOR SMALL BUSINESSES FROM KOGAN PAGE

BDO Stoy Hayward Guide to the Family Business, 3rd edition, Peter Leach
The Business Plan Workbook, 3rd edition, Colin Barrow and Robert Brown
Cheque's in the Post: Credit Control for the Small Business, Andrea Shavick
Do Your Own Bookeeping, Max Pullen
Do Your Own Market Research, 3rd edition, Paul Hague
E-business for the Small Business, John G Fisher
Financial Management for the Small Business, 4th edition, Colin Barrow
Getting Started in Export: A Practical Guide, 2nd edition, Roger Bennett

Getting Started in Importing, 2nd edition, John Wilson
How to Prepare a Business Plan, 3rd edition, Edward Blackwell
How to Set Up and Run Your Own Business, 16th edition, Ed. Helen Kogan
Practical Marketing and PR for the Small Business, 1998, 2nd edition, Moi Ali
Running a Home Based Business, Diane Baker
Start Your Own Business in 30 Days, Gary Grappo
Start Up and Run Your Own Business, Jonathan Reuvid and Roderick Millar
Successful Marketing for Small Business, 5th edition, Dave Patten
Top 200 Websites for Small Business, Sarah Lee

A SELECTION FROM THE KOGAN PAGE CAREERS SERIES

Careers in Art and Design, 8th edition, Noel Chapman
Careers in Catering, Hotel Administration and Management, 5th edition, Russell Joseph
Careers in Computing and Information Technology, 2nd edition, David Yardley
Careers in Fashion, 5th edition, Noel Chapman
Careers in Journalism, 8th edition, Simon Kent
Careers using Languages, 9th edition, Edda Ostarhild
Careers in Retailing, 1997, Loulou Brown
Careers in the Travel Industry, 6th edition, Verité Reily Collins
Careers Working Outdoors, 8th edition, Allan Shepherd

To order Kogan Page books contact:

Littlehampton Book Services
PO Box 53
Littlehampton BN17 7BU
Tel: 01903 828 800
Fax: 01903 828 802
E-mail: orders@lbsltd.co.uk

Or order through the Kogan Page Web site: www.kogan-page.co.uk

Index

References to addresses of organizations are in *italics*.

INDEX OF ADVERTISERS